#9183220

WITHDRAWN

# THE OTHER SIDE OF THE REPORT CARD:

**GOOD YEAR ® EDUCATION SERIES**
Theodore W. Hipple, Editor

 **Good Year Books**

are available for preschool through grade 12 and for every basic curriculum subject plus many enrichment areas. For more Good Year Books, contact your local bookseller or educational dealer. For a complete catalog with information about other Good Year Books, please write:

**Good Year Books**
Department GYB
1900 East Lake Avenue
Glenview, Illinois 60025

# THE OTHER SIDE OF THE REPORT CARD: A HOW-TO-DO-IT PROGRAM FOR AFFECTIVE EDUCATION.

LARRY CHASE

**Scott, Foresman and Company**
Glenview, Illinois, London

ISBN 0-673-16408-X

Copyright © 1975 Scott, Foresman and Company.
Printed in the United States of America

171819202122232425–KPF –98979695949392919089

*This Book Is Dedicated to*
*CARLTON CHASE, Sr., my father.*

*Dad, how come as I get older,*
*you seem smarter?*

# ACKNOWLEDGMENTS

Many people have had a hand in making this book a reality. Some had a hand in the book itself, and others had a hand in the author's psychosocial development. The "thank yous" below are the ones I feel strongest about right now. For the rest of you . . . you know who you are.

Thank you Tim for having faith in me and teaching me that there are no big leagues.

Thank you Jean, Marilyn, and Grace for having class—class tells.

**Thank you Wayne for giving me perspective.**

**Thank you Rod for telling me about this publisher.**

Thank you Dave for supporting my book.

Thank you Jackie. (I always thought editors were bad guys.)

Thank you Betty for loving me and never hassling me to "be" somebody.

# CONTENTS

# EDITOR'S INTRODUCTION

Affective education has come of age. No longer must teachers feel that they are short-changing subject matter when they organize class activities that center on values, attitudes, feelings of self-worth, interpersonal communication, and the like. These kinds of activities, they now realize, help pupils approach the most significant goal of all education—self-knowledge—in ways that traditional lessons in traditional disciplines seldom do.

It is not that a knowledge of Boyle's law, of Macbeth's tragic flaw, or of the trips of the explorers is unimportant. It is rather that this kind of learning has for so long dominated the content of elementary and secondary education that attention to students' self-concepts, to their relations with others, to the opinions they profess, the values they cherish, the beliefs they espouse has been all but ignored amid the harried and hurried struggle to acquire more knowledge of the cognitive sort.

The time for change is upon us—a time of Watergate, of racial unrest, of doubt and concern about our nation's commitment to the support and defense of other countries, of marital disharmony of an unprecedented degree, of black/white, rich/poor, old/young, white collar/blue collar dichotomies.

The critical question for practicing teachers, therefore, is not *whether* affective education should occur but *how* affective education is to occur. And they have every right to ask this question. Their preparation for teaching focused on the accumulation of knowledge that, once degreed and certificated, they would pass along to their pupils. They now realize how limited such a preparation was, and how ill-equipped they are to lead pupils into the exciting potential of affective education. This book was written for these teachers. It shows them *a*—not *the*—way; indeed, it provides a whole series of ways. For some of these teachers it will provide a sound and scholarly support for what they are already attempting to do; for many it will be a stimulus to their trying to move into affective education; for most it will be these things—support and stimulus—and, most important of all, a guide that is clear, precise, and above all else, sensitive.

*The Other Side of the Report Card* offers much, too, to the pre-service teacher, to the young person whose healthy idealism is being strained by what he remembers of his own elementary and secondary education and what he sees as he visits classrooms and observes students. He knows, intuitively perhaps, how vital affective education is. He knows how much he wants to be a part of it. What he does not know is the "how." This book provides the answer, the rationale for affective education and the methods for incorporating this kind of study into any classroom in any subject or grade level.

*The Other Side of the Report Card* is an important and useful book. The devotion of its author, Larry Chase, and his concern for helping teachers help pupils, are apparent throughout. To readers I can only say: Read it carefully. Use it often. You will be glad you did.

*Theodore W. Hipple*
**Editor**
**Good Year ⓇSeries in Education**

# PREFACE

The point of this book is that the social and emotional development of children is as much the business of public schools as are reading and writing and arithmetic. Those of us who are privileged to work with children are accountable to them—accountable for at least attempting to teach them the survival skills necessary to make it through the last quarter of the twentieth century. Those skills include how to relate, how to be responsible, how to choose, how to cope with problems, how to love, and how to think.

In addition, we now know that the degree to which any child can learn in the traditional subject areas is a function of his self-esteem.

This book is a smorgasbord of ways to help children learn some of the survival skills they need today and tomorrow. It was written because of my conviction that a teacher in a classroom *can* significantly affect the social and emotional growth of students in positive, healthful ways. The activities, directions, and topics described in this book are relevant. They have all been used with kids and grownups, and most have worked most of the time.

These ideas represent the snyergy of the ideas of all the teachers I've worked with, all the workshops I've attended, all the books I've read, and, mostly, the thousands of kids I've rapped with in circles. That makes me the culminator, cultivator, and communicator of the ideas—not the source.

If you like these ideas, please take them and change them for your situation and your kids. This is not a package deal. Pick and choose the activities that suit your needs.

You could make this book the basis for a curriculum of affect that would take two to four years to complete.

These units could be used to build rapport and develop the group cohesiveness you need to accomplish your classroom goals.

These activities could become the training program for teachers wishing to develop programs in the affective domain.

This book could become the course outline for a course on self-awareness for teachers-to-be.

Finally, this is a book of tools. The affective techniques here are not the goal. The goal is to have schools in which teachers and students relate as authentic, caring, sympathetic people. It is my hope that this book will contribute to the accomplishment of that goal.

*Larry Chase*

# 1

# WHY AFFECTIVE EDUCATION?

When I go to an institute day session or to an introductory workshop on affective education, or especially when I address a P.T.A. about the topic of this book, someone always says, "What is this effective* education?" Someone else will usually say, "Seriously, what do you do?" I have developed different one-sentence responses to try to get across the idea of what affective education is without going into heavy educator talk. So I usually say, "I teach teachers how to like kids," or "You know the stuff on the other side of the report card? Well, we're trying to help kids not get check marks." If I'm speaking in an area where people are aware of current popular psychology I say, "You know the ideas in *I'm OK–You're OK*? Well, this is a how-to-do-it program in OKness." Most people get the idea right away when I say that—especially the part about the report card. Everybody has gone to school, received report cards, and experienced anxiety over the "other side." When I was going to school, some people lived in fear that they would actually get a check, while others, like me, kept score and had contests to see who could get the most checks. Getting checks is a great way to get attention.

Most schools give out report cards. Progressive schools give out progressive-looking and progressive-sounding ones called behavior check lists, progressive reports, behavioral objective assessments, and the like. They often disguise the purpose of the report card by replacing A, B, and C grades with happy faces and sad faces or by using numbers instead of letters. Traditional schools, such as Stockton School in Chicago, where I went, used a report card like the one on the cover. Every report card I have ever seen, regardless of the cover-up, has had the same purpose and has been organized in the same way. The purpose of report cards is to tell parents what the teachers think of the kids. The cards always have a part devoted to evaluating the child in terms of what he knows about reading, math, social studies and other academic subjects. Then there is always a part, usually the other half, that tells what the teacher thinks of the child's attitudes, social habits, emotional stability, and so on. This part usually contains statements like "works well with others," "completes work," "plays with other children," "contributes to class discussion," "attempts tasks," and the catch-all, "accepts responsibility."

Now, half the report card is devoted to these social and emotional concerns. Teachers spend at least half their time dealing with these kinds of problems.† Parents continually say that "discipline" is the most important thing they want from the schools, and, year after year, boards of education make philosophy statements that indicate their concern with social and emotional objectives.

A rather conservative school system near my house recently up-dated its district philosophy of education. The objectives these average, middle-

---

*The word "affect," meaning feelings, attitudes, values and the like, just isn't a well-known word. That's why people keep hearing me say "effective."

†Interaction analysis data on student-teacher verbal behavior consistently support the idea that teachers spend much more time than they think they do dealing with problems related not to academics but to order, control, following directions, and the like.

class, suburban board members decided upon as the basic elements of a good education were:

1. Mastery of the basic skills of communication and computation.
2. Acquisition of the knowledge and skills necessary for a general education.
3. Acquisition of the skills and attitudes required for independent learning.
4. Discovery and cultivation of creative talents.
5. Development of a positive attitude of self-worth.
6. Examination of moral and ethical values.
7. Acquisition of the rights, responsibilities, and obligations of participation in the family, community, nation, the world.
8. Knowledge of ways through which people can understand and accept each other.

I often ask teachers and parents to rank these objectives in order of importance, and the ones that relate most directly to social and emotional goals are almost always listed as most important.

When I look around at what actually goes on in teacher training programs, in in-service education, in financial allocation for programs in local district, and in time allotments for subject matter, I notice that in spite of our verbal philosophies we are guilty of not putting our money where our collective mouth is.

What I am suggesting here is that we do for social and emotional growth what we have done so well with reading. What this country needs is not a "Right to Read" program but a "Right to Feel Good About Yourself" program. Imagine what would happen if the government made that kind of commitment! By 1980 every public school would have a program designed to teach children how to understand themselves and others and how to make decisions, set goals, like themselves, cope with normal problems, clarify values and accomplish all the other objectives contained in the board of education's philosophy, including an understanding of their rights and obligations as human beings and as citizens.

I have a story I tell at workshops that I got from Jim Ballard, a very "super" consultant in affective education: If you were walking down the street with a friend and you saw a clever advertisement, you might say to your friend, "Look at that sign. Isn't it clever?" If, in response, your friend were to say, "Tell me what it says. I can't read it. I don't know how to read," you would be shocked. If your friend were then to tell you that he went to a school where students weren't taught reading—that they played a lot and had groovy discussions but did no reading—you might become quite angry. After all, don't those school people know how important reading is if a person is going to make it in life?*

If, however, you were walking with friends and you were to turn to one friend and say, "How are you doing?" and be met with "Hey, kiss off. Quit bugging me, I can handle my own problem," you would probably be upset.

_____
*For "make it" you may substitute be happy, fit in, adjust, succeed, get a job, survive, etc.

But I doubt whether you would wonder where he went to school. You wouldn't expect school to teach people how to cope with bad feelings, how to tell others when they're upset, or how to listen for feelings. Schools just don't do that—it's not their job. How important for having a happy life is understanding yourself, liking yourself, and knowing how to get along with others? Are these things as important as reading?

Boards of education don't include affective objectives as only July 4th type rhetoric. I think they really believe that these objectives are important. What most boards don't know when they write their philosophies is that there exists a theory and a technology for accomplishing those objectives, just as there is a technology for teaching reading. Call it citizenship education, call it the living social studies, call it democracy, or call it basic skills time.* What it is, is *affective education—the other side of the report card.*

## THE BACKGROUND OF AFFECTIVE EDUCATION

Affective education has become a valid field of study. Colleges and universities are offering courses specifically devoted to the subject, and more and more studies are being done in which researchers are attempting to measure affective changes. Not too long ago, attempts to measure "self-concept" and other such "mystical" constructs were included in the category of "soft" research projects that were below the attention of serious scholars. Affective education has gained respectability as a serious topic of study because educators' attitudes have changed from a focus on highly accurate measurement of often insignificant subjects, to a position of willingness to accept less rigorous measurements, knowing that the subject matter of their study, affective development, is important and needs to be studied now, even as the needed instruments of measurement are still being developed and refined.

Affective education today represents a marriage between numerous theorists in the humanistic psychology movement and educators who have been able to translate humanistic theories into curriculum programs for children. I will not attempt a detailed explanation of the chronology that brought us to this point. The theorists and their theories are all referred to in the bibliography. Generally, though, affective education has been an offshoot of the human potential movement with its emphasis on encounter groups, sensitivity training, group dynamics, and personal growth. That movement was, and is, an offshoot of the growing influence of the humanistic psychologists, namely Abraham Maslow, Carl Rogers, Rollo May, Erich Fromm, Arthur Combs, Haim Ginott, Karen Horney, Erik Erickson, William Glasser, and others.

Despite great differences between the theories of these psychologists, they all accept certain basic assumptions about man that are crucial to their theories and that make affective education sensible. They all believe that, to one degree or another, man has control over his destiny. This belief stands

---

*In one school with which I work, several teachers who are using the units in this book call affective education "basic skills." Well, it is a basic skill, you know.

in stark contrast to the psychoanalytic theory, which holds that unconscious drives motivate behavior, and the behavioristic theory, which holds that all human behavior is a response to specific stimuli beyond the control of the person. The humanistic theorists conclude that people can become aware of and control the forces affecting them, can make choices, can respond freely and intelligently, can solve their problems, and can grow toward becoming fully functioning (Rogers), self-actualized (Maslow), integrated (Perls) people.*

One of the fundamental ideas in humanistic psychology is the notion of positive mental helath. Traditionally mental health was seen as a problem of adjustment. This approach concentrated on people who were considered to be ineffective or "sick" and helped them to become adjusted and "normal." The models today, however, are successful people. In the service of the idea of positive mental health, affective education programs attempt to help students become clear about who they are, what they want out of life, and how they can get it without hurting others. Contrast this approach with the idea of adjustment to a rather mediocre concept of the "normal" person.

Throughout the 1950s and 1960s techniques were developed to help adults become self-actualized. Growth centers like National Training Labs (Bethel, Maine), Esalen (Big Sur), Kairos (Southern California) and Oasis (Chicago) became clearing houses for people who wanted to work on their personal growth. It was inevitable that someone would realize that these ideas could have much greater impact if a way could be found to adapt them and sell them to the public schools.

Think about that! Just about everybody goes through the public schools. What if, as a regular part of education, boys and girls had experiences that helped them feel good about themselves, become aware of themselves and others, and develop communication and problem-solving skills to help them cope with things in general?

Enter affective education. Many theoretical models for teaching affective education have been developed. This book is one. Following are descriptions of some other affective education programs that are widely used.

## The Human Development Program

The "human development" approach to affective education employs the vehicle of the circle discussion, or "magic circle," to help children become aware of their feelings, thoughts, and behaviors, to develop self-confidence, and to become interpersonally competent. It consists of a theory manual that explains in detail why certain things are done in the circle, daily lesson guides that explain each day's discussion topic to the teacher, rating scales for evaluating the program, and a training workshop for teachers designed to prepare them to conduct the "magic circle." This program is by far the best-packaged affective education program for elementary-school teachers that I have experienced. The key to the successful use of this program is the workship training, which prevents misuse of the program materials.

---

*I'm sure behaviorists and psychoanalysts don't see it that simply. I know there is more there—but in one paragraph?

## Values Clarification

The "values clarification" approach is based on the value theory first presented in the book *Values and Teaching* by Simon, Harmin, and Raths. Since that book was first published, in 1966, the authors and their students have developed hundreds of strategies for helping people clarify their values. Merrill Harmin of Southern Illinois University, Sidney Simon of the University of Massachusetts, Lee Howe of Temple University, and Howard Kirschenbaum of the Adirondack Humanistic Mountain Retreat have been the primary proponents of this approach. The basic idea of this approach is that most of us aren't very clear about our values. For example, we often say we value something when our behavior indicates we value something else. Through the value-clarifying process people become more responsible, more self-directed, more willing to stand up for their beliefs, more self-confident, and more independent. The components of the "values clarification" approach to affective education are the books and pamphlets containing the value theory and the strategies— the best one being *Values Clarification* by Simon, Howe, and Kirschenbaum, and the second best being *Reality Games* by Sax and Hollander. *Values Clarification* is the best book on the market for the practitioner who wants a minimum of theory and lots of ideas for classroom activities. Many of the people I mentioned, as well as their lesser known but equally competent colleagues, conduct workshops around the country to teach people about values clarification. These workshops are great fun and very interesting for the participants in terms of their own lives.

## Schools Without Failure

The "schools without failure" approach grew out of the writing of William Glasser. He wrote a book with that title that presented a series of things that schools could do to promote positive self-concept development and to improve social development in children.

Essentially, he said that if teachers would get personally involved with students, teach things that were relevant, and promote thinking rather than memorizing, most school failure could be eliminated.

The schools without failure process begins with a school workship during which Glasser's ideas are presented and teachers are taught how to begin *class meetings.* * The class meeting is the vehicle Glasser pushes as the systematic way to develop thinking, get involved, and make school more relevant. Class meetings are not unlike the circle discussions of the human development program or the values clarification groups.

Another significant component of the schools without failure approach is the film library Glasser and his associates have made available for rental or purchase. These films and descriptions of their content are listed in Appendix B.

---

*A detailed explanation of the class meeting concept—how it is different from other group methods as well as how to do it—is included in Chapter 4.

## Confluent Education

The "confluent education" approach was devised by George Isaac Brown of the University of California at Berkeley and his colleagues as they developed curriculum materials in affective education under a Ford Foundation grant. Brown's book, *Human Teaching for Human Learning,* contains the theory behind this approach as well as descriptions of techniques employed to accomplish confluent objectives. The essential idea is that when the mind and body are both involved in learning, the learning is more effective. The techniques developed by Brown and his colleagues employ ideas from Gestalt therapy and other humanistic theories and apply these ideas to traditional subject-matter content to make the learning more personal. A first-grade teacher starting a unit on the body begins by having the students go on a fantasy trip through their own bodies. Members of a high-school class about to study *The Red Badge of Courage* discuss a time when they felt cowardly or courageous, as a prelude to reading about the hero's experiences.

Although the term "confluent education" has been picked up by many practioners of affective education, Brown's ideas are not nearly as widely practiced as some of the others already mentioned. This is partly because some of the techniques in his book seem really "heavy," and many classroom teachers are probably afraid to try some of the techniques because of their own lack of training.

## Teacher Effectiveness Training

"Teacher effectiveness training" is primarily an in-service training approach. It is based on the ideas contained in Thomas Gordon's *Parent Effectiveness Training.* Gordon has outlined a plan by which parents and teachers can communicate more effectively with children and by which most of the discipline problems that plague our schools can be eliminated. The training for teachers includes learning how to listen, how to structure environments to avoid hassles, how to negotiate, how to decide who owns the problem, how to use ownership language ("I-messages"), and just generally how to solve problems without anybody losing.

The skills teachers learn during a T.E.T. course are helpful regardless of which affective education program they are using.

## Transactional Analysis

The "transactional analysis" approach consists of teaching students about the now very popular concepts contained in *I'm OK—You're OK* by T. A. Harris. It is a less formal program than some of the others discussed here. What has happened is that many people interested in T.A. have developed activities to teach the concepts and have organized workshops to teach teachers about it. One of the better books on the subject for teachers is *T.A. for Kids* by Alvyn M. Freed. He has also written *T.A. for Tots,* aimed at the preschool child.

### Curriculum Materials

There are numerous commercial programs in affective education that a school can purchase and use. Many of the larger textbook companies have group guidance programs in this area, using student texts, filmstrips, records, puppets, and role-playing to teach students about getting along with others and understanding themselves. A comparison of three rather popular programs is contained in Table 1. Others include *Dimensions in Personality* (Pflaum); The Duso Materials; *Moods and Emotions* (David C. Cook Publishing Company); and the Peabody Language Program for primary youngsters. The problem with these materials is that without proper teacher training, they are used in the same way that has produced lists of "do bees" and "don't bees," subtly coercing students into the "right" way to feel and act. With proper teacher training these materials can be used effectively in an affective education program. One suggestion for companies selling these programs is to hire people to conduct affective education workshops and sell the materials. Holt, Rinehart, and Winston has done this with Bill Martin Jr., author of *The Sounds of Language* reading series, an "affective" approach to reading.

### SUMMARY

Affective education is affective education. You can use many different theoretical approaches, isolate one aspect of affective development, and focus on it (as in values education), or you can emphasize certain social processes over others. You can sit in a circle or a square, or have small groups or large groups, but it is all the same trip. Affective education is people figuring out together what it means to be a human being and learning how to be a better one. . . . It's telling kids what adults are afraid of. . . . It's figuring out a way to get big kids to stop bullying little kids. . . . It's sitting in a circle. . . . It's saying, "I feel angry when you throw your book," instead of "Billy, you are disturbing everyone. If you don't like what we are doing go to the office." . . . It's saying, "You feel like no one in the class likes you," instead of "No, Bill, I'm sure you're wrong. We like you—we like all the students." . . . It's acknowledging that kids have to know "who they are" before they can be concerned with "where they are." . . . It's treating kids the way you would treat guests in your home.

It is, most simply, a prescription for a certain kind of interaction between teachers and their students that emphasizes sharing, acceptance, responsibility, and interdependence.

It is *not*, by the way, playing junior psychologist . . . an invasion of privacy . . . tricking kids into being good . . . something to do on Friday at 3:00 p.m. because there is no construction paper . . . permissiveness in action . . . a substitute for classroom management . . . an attempt to make everybody alike . . . sensitivity training . . . a creative way to teach listening skills . . . this year's educational fad . . . an attempt to make teachers "buddies."

Educators have assumed that social and emotional development just

## Table 1 COMPARISON OF AFFECTIVE EDUCATION PROGRAMS

| TITLE | SRA—FOCUS ON SELF DEVELOPMENT | EDUCATION IN HUMAN BEHAVIOR (OJEMAN) | STECK-VAUGHN: HUMAN VALUES SERIES |
|---|---|---|---|
| **OBJECTIVES** | Three developmental programs: Stage One—Awareness (K-2) Stage Two—Responding (2-4) Stage Three—Involvement (4-6) The program emphasizes the child's understanding of self, others, and his environment. | A program designed to help children: 1. Understand why people act as they do. 2. Become more aware of feelings and ideas. 3. Experience vicariously the feelings and viewpoints of others. 4. To be able to understand, appreciate, and meet their developmental needs. | The most influential factor in the development of an individual's intellectual potential involves his attaining realistic self-esteem and respect for others in his attempts to satisfy his needs and wants. Done through: 1. Increased reading comprehension. 2. Vocabulary enrichment. 3. Instruction in moral practice and ethical standards. 4. Enhancement of the child's mental health. 5. Developing social skills. 6. Gaining awareness of the goal-directedness of human behavior. |
| **CONTENT** | Self-concept development, awareness of environment, socializing, sharing, problem-solving abilities, emotions, family relationships, group rights, justice, conflict. | Adjustment to school, feelings, making choices, meeting failure, seeing another's viewpoint, problem solving, accepting one's physical self, respect for others, and daydreaming. | Respect, power, wealth, and enlightenment, skills, well-being, rectitude, affection. |
| **METHOD** | Class or group discussions revolving around filmstrips, cassettes, stories, photo boards, artwork, and role-playing. | Discussions and role-playing based on narratives read by the teacher. Lesson plans are also provided for implementation of a casual approach in curriculum areas, such as social studies, language arts, etc. | Discussions based on story situations involving the character's experiences, similar to a basal reading program. |
| **GRADE** | K-6 | K-10 | K-6 |
| **COST** | Media Kits: $102-$116 25 Pupil Activity Books: $11-$12 | Teacher's Handbook: $3.50-$7.00 Pupil Books: $.90-$1.50 each | Teacher's Guide: $3.50 Pupil Texts: $106 for class of 30 |

happen. They expect eleven-year-old boys to lie about their true feelings and to engage in endless rounds of name calling and other put-downs. They have equated "behavior that is usual" with "normality." The idea of affective education is that social and emotional growth don't "just happen." They are learned, as reading is learned. Therefore, they can be taught. The activities in this book can be used to teach them.

Chapter 2 is a step-by-step plan for beginning to have awareness sessions with children.

Chapter 3 is the heart of the book. It contains the units I have developed to teach children about the stuff on the other side of the report card.

Chapter 4 goes into some detail to explain how I develop units in affective education and includes quite a bit of unrefined data for units yet to be developed.

Chapter 5 is the "what ifs" section. In it I consider some of the common problems that come up when leading awareness sessions, along with suggestions for dealing with them.

Chapter 6 talks about evaluating affective education programs.

Finally, a bibliography and a list of affective films are included as appendices.

# 2

# BEGINNING AWARENESS SESSIONS

If you have led group discussions for a year or more, the guidelines in this chapter will help remind you of the real reason you are doing certain things. If you are just beginning to lead awareness sessions, it is important that you read and reread these pages of instructions several times until you know exactly what these activities are for, what your role is, and how to help your group progress toward self-understanding. This chapter is designed to lead you by the hand through the transition period of beginning to teach kids how to be responsible.*

## YOU

The most important thing to remember as you begin to facilitate these group activities is that what happens in your group, the behavior of the boys and girls in your group, is primarily a function of *your* behavior. Sometimes it's difficult for us to believe that. Some of us begin with groups that are made up of children who are very highly motivated at the start, who respond very easily to our commands, and who look forward to the opportunity to talk to each other. Other groups begin with much more resistance to discussion on the part of the children. In both cases, however, if the groups are to make progress and begin to develop the attitudes that you hope they will, your behavior is crucial. It is not easy for a leader to consistently behave in ways that will allow the group to progress and grow in the development of positive attitudes. As you begin working with the group, you will probably err by being too strict or too permissive. It is difficult to learn just the right balance of openness, acceptance, and strictness that will result in helping the children to have meaningful experiences and really learn about themselves and others. It will take time for you to become comfortable as a group leader, especially if your normal classroom style is very different from the style described below. But that's O.K.—take the time. Start slowly and be successful.

## THE PURPOSE

You should have clearly in mind the overall purpose of your program. You should have in mind the long-term objectives of your group activities and the specific day-to-day objective for each experience. One of your constant jobs as a leader is to try to build in the continuity to the experiences so that each activity builds on the previous one toward your overall goals. This is not an easy task, but these directions are designed to help you master it. (If you don't know why you're doing something, don't do it.)

This program is based on one relatively simple idea: If children can be encouraged to participate in meaningful, enjoyable discussions and group activities with a trained teacher-leader as their guide, and if these discussions

---

*My experience tells me that anything new takes three weeks to become part of me—moving to a new house, changing jobs, using a new reading series, or leading groups. While some kids will respond right away, it will take three weeks for you and the class to be comfortable with this new way of relating.

encourage the children to talk about themselves, about getting along with each other, about growing up, about liking themselves, and about developing positive attitudes toward school and life in general, then eventually these children will develop positive self-concepts and become aware of their unique potentials as healthy human beings. They will learn how to get along with each other and, in the long run, will achieve more and behave better in school. In short, the group activities are designed to help them and *you* become happier.

## TWO MAIN SKILLS
With that overall purpose in mind, you should understand that in every group there are two things occurring at the same time. The first and most important thing that is going on is the process you are engaged in. This process consists of the accepting, but serious, interaction that is going on between you and the students and between the students and each other. Regardless of the activity, your attitude toward students should, as much as possible, be one of unconditional acceptance. By that I mean that you should try to develop the ability to accept unconditionally—without value judging, without looking shocked, and without looking overly pleased—every contribution a member makes. What you're trying to get across to the students by your acceptance of them is that they are O.K.—that you like them and accept them just as they are. If you're successful in developing this attitude of acceptance, the children will be much more likely to participate in the discussions and to talk freely about their real concerns—not to just try to snow you and tell you what they think you want to hear.

Another part of this process is listening. You model good listening by listening to the children. You should consistently try to provide this modeling for the children by your nonverbal messages to them—the way you sit, your facial expressions, your hand motions—as well as by your verbal interactions. You should be listening to what they say, and you should also be listening for feelings—for the things they are saying that aren't in the words they are using. The activities in this book have a built-in mechanism for giving children feedback that tells them they have been listened to. Whenever you have a remembering session in which you and the children remember what other people have said in the circle, you teach listening. You encourage the children to become good listeners by asking them to be aware of what their classmates are saying and to reflect back to their classmates, upon your cue, what they heard them say. These two skills of acceptance and listening are foundations for the entire program.

## RISK TAKING
You need to remember that every time a child says something in your circle he is taking a risk. He is taking the risk that what he says won't be accepted, that he will be laughed at, or that what he has to say will not be considered an important contribution.

The growth of each student, as well as of the group as a whole, will occur as students discover that they are able to risk more easily and more often in the group. As students progress in this way, they will be willing to discuss many things that, earlier, they would have been too suspicious or distrustful to discuss. They will know that during this class, if no other, they can tell their opinions and feelings without being ridiculed or ignored.

## SUBJECT MATTER

In addition to the process I just described, which is going on in the group regardless of what you are talking about, the group is also concerned with subject matter. The subject matter for these discussions is the lives of the students. I have attempted to spell out, very specifically, units of study in the areas of social and emotional development that deal with the relevant concerns of children in elementary school and junior high school. I've tried to come up with key ideas for cues upon which the students can do some serious thinking. These units of study have been organized so that, in most cases, they build on each other, enabling students to discuss, in gradually more sophisticated ways, issues related to growing up. I have attempted to outline the subject matter so that it can be easily followed.

## THE FIRST SESSION

You are going to be meeting with a group of children for the first time. You meet with them in a classroom, in a hall, in a learning center, in a closet, under a table, or on the lawn. As quickly and efficiently as you can, you get them seated in a circle. This circle could be on the floor or on chairs, but it has to be a circle—not an oval or a square. The reason for the circle is that everybody has equal status—all members of the circle can see and communicate with each other equally well. It is a closed, rather perfect communication system. If you are going to err on the first day, make it be in the direction of being too strict. Make sure that the children are in the circle and that they are quiet so they can hear initial directions and an explanation of what you are going to do.*

### Introducing the Group Concept

You must use your own style for introducing the idea of the group and getting it going, but the following suggestions have been tried many times and have been found to be successful for other teachers. If they feel good for you, use them. If they feel phony or inappropriate, use a different method.

### The First Activity

After the children are seated and quiet, say, "The group that we are sitting together in this morning will be meeting together like this for the whole year. Hopefully, during these discussions we can talk about interesting things and

---

*See page 26 for specific directions on using the inner-outer circle technique.

get to know each other better and just have an enjoyable, interesting discussion each day. We will probably have to develop some rules as we go along so that we can interact with each other. I'd like to start with just a few very simple rules and make sure you understand them before we go on.

"The first rule I want you to understand is that in this group, at all times, anyone can say anything he wants about what we are talking about and not get put down. By that I do not mean that it's O.K. to make fun of another person, to tease them, or to laugh at what they say if you don't agree with it or if you think it's silly. I'm going to be very strict in enforcing that rule and it is important to me that you understand that.

"A second thing that I think we have to have in our group is the understanding that everybody gets listened to. I'm going to be doing things in our group to show that we listen to each other, so I'll be asking you to remember what other people say. I would like for everyone to feel that whatever he says, we will listen to it. I certainly hope that you will listen to what I say.

"A third thing about our group is that everyone who wants a turn can have one. If time is a problem and five or ten people want to talk about the same thing, we may not be able to get to everyone that day; but I will try very hard to see to it that everybody that wants a turn gets one."

Following this kind of an introductory statement about the purpose of the group sessions, you might want to allow five or ten minutes of inter-action on the part of the students as a response to what you said. After enough appropriate comments have been made by the students, say the following: "Some of you right now may really like the idea of these discussions just based on what I've said, and some of you may at this point think that the whole idea is pretty dumb. What I would really like you to do is give it a chance.* I'd like you to give it a couple of weeks to really see what you can get out of it; try to participate with us and just watch what happens. At the end of that time we'll talk about our discussion and talk about what we like about it, what we don't like about it, and how we can make it better. It would be very important to me if each of you would make a promise to yourself that you will give this idea at least a couple of weeks before you make a decision on whether you like it or not. O.K.? O.K."

If time permits during this first session, follow your introduction with an easy-to-talk-about introductory topic like "something neat that happened to me over the weekend" or "something that makes me feel good." You might wish to end this circle the first day with an incomplete sentence. This technique is described elsewhere in the book, but you might take a sentence like "On Saturday mornings I like to . . ." or "If I were President I'd . . ." or "My favorite color is . . ." or "My favorite song is . . ." or "My favorite TV show is . . ." or "The dumbest commercial on TV is . . ." The reason for ending the session this way is to have the students going away laughing or just having a funny kind of feeling that what they did today was enjoyable.

*This statement probably isn't necessary below sixth grade.

They'll remember the directions and they'll remember that your overall tone was serious, but to the extent the children can identify the group as a fun kind of place to be, you will be able to get them into the process more quickly.

**Evaluate**

After the session, take a few minutes to think about what happened. See if you can evaluate how you looked to the students. Did you come on too strong? Were you too strict? Did you confuse them by trying to say too much? If you did get into the group process itself by talking about a topic, did you accept what was said without judging it? Did you reflect what you heard by giving it right back to the student after he said it or by having someone else give it back to him? Evaluate just these two things.

Another word of advice for you, especially if you're a new group leader, is to trust the cues and the activities that are outlined for you in the book. Eventually you will be developing your own style—you will have your favorite strategies that work for you, you will eliminate certain activities that just won't fit when you're doing a group, you will come up with new ways for interacting with kids, and you will come up with your own topics that you think really fit with the program. This is as it should be. But for the first four, five, or six months that you're doing this program, really try to follow the subject-matter cues that are laid out for you in the units. If you can concentrate on developing your process skills—your techniques as a group leader—and not worry about what to talk about in the circle, you will be able to improve those skills more quickly.

**THE SECOND SESSION**

You are now ready to meet with the same group a second time. At this point, it is very important that you learn the students' names. If you don't know their first names by now, make that your goal at the beginning of the second circle discussion. There are many ways to do it. One way that works for many people is to start by saying, "Today I would like to try to learn your names before I do anything else, so what I am going to do is go around the circle and say your names and try to connect them to each other in a string and see if I can go all the way around and remember them." Then start with the person on your left. Say, "What's your name? Bill? O.K., Bill. Next, Mary. O.K., Mary, Bill. Next, Susie. Susie, Mary, Bill. Next, Fred. Fred, Susie, Mary, Bill." Go all the way around the circle until you know all the names. Believe it or not, just the act of having their names said over and over again in the circle has a tremendous impact on the self-esteem of children. You will find them very happy, animated, and ready to go by the time you finish trying to learn their names.

The next important thing to do before you begin doing anything new is to remember what happened the last time you met.* Even though this is

*Beginning this way builds continuity into the group and will get them through the transition phase quicker.

only the second session, you already have a history with this group. You've spent twenty-five minutes with them and they have not forgotten it. So begin this part of the circle by saying, "Who can remember some of the things that were said the last time we met?" Make sure they raise their hands, call on them one at a time, and allow them to remember one or two things that were said. What you're after is something that you said or something another child said. It's not necessary, at this point, to have them remember everything, as long as three or four different children remember something and all of them seem to get back into the mood by remembering what it was like.

Then say, "How many of you have ever wished for something to happen or just wished that you had a certain thing or that you could go to a certain place?" (Some hands should go up as students think about your questions.) Today I am going to give you a chance to tell us something you would like to wish for." If no hands go up right away, share a wish you have. Expect someone to say, "I wish I had a million wishes." If someone does, laugh with him and then tell the group that that kind of wish is not fair. Watch the clock closely. Allow students to share wishes until there are just a few minutes left. Then have children remember what people said. Finish by going around the circle with this sentence stub: "I wish . . ."

One thing to remember at this point, and to keep in mind throughout the year, is that you should not usually begin a group discussion by saying, "Today's topic is . . ." This approach is cold and rigid, and it is easy for children to get uptight and tense when you introduce a topic this way. One of the most common problems of leading awareness groups with older children is getting them to talk, and a poor introduction technique is probably the main reason children find it difficult to talk. There are many ways to introduce a topic gently. I will describe just a couple here; elsewhere in this book other ways are described. Let's say the topic is "If I had three wishes . . ." You might begin by saying, "How many of you have ever wished for something so much that you thought about it all day long?" Ask for a raise of hands. Or you can say, "How many of you have ever wished for something and had your wish come true?" Then ask maybe a third question, very generally, and have them raise their hands in response. Following that, say, "Well, I was thinking today we might think about wishes and each of you could think of two or three things you would like to wish for—as long as one of the wishes is not 'I wish I had a million wishes.' Then, if you'd like to tell us about something you'd like to wish for, you can." Another way to introduce a topic, other than asking questions, is to just look puzzled about something and say, "You know, I was thinking," (let's say the topic is "something I do that bugs my parents") "that a lot of times I do little things at hime, or even at school, and I can tell it bothers other people. Like, I do this thing where I tap a pencil all the time—yes, just tap the pencil, tap the pencil, and I can tell that some of the people who are around me really get bothered by it. I was thinking that these little habits would be a good thing to talk about. I was wondering how many of you can think of something you do that, let's say, bugs your parents. Something that you do—not any big thing—that really bugs them. Who'd like to go first? Who'd like to talk about that?"

Another effective way to begin is with the unfinished sentence. With this method, you whip a sentence stub around the circle and then take the topic of the sentence whip and make it the discussion topic. For example, if you were to go around the circle and do a very quick whip, you might say, "Let's go all the way around the circle. I'll start. I would like you to finish this sentence. 'The worst kind of punishment I could ever give my child would be . . .' " Typical responses might be: "to not let him go out," "to beat him," or "to make him go to school on Saturday." Let all the kids respond to the stub. After everyone has done so, you say, "Let's think about that in a more general way. Think about the worst punishment you ever received and what it was like." Again, you're into the discussion, they've already talked about it, they've begun to think about it, and you haven't had to say, "Today's topic is . . ." Once you're into the circle discussion about today's topic, simplify your interaction with the group.* But make sure you take a turn—whatever the topic is, share something real and personal about your life. Before and after you've done so, be very aware of how you listen. Make sure that you listen to every person who shares. Make sure you reflect what each person has said or the essence of what he has said before you go on to another person. Also, make sure that, before the circle is over, you ask the children to remember what others have said. See to it that all children that participated that day are remembered. At this point in the group don't get anxious about whether everybody has participated. If half the group, or even slightly fewer, have participated, fine. The program builds slowly, and within a couple of weeks you'll have everybody, or almost everybody, participating on a regular basis.

**Evaluate Again**

Now that your second group session is finished, evaluate again. Continue to evaluate yourself on the two most important points. Were you able to accept what was said by the members with a minimum of valuing, either positive or negative, and did you model effective listening behavior throughout the circle? Those are the two most important leadership skills needed for the circle discussion process. Also, evaluate some very physical things. Were the students in a circle? How long did it take you to get them in a circle at the beginning of the meeting? Could you speed that up? Were you too strict? Were you too permissive? Did you allow too much cross-talking? Were there statements made by children that were ridiculing to others and that you allowed to go unchecked?

It will take time before you eventually eliminate all the negative things in the group and build the positive skills. You should be evaluating each dis-

---

*I emphasize the circle here because, regardless of the activity, you will end up processing it in a circle.

cussion for at least a few minutes to keep aware of where you're going with the process.

## THE THIRD SESSION

You're now ready to begin your third session with the children. What you're doing by the third session is really establishing a pattern of interactions that the kids will expect from now on and will look forward to. That pattern ought to have a beginning, during which you remember a few of the things that were talked about the previous day to connect what you're doing today with what you did. It involves an introduction into today's area of concern, which may consist of questions from students, a sentence stub, an informal story on your part, or whatever you decide to use to introduce it. It will then involve the body of the group activity, which is the contributions of the members and the attention of the other members and of the teacher to what is being said. This is followed by the ending of the group, which usually involves, once again, remembering what was said and done that day and often by some kind of summarizing statement by the teacher about the meaning of it all. For example, if you have just had a discussion about "something I used to be afraid of but am not any longer" and it was apparent that many of the children used to be afraid of the dark but are not anymore, you might say, "It sounds to me today like many of the people used to be afraid of the dark but aren't anymore. That's probably part of growing up—that we become less afraid of some things and more afraid of things that could really hurt us. For example, as little kids none of you were afraid of cars, but today many of you are afraid of getting killed in a car accident. You ought to be afraid of that because it is a very real possibility. Hopefully, being afraid of it will encourage all of us to wear seat belts. They make our fears less likely to be realized."

To begin the third session, spend five minutes remembering what was done during the first two sessions. Focus on having the contributions of specific members restated. You are teaching them that others will not forget what they say. Introduce the topic for today by saying, "Think about something someone does that bugs you. Maybe it's a little thing someone does, like turning the TV channel knob, or taking your hat, or making a face. I'll share mine first." Then share something someone does that bugs you. Spend ten to fifteen minutes eliciting stories concerning all the different things that bug the group members. Concentrate on accepting their statements without judging them and reflect back the essence of what they say. Listen for the feelings expressed by each person and respond to them, if possible.

When five minutes are left, recap all responses. Make sure everyone has been remembered. Tell those who didn't get a chance to talk that you will be sure to get to them next time. Thank all the group members for their participation.

## THE FOURTH SESSION

The purpose of this session is to build a positive group feeling, and to encourage a sense of sharing among group members. Begin this session by passing out to each student the activity form, "This Is Me." Tell students that today's activity will invilve filling out the form. Say, "I'd like you to take five or ten minutes to fill out this form as well as you can." After all group members have filled it out, tell them to form dyads (groups of two) to discuss their forms. Allow each group of two to spend ten to fifteen minutes sharing. Bring the whole group back together for the last few minutes. Have each student tell one new thing he has learned about his partner from this activity. Another way to have students introduce their partners is by saying three or four adjectives that

# THIS IS ME

Name _____    Address _____

Height _____    Color of Hair and Eyes _____

Do you have any brothers or sisters?

_____

   How many? _____

   How old are they? _____

What is your favorite TV show?

_____

What is your favorite thing to eat?

_____

What games do you like to play?

_____

_____

_____

What is your favorite song?

_____

Do you have any hobbies?

_____

_____

_____

What is your favorite color? _____

What are your favorite books?

_____

_____

_____

Do you have a pet? _____ If so, what is it? If not, what kind would you like?

_____

_____

_____

What is your favorite movie?

_____

If you could go anywhere in the world, where would you go?

_____

Where have you gone on a trip that you liked?

_____

_____

What are two things you believe in?

_____

_____

describe him. Even more interesting: "If my partner were a color he'd be . . ."
If my partner were a car he'd be . . ." Spend the last few minutes discussing
the forms in the large group.

## TYPICAL PROBLEMS

As you continue to lead the activities, you will encounter two typical problems that you will constantly be dealing with. One of these is the withdrawn
child—the child who won't participate, the child who doesn't seem to be
part of the group. The second problem is the disruptive child—the child who
has a tendency to put down other children, who wants to get all the attention
all the time. In this introduction I will describe very briefly what to do with
those problems. Later on, in Chapter 5, there are some more instructions for
dealing with the specific problems of withdrawn children and disruptive
children.

### The Withdrawn Child

There are probably as many ways to draw out withdrawn children as there are
group leaders. The first way is to involve him nonverbally. Indicate by where
you sit that you know he's there. For example, sit next to him, touch him
occasionally, look at him, and smile. Following someone's contribution to
the group you might look at the shy child and nod, signifying, "We both
heard that" by your look. These signs of nonverbal support can very subtly
give the message: "It's O.K.—if you feel like talking, I'll protect you." That,
by itself, can do the job.

Another way to involve the withdrawn child is to call on him to remember what others have said. Sometimes children don't participate because
they fear the sound of their own voice or they don't know how it will sound.
If you give them something to say, some task they can handle—like remembering what's just been said—they can know that what they're saying is
right. Whey they have finished, praise them for it. You might say something
like, "Boy, you really remembered—you remembered what Billy said. Thank
you." That kind of interaction can get them more involved in the group.

Another technique that can be used with the withdrawn child, if the
topic is appropriate (like "three wishes" or "the time I had a good feeling"),
is to have someone else guess what the child's response would be. If you
know there is someone in the circle who is the child's close friend, or who
at least knows him well, you might ask, "May I have [friend's name] guess
what would make you feel good?" or ". . . what you would wish for?" or
". . . what you like about school?" or ". . . what bugs your mother"? If
the child says yes, then ask his friend to try to guess what the answer
would be. The only concern you have here is that the person who does the
guessing be seriously trying to guess and not trying to say something funny
to get attention. Following the guess, you can ask the shy child whether it's
right, and if he says yes, you can either ask him to tell you more about it or
you can just say, "O.K., very good."

## The Disruptive Child

The disruptive child, in class as well as in the circle, gets much more attention than the other children. Often, that is just what the child wants, and by giving him this attention you can reinforce his actions, encouraging him to continue behaving in this manner. The point of the group is to try to encourage the disruptive child to behave in a different manner. Again, there are many ways to handle this kind of child. The simplest, and most specific, is to ignore negative behavior and reward positive behavior. To the extent that it is possible, ignore the negative asides and comments of the disrupter, but reward him when he does or says anything that is supportive, helpful, and contributing to the circle. Eventually the child will realize, "I'm not getting attention when I do bad things but I am getting attention, and plenty of it, when I do the right thing." He will then be less likely to be disruptive.

Sometimes, however, the reward method doesn't work—sometimes you just can't ignore his negative behavior. When this is the case, there are other things you can do. When someone is contributing to the circle in a positive way and someone else is behaving disruptively at the same time, it is very apparent to the group. A good way to handle this situation is to deal nonverbally with the needs of the disrupter while you continue to keep the focus of the circle on the child who is sharing. It is important to remember that everything a child does in the circle springs out of his feelings about himself. It is very possible the child who is disrupting the circle is trying to say in his own way, "I don't think you really accept me," or "I don't think I'll get a turn," or "I don't think I'll get attention in this group, even though you said I would, and I need more proof." What you need to do is give him that proof without rewarding his negative behavior. What you might do is look at the child, open your hand, touch him, and indicate, "Hey, calm down. I see you. I'll get to you. Stay with us for a while and everything will be O.K.," without really saying it out loud. You can also ask the disruptive child to move from where he is sitting and sit next to you, or you might move your seat next to him. Then you can make closer physical contact with that child.

If you have to stop the ongoing activity to deal with this disruptive influence, it is important that you say something like, "Hey, I really want to hear what you're saying, but something is happening right now that I have to deal with. Just hold on for a minute; we'll be right back to you." Don't do that all the time but, if you have to do it, make sure then that you really deal in a confronting but gentle way—with the negative behavior.*

If you stop the circle to deal with negative behavior, you might say to the whole group, "What happened right now?" Then let the people in the group raise their hands and say what happened—let them name the disruptive behavior: "Billy laughed." "Billy shouted out." "Billy hit Tommy." "Mary hit Bill." If Billy is the problem, and the group has just named his behavior,

*The worst possible way to deal with negative behavior is to nag—to say "stop that" or "shut up" over and over without following through.

you might look at him and say, "Yes Billy, did you hear that?" As he responds say, "O.K., can we go on now?" Get him to say, "Yeah, O.K., you can go on." Try to avoid preaching, try to avoid giving lectures to individuals. If this approach is coupled with the physical approach (in which you sit close to him), you should be able to eliminate the disruptive behavior.

You might want to ask the person who is causing the disturbance to stay after class so you can talk to him. Make it clear that the point is not punishment but that you would like to talk to him about what happened in the circle. Then do talk to him. When you talk, try to get him to respond on a private basis about where his behavior is coming from and what is happening to make him behave in this manner. See if you can work out a contract to get him to change his behavior.*

As a group leader, your ultimate weapon when dealing with disruptive behavior is to ask the child to leave the group for that day. Remember, though, it is much more important *how* you ask him to leave than whether you do it or not. It is quite possible to ask a child to leave a group and have him like it—have him go away feeling really good about himself. However, it is also possible to ruin any chance for developing rapport. It is best to make it clear to the child that you like him and that you really like it when he participates in the circle and does the right thing, but that you can't handle it when he does certain things. Let him know that it is just not possible for you to continue as a leader when he behaves in a disruptive way and that you're asking him to leave because you have tried other things and they haven't worked.

You should have a specific place established where he can go—to the office, to another part of the room, to another room—but it should be someplace very clear to him. You say, "I'd like you to go there, and whenever you think you can behave in the circle and within the rules of the circle, you can come back. You can come back tomorrow. If you come back then, I will assume that you know what your return means." What you really are saying to the child, in every one of these interactions, is, "You're O.K., your being in the circle is O.K., and your contributing is O.K., but sometimes you do things that aren't O.K. If you eliminate those things, then you can participate in the activities."

Another simple technique for dealing with disruptive behavior is to name it yourself. Instead of threatening ("If you don't stop that I'll . . ."), say, "Billy, you're laughing at me," "Billy, you're punching Tom," or "Billy, you're shouting." Just naming the behavior, without judging it, can have a therapeutic effect. Believe it—use it in the classroom. You don't have to threaten or preach. Just let the child know, "I see you, I see what you're doing." Then reward the child when he does acceptable things.†

---

*The steps of reality therapy work very well here: (1) Ask him what he was doing. (2) Ask if it is helping. (3) Together, make a plan not to do it anymore. (4) Make a commitment—no excuses. (5) Let him know you won't punish (reject) him.
†Janet Lederman's great book *Anger in the Rocking Chair* develops this technique much further.

# QUESTIONING TECHNIQUES IN THE CIRCLE

The kinds of questions the teacher asks can get one child to go into an experience and to think about it more seriously, or they can get a whole group to examine something more deeply. Questioning can have a helpful or negative effect on the group. The main axiom is: Avoid all questions that might make children feel defensive or feel that they have to justify what they did. In almost all situations questions that ask *why* do that. There are some times when you can ask a why question without making a child feel defensive, but generally this is not the case. Try to avoid questions that begin with why—especially if a child is talking about a feeling. People don't always know why they have certain feelings—they just have them. The point of these sessions is to get the kids to know that it's O.K. to have feelings, both good and bad ones.

Open-ended questions encourage the child to go further into the experience. Some of the stock questions are:

1. Would you like to tell us more about that?
2. What was it like for you when such and such was happening?
3. Was that feeling all good?
4. Was that feeling all bad?
5. Were there good and bad feelings mixed together?

Try not to give the child the feeling that he is being grilled.

Another good questioning technique, which is really a part of the listening technique as well, is to simply respond to the child's statement by saying something like, "You really sounded excited when you told that," "You seem to have really felt strongly about that," or "It sounds to me like you have never really gotten over that bad thing." Again, by reflecting back you're opening the door to the child and saying to him, "If you want to talk more about it, we are going to listen to you."

Clarifying questions, which ask the child to clarify an experience or feeling in his own mind, are important. Examples of clarifying questions are:

1. What did you do when that happened?
2. What led up to that experience?
3. Is there any other reason he might have said or done that?
4. Do you think many people feel that way?
5. How do you know that is a good feeling?
6. Have you felt that way for a long time?
7. If you were older (younger), a boy (a girl), would that have happened?
8. Was it your decision to do that?
9. What would have been the situation if such and such had happened?
10. What must you assume, believe, or accept in order to do that?
11. Do any of you have any questions you'd like to ask Bill?

## GETTING MORE HELP

It takes a year to become really comfortable leading awareness sessions. If you have another teacher working with you, support the hell out of each other. Give each other feedback. Keep track of strategies that have worked. If you have access to some kind of workshop training, get it. Refer to Chapter 5 for help with some common problems. Have your own "What if" sessions with others who are using the activities and add to the list. And most of all, *trust your feelings* about what is appropriate.

If you are trying to conduct these awareness sessions with thirty students, you might want to try using the inner-outer circle technique, described next.

## GUIDELINES FOR USING THE INNER-OUTER CIRCLE TECHNIQUES

Once the decision has been made to work with students in a group discussion, the problem shifts to one of getting started. The problem of arranging the class physically and getting the students "ready" for the experience is an important one. Too often we just begin and then get discouraged when our great ideas get bogged down in ticky-tacky details. The first point about group discussions is that they are no replacement for good classroom management techniques or for classroom discipline. As teachers, we are constantly grouping students for instruction. Arranging the class for the group discussion is no different except that the particular kind of arrangement may be new to them. The inner-outer circle technique can and does work with elementary-school students. In fact, among many different methods that have been tried for working with large groups, the inner-outer circle method has proved the most effective. Following are the specific steps that should be taken if you desire to get your class going on group discussions.

### Day 1    Whole-Class Orientation

1.  Explain that tomorrow you are going to begin discussions, involving the whole class, about things that are important to you. Say, "The first couple of days we are going to be concentrating on how the group will work. We will do that until everyone is able to understand how to participate in the discussions."
2.  Add anything that is appropriate for your particular group.

### Day 2    Getting into the Group

1.  Tell the class the following: "today we are going to be starting our group discussions. Will the following students please sit with me over here in a circle?" (Make sure there is room. The floor or chairs will do.) "The following people will sit in a larger circle around the smaller one." (Name all the remaining class members and don't go on until everyone is seated

properly.) "The job of the inner-circle people today will be to think about the topic we discuss and to tell what you feel about it. The job of the outer circle is to *listen* carefully to what is said, to think about what you would say about the topic, and to observe what is going on in the inner circle."

2. Have each person in the inner circle introduce himself and tell something he likes to do, like swimming or watching TV.
3. Ask people in the outer circle to remember what was said.
4. Rememberers should call the person by name and say something like "I remember Mary said she liked swimming."
5. Thank the rememberer in some way and then call on another student. To be called on, a student must raise his hand. Only one student talks at a time.
6. After all the inner-circle people have been remembered, have the groups switch places. Repeat the same procedure for the new group. End the circle.

## Day 3  Reviewing the Rules and Starting Slowly

1. Ask the students to review the rules for conducting the discussion. Also ask the students to explain the procedures for getting into the group.

2. Today have the kids who were in yesterday's outer circle be inside first. Don't start the discussion until everyone is seated properly.

3. Start by having some outer-circle students remember what some people said yesterday.

4. Introduce the concept of the open space or open chair. Tell the group, "We are going to leave an open space in the inner circle. It is for a visitor from the outer circle who wants to share an experience with us and just can't wait until his group is inside. If you want to share, you may quietly get up from your place and sit in the empty space. I will know you have something and I will call on you as soon as I can. After you have your turn, you may quietly get up and go back to your place in the outer circle." (Have several students practice getting up and coming into the inner circle until you feel they all understand the procedure.)

5. Today do a very simple topic, like "If I had one wish . . ." Make sure you ask the outer circle to remember what the wishes were. If time permits, have the groups switch after about ten minutes and repeat the process.

## Day 4  Finally Getting into the Process, Maybe

1. Ask class members to review the rules of conducting the discussion and for getting into the circle. Ask them whether they think they are ready to get more into the discussions or whether they need to concentrate more on the procedure. If they indicate they are ready to go, ask the people who were in the inner circle on the first day (group A) to form the inner circle as quickly as possible. After the inner circle is set, ask the outer circle (group B) to get into its group.

2. Make sure you leave the open space for the outer-circle people to come in.

3. Start by remembering a few of the wishes from yesterday; then introduce the first topic from the program.

4. After about three people have shared on the topic, stop and ask the outer circle to remember what they said. (When you do this, you are reinforcing the outer circle as an integral part of the process.)

5. If no one comes from the outside to the open space, ask them to think about why. Encourage someone who would like to come in but who might be shy about standing up and being watched.

6. Make certain that all those who share are remembered. Summarize the discussion by commenting on what you heard people saying today. An example of what you might say is, "I heard many people telling things that make them feel good. Some, like Bill and Carl and I, feel good doing sports, while others like to be alone. It's nice that we feel good doing so many different things."

7. Before you quit, ask them whether they thought it went well today.

## Day 5  Into the Process

1. Today start with group B in the inner circle. After they are seated ask group A to get into the outer circle. This will be the regular set-up—alternating on different days.
2. Don't use the same topic as yesterday. Go on to the second topic in the program. Start by remembering some of what was said yesterday.
3. Remember the open chair or space.

## GENERAL GUIDELINES

1. If your class is seated in a large circle for the regular class, it is much easier to get them seated for the discussion. All you have to do is have the inner group come down to the floor in the middle of the room.
2. Make sure that students who are potential discipline problems are separated from one another as much as possible.
3. Each day you should sit someplace different—one day next to a discipline problem, the next day by a withdrawn child, and so forth.
4. Try to let vocal students know, by sending a nonverbal signal (a nod, a glance, or a smile), that you will give them attention.
5. IT TAKES TIME—especially with older students, who find it difficult to trust adults. Don't be surprised if it takes a month before everyone really feels comfortable with the whole idea. It will happen.
6. During the first several weeks, be very conscious of students who are testing the limits and who are ready, but reluctant, to jump into the group without an invitation. This will happen a lot in the beginning. Some students will test the limits by making inappropriate comments. Always appeal to the highest motives of the students, not the lowest. Tell a student who makes an inappropriate comment that you don't think he really meant to say it. If he persists—accept it.
7. Make sure you are a participant as well as a leader.
8. No discussion should end without summarizing what has been said. Sometimes the summary will be the most important part of the discussion, and sometimes it will be unimportant, but always do it.
9. Every few days, ask students to evaluate what is happening in the discussion.

Feel free to modify these rigid directions for getting started. Possible modifications:

1. Allow outer-circle people to participate directly from where they are without having to come into the inner circle.
2. Have outer-circle members observe certain people and give feedback on what they see.
3. Have students talk without raising their hands.

The circle is an accepting environment, but destructive behavior, such as ridicule or overt disruption, should not be accepted or allowed to continue. Leaders can deal with the needs of disrupters while keeping the focus on the individuals positively participating. If a leader gets maneuvered into dealing with negative attention-getting, the others may decide that's the best way to get attention. Leaders should try to deal with the interrupter's feelings non-verbally. It usually helps to speak directly to the child about his actions—to try to make him aware of his motives while avoiding analysis or harsh punishment.

If these techniques have no immediate effect, remind the disrupter that his presence is desired but that his disruptive behavior will not be accepted. He may remain as a part of the group, but his misbehavior must leave. If he can separate his negative behavior from the group, he stays; if he can't, they both leave. After the group, talk to the student and let him know you want him in the group. The goal is always to get the student back into the group as soon as possible.

Students are so anxious for an opportunity to communicate with their teachers and peers that seldom will they continue to disrupt a circle discussion. Shortly, the discussions will be so widely accepted by students that peer pressure will prevent most disruptions.

# 3

# THE
# UNITS

This chapter consists of twenty-four awareness units. Most of the units are built around a theme or concern that is meaningful to elementary-school children. A few of the units are centered around concerns of teachers. If you begin using this program and follow the directions closely, it will take you about a year to complete the units. All of the units contained here have been used with real-live kids at least once. Some have worked well—the sensory awareness one, for example; and a couple need some help—the study skills one, for example.

These units represent my ideas for actualizing affective education. I can make these units work as they are. You may have to change them to make them work for you. Go with your feelings about the appropriateness of an activity. Most of the activities are just gimmicks to generate data anyway. The important part of the program is the *real* encounter between you and your class as you discuss what happened. A few other hints on beginning this program:

(1) Trust the process. Time is the only variable. If your overall classroom climate encourages trust and openness and shared decision making, the activities will go better. (2) Don't assume that kids who aren't active aren't involved. People have their own styles of participation. Kids grow at different rates—let them be. Always give kids the real option to pass. (3) If you aren't sure of an activity, try it on your friends first. Make sure you have support before you get seriously into these activities. (4) Share of yourself—a lot. (5) If people want to come in and see what's going on, first ask the kids. Second, make the visitors get involved. (6) Keep a personal diary of how each session goes. Later you can publish it. (7) Remember, the real content of these activities is the people involved. Be prepared to chuck an activity when something here and now requires it. (8) Read *The Geranium on the Windowsill Just Died but Teacher You Went Right On* by Albert Cullum.

Have fun. If these sessions aren't fun, forget it.

# FRIENDSHIP

## Objectives
Students will:

a.  Analyze how people make friends.
b.  Take a stand on how they feel as friends.
c.  Identify the most important qualities in a friend.
d.  Compare their own qualities to those of an ideal friend.

## Activity 1
*Purpose:* To introduce the concept of friendship in the group; to begin to identify what friends are.

*Process:* After students are seated in a circle and are ready to begin, ask them the following questions:

1.  How many of you have a best friend?
2.  How many of you have a friend now that you used to not like?
3.  How many of you have a good friend of the opposite sex?
4.  How many of you have had a fight or argument with a friend recently?
5.  How many of you have a brother or sister who is also your friend?

Tell the students to vote "yes" by raising their hands and "no" by putting their thumbs down. After they have responded to your questions, say, "For the next several sessions, we are going to be thinking and talking about friends. Right now I'd like you to close your eyes for a minute and think of someone who is now or who used to be a friend." (Make sure they close their eyes.) After about twenty-five seconds say, "Who would like to tell us about a friend and about how you know this person is your friend?"

The main discussion is now on, and you should try to keep it in the area of telling about a friend: how the kid knows his friend is a friend, how they met, and so forth. Reflect back the contributions as they are made to you. Watch the clock, and when there are five minutes left, cut off the discussion and ask the students to remember what others have said. (Have noncontributors do the remembering.) If you have a minute left at the end, have the kids whip the following sentence stub around the circle: "A friend is . . ."

Tell them as they leave that you will be talking more about friends next time.

## Activity 2

*Purpose:* To become aware of how we make friends.

*Process:* Begin today's lesson by saying, "Who remembers what we did the last time we met?" Encourage five or six comments about the previous session, then say, "Today we are going to think about friends in a different way than before. I want you to think about a friend who you have now or used to have and remember when you first met. Was it an accident? Did you start it? Did the other person? Think of other things like this."

As students share their stories, encourage them to talk about what they did to develop the friendship. Ask them if any risk was involved. To involve reluctant members, call on them by saying, "Billy, can you name a person who is your friend or who used to be?" After he answers, say, "Tell me how you met—what season it was, how long ago, and so on."

Make certain that you leave time to remember what has been said. Before the students leave, summarize what has been said about meeting friends. For example: "Most of us seemed to meet our friends in the summer," or "It seems we usually met our friends accidentally."

## Activity 3

*Purpose:* To establish personal priorities for qualities in a friend.

*Process:* Begin the lesson by having five or six students remember what was discussed at the previous session. Then say, "Today I want you to think about what is the most important quality in a friend. I will name three qualities and you decide how you would rank them: generosity, loyalty, and honesty."

Call on different members to tell their ranking and ask them to explain
why they ranked them that way. Discuss the ranking for ten or fifteen minutes,
then say, "O.K., everyone stand up." Point to one place in the room and say,
"If you think you are more loyal than honest, go stand there. If you think
you are more honest than loyal, go stand there." (Make sure the spaces are
not too far apart.) Pretend you have a microphone and ask a couple of people
in each group, "Excuse me, sir, why are you here?" Get a few opinions and
then have them sit down in the circle again. Spend the last five minutes remembering what has been said. Summarize the ranking by saying how many
felt a certain way.

**Activity 4**

*Purpose:* To encourage group members to look at themselves through the eyes of others.

*Process:* Each person should have a piece of scrap paper or a 3 × 5 card. Begin by remembering what happened last time, then say, "On the paper, write the name of your best friend in the world right now. Under his or her name, write three words that end in 'able' that you think describe your friend." After they do so, ask whether anyone would like to share his words. Discuss this for ten minutes at most, then say, "Somewhere on your paper write your name; under it make four columns. In column one write BF. Under that heading list three words ending in 'y' that your best friend would use to describe you." Give them thirty seconds. "Next, write WE in the second column. List three words ending in 'able' that your worst enemy would say about you. In column three, write TEACH, for your favorite teacher, and write three words ending in 'ing' that he or she would really use to describe you. In column four, write ME, and list three words that you think describe you." Spend any remaining time reading and comparing lists.

**Activity 5**

*Purpose:* To synthesize the past four discussions into thoughts about ideal friends.

*Process:* You will need one felt marker and one piece of butcher paper five feet long. Begin by asking for a volunteer to lie down on the paper. You or someone should draw the outline of his body on the paper. After you have the outline made, tell the group, "We have here the outline of the perfect friend. I want you to think about what the perfect friend would be like. I will write words and sentences on different parts of the outline. I will start, to give you the idea. I think the perfect friend should have a good sense of humor and I'll draw a happy face on the outline. Use your own imagination to complete the outline."

If you have enough paper, allow students to pick partners and do the activity in pairs, taking turns outlining bodies and then helping each other fill in the drawings. If you do it this way, put up the finished outlines around the room.

Some ideas:

1. Draw a line down the center and make half a boy friend and half a girl friend.
2. Put feeling words by the heart.
3. Put thoughts and ideas by the brain.
4. Put things he can do by the hands and feet.

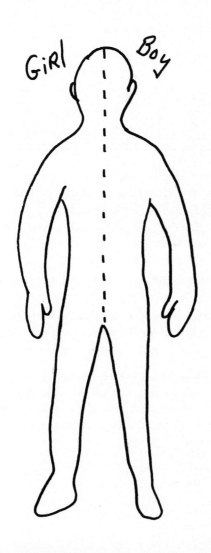

**Objectives**
Students will:

a. Accept that fear is a universal human problem.
b. Distinguish between realistic and unrealistic fears.
c. Identify fears they have overcome.
d. Establish a plan for overcoming at least one inappropriate fear.

**Activity 1**
*Purpose:* To experience a fantasy trip; to prepare for a series of discussions about fear.
*Process:* Begin the discussion by asking students if they know what a fantasy trip is. Tell them that today they are going to take a fantasy trip. Tell them to relax as much as possible and then lead them on the following trip:

> "Close your eyes. . . . Go back to a time when you were little . . . when you were very, very happy. Maybe you'll go back to just one day . . . or you might picture a summer or a whole year. Go there and feel what it is like to be there. Be aware of the things you see, hear, and smell. Just stay there for awhile."

Give them two minutes. Then say, "You can open your eyes whenever you wish." Have the group members discuss their childhood experiences for the rest of the session. Make sure you use the last five minutes to remember what was said.

(*CAUTION: Occasionally a child will have had a very negative early child-hood. Do this activity after you have gotten to know the students well.*)

## Activity 2

*Purpose:* To become aware that all of us have many realistic fears; to intervene into the delusion of the uniqueness of fears that bother many students.

*Process:* Begin the session by asking the following questions: How many of you are afraid of heights? Worry about dying? Are careful about eating uncooked meat? Wear seat belts? (Add your own additional questions.) Then say that today's discussion topic is "a fear I have that I am glad about." You may have to give examples to get students started. As they share their fears, ask them whether they think the fears are realistic. Do they hope that their children will be afraid of the same thing? On some examples that might be questionable, ask the whole group whether they think the fear is reasonable or unreasonable. For example, if a child says he is afraid of large, unchained, vicious-looking dogs, that is quite reasonable; but if he is afraid of all dogs, that might not be reasonable or realistic. Accept every contribution without judgment, but let the group members give their evaluations as well. Spend the last few minutes remembering.

## Activity 3

*Purpose:* To increase awareness of unrealistic fears.

*Process:* After you rehash yesterday's discussion, tell students that today's topic is "something I'm afraid of." Let them know that it takes courage to talk about something you are afraid of, and model the kind of interaction you want by going first. As they share fears, help them become aware that many of us share the same fears and that it is O.K. to be afraid of something, even if you think the fear is silly. It is important, however, to be honest with yourself about what your fears are. (If you share first, and more than once, you will be modeling the kind of risk taking required.)

## Activity 4

*Purpose:* To publicly confirm our own fear concept; to increase our awareness of how we overcome fears.

*Process:* Put a long line on the board, and for end points use Fraidy Cat Freddie and Fearless Fosdick. Use your and student imaginations to describe the extremes. Ask for volunteers to put themselves up on the board. When at least half have done so, get the rest involved by asking how many are more fearful than (pick the person nearest the center) and how many are less fearful than (same person for the rest of the discussion). Ask them to discuss "something I used to be afraid of and now I am not" or "something my little brother or sister is afraid of that I am not." Encourage generalizations about changing fears: "Why I'm not afraid of certain things any more."

**Activity 5**

*Purpose:* To complete the unit on fear; to identify action steps to overcome fears.

*Process:* Continue the previous discussion, and when the students are done, tell them that they are a panel of fear experts who are going to discuss the best way for overcoming a certain fear. You can make up examples and discuss them, or you can let kids use fears they have right now that they can't overcome. If they don't bring up the idea of confronting fears, then you should bring it up. Some common examples for discussion are: fear of tests, fear of the dark, fear of animals, fear of dying, fear of being laughed at, fear of heights, fear of water, and fear of closed-in spaces.

Everyone has fears, but some fears become serious even though the real risk is not serious. These fears are called phobias. Some common phobias are listed below. Encourage students to make up phobia names for their own special fears.

Some common phobias:

aerophobia—fear of high places
agoraphobia—fear of open spaces

algophobia—fear of pain
astraphobia—fear of storms (thunder and lightning)
claustrophobia—fear of closed places
hemophobia—fear of blood
mypaphobia—fear of guns
monophobia—fear of being alone
nyctophobia—fear of darkness
ochlophobia—fear of crowds
pathophobia—fear of disease
pyrophobia—fear of fire
zoophobia—fear of animals

## Additional Activities

1. Have students define names of phobias.
2. Make up a phobia, name it, and describe it.
3. Trust fall. Pick a friend and let him catch you as you fall backward with your eyes closed. Discuss how it felt.
4. Discuss fears of blind people, invalids, and so forth.
5. Role-play: falling, facing a phobia, a roller-coaster ride, a practical joke.
6. Make two lists of fears—fears you would openly admit and fears that are secretive. Compile and share.
7. List various emotions. Pose situations, then have students express each emotion involved.
8. Provide each student with cards for several emotions. Pose situations, and have students hold up cards showing each emotion they feel and explain why they feel that way.
9. Get a record of Halloween-type sounds (no words or music). As the class listens, write down sounds, then the types of fears they suggest.
10. Become someone else's fear and act it out.
11. Divide the class, grouping and regrouping according to the fears they possess.
12. Show films: *"Run," "A Night On Bald Mountain," "Occurrence at Owl Creek Bridge."*

## Additional Discussion Topics

How do you feel when you're afraid?
A time someone scared me.
A time I dared someone and they got hurt.
A time I scared someone else.
A time I didn't do something because I was afraid.
A time I was afraid to do something but did it anyway.
A time I was afraid and people made fun of me.
A time I wasn't afraid and should have been.

Things I should be afraid of.
Something I'm afraid of but shouldn't be.
A fear I have overcome.
A fear I have not overcome.
A time I was afraid of something new.
A time I was afraid of another person.
Things that scare me that aren't real.
What I do when I'm afraid.
A time when I like to be scared (Haunted houses, roller coasters).
I am afraid when . . .
My worst fear is . . .
Some people fear . . .
Fears I have during the night, but not in the day.
I am not ashamed of fearing . . .
I used to be afraid of —— but now I'm not.
Some unreasonable fears are . . .
These fears are reasonable because . . .
One fear I cannot outgrow.
A fear I pretend I don't have, but I really do.
When I forced myself to —— I was no longer afraid

## Objectives

Students will:

a. Identify pleasurable and unpleasurable sensory experiences.
b. Increase awareness of common sensory pleasures shared by others.
c. Become sensitive to how it would feel to be without particular senses.
d. Discuss how communication is affected by retelling stories.
e. Become aware that perception is different for each person.
f. Learn how each sense contributes to knowledge of reality.
g. Experience staying in the here and now.
h. Develop a greater respect for their own sensory powers.

## Activity 1

*Purpose:* To become aware of the importance of using our senses; to practice focusing on individual senses and sharpening our ability to use our senses.

*Process:* Because this is the beginning of a ten-session unit on sensory awareness, you should start slowly. Begin the session by talking about the senses in general. Give each person two sheets of paper and tell him that for the whole session he is to sit quietly some place in the room and make a list of his ten favorite things to see, hear, smell, taste, and touch. (If a student finishes, he should list five or ten things he hates to see, hear, smell, taste, or touch.)

Spend the session completing your own list, and collect the completed lists before the students leave. (File the lists in the folders you have for each child.)

### Activity 2
*Purpose:* To experience increased dependence on hearing, smell, and touch; to experience dependency and control in a safe environment.
*Process:* You will need to have blindfolds for all the group members. Begin the session by explaining the reason for a blind walk and asking for the group's help in making it work. Have the group line up in two lines facing each other. Pick one line to be blind first and give the members blindfolds. After they are

all blind, tell the sighted people to pick a partner, but not necessarily the one across from them. The directions are: for five minutes the blind person is to be led around by the sighted one. (There can be no talking and no peeking.) Either the room or the hall can be used as the area for the walk. (Go outside, if possible.) Tell the leaders to try to give the blind person as many sensory experiences as possible. After five minutes, quietly stop them and bring them back. Get them back in line facing each other and have the leaders mix up so that the blind people won't know who their leaders were. Don't allow any discussion at this point. Give the blindfolds to the former leaders and have them put them on. Follow the same process as before. No talking and no peeking. Make sure students understand that they are not to push or trick each other during the activity.

After five minutes have passed and the group members have come back to the starting point, tell them to sit down. Allow members to discuss the blind walk. Allow people to make statements only about their own experience. No analyzing, guessing leaders, and so on. You might force them into cooperating by telling them they can only make statements that begin with I felt, I heard, I smelled, I tasted, or I thought. After they have run out of statements, ask them to discuss "what it would be like to be blind all the time."

## Activity 4
*Purpose:* To experience an entire discussion as a blind person would.
*Process:* Begin this session by having several students remember what happened yesterday. Tell them that you have decided it might be interesting to conduct an entire discussion as blind persons. Everyone is to be blindfolded for the entire period. After the blindfolds are in place, pick a topic to discuss. Members will have to decide on how to conduct the discussion. They might want to talk about blindness or about being in the dark or maybe just about favorite TV shows. Use your imagination to think of things to discuss. When three or four minutes are left, take off the blindfolds and discuss the experience. (Encourage students to write in their diaries about the experience.)

## Activity 5
*Purpose:* To become sensitive to all the layers of sound that we normally miss; to experience hearing our own voice.
*Process:* For the first five minutes of the session instruct the group members to sit silently and completely still and to listen to everything. They may use pencil and paper to record what they hear.

After the five minutes is up, discuss for five more minutes the layers of sound present in the room. Have students share their lists to see whether any sounds were heard by just one person. Discuss how we tune out sounds we don't want to hear, such as teachers, mother, and so on.

At this point, turn on your tape recorder (check the sound reproduction before you begin) and have each person introduce himself by saying, "Hello tape recorder, I'm——and I feel——." You may choose to use some other ritual-type response, but make certain everyone says the same thing. After everyone (including you) has recorded his voice, play the tape back; then discuss how your voice sounds to you. Why does it sound different to you but the same to others? Discuss the properties of sound, how it travels, and so forth. Have students discuss whether or not they like their own voices.

### Activity 6

*Purpose:* To demonstrate how easy it is to mess up a verbal message when passing it to another person; to become aware of how rumors get started. *Process:* This activity is an old one. It is called "Rumor Clinic" or "Telephone." Pick a reasonable passage from a book, magazine, or newspaper and make two copies of it. Give one copy to the person on your right and one to the person on your left. They should read the article and then whisper the story to the person next to them. Continue this process until one person gets both messages whispered to him. That person should tell the two stories as he heard them, and then he should read to the group the actual written account that you gave to the persons on your right and left. Then have the group discuss "a time someone told me a rumor and it wasn't true" or "when I started a rumor."

### Activity 7

*Purpose:* To become aware of how our senses can be tricked by reality; to reinforce the notion that, in terms of perception, we have no common world. *Process:* Without saying anything, hold up the diagram on page 47 and say, "How many squares do you see?" Give the students a few seconds to look at it, and then get several responses. As they argue to convince each other of the answer, tell them the question was "How many squares do you see?" not "How many are there?" All answers are correct from the point of view of the person giving the answer. Next, pass around the room the page with the different optical illusions (p. 48). As people tell what they see, let them know that they can be tricked into seeing what really isn't true: Figure 1 can be seen as either a chalice or two faces looking at each other. Figure 2 can be seen as a young woman or an old one. Figure 3 is different things to different people. In Figure 4, ask which line is longest and which is shortest. (All are equal.) In Figure 5, ask which stick is longer, then reveal that the sticks are telephone poles and ask for reactions.

After the discussion dies down, ask the following questions and discuss them:

1.    Are there some times when people *could* see the same thing but really see different things? (Accidents, fights, games, and so forth.)
2.    What influences how we perceive a situation?

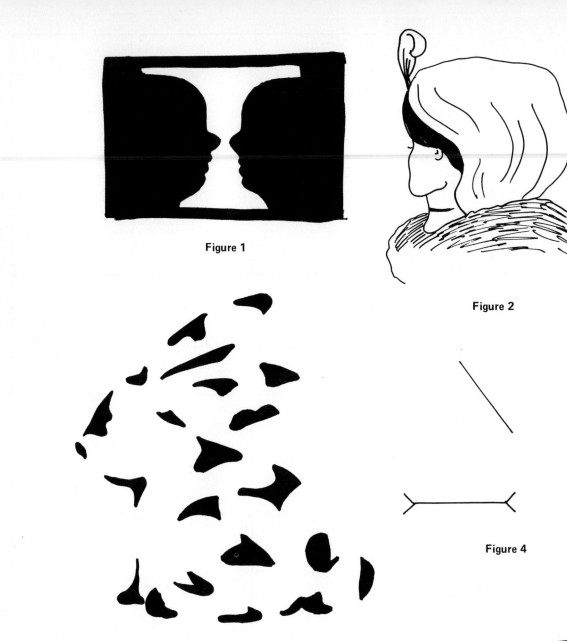

Figure 1

Figure 2

Figure 3

Figure 4

Figure 5

3. What would happen if an umpire were secretly in favor of one team?
4. What is a bias?
5. What is long hair? Do you and your parents agree?

Let the group spend the rest of the time discussing how different perceptions can cause problems. (Obviously, this session could expand into several. If it feels good, let it.)

## Activity 8

*Purpose:* To increase student awareness of the connection between smell and memory.

*Process:* Begin today's session by saying, "Did you ever smell something that took you right back to an experience you had long ago?" Give students an example by sharing a personal smell experience of your own. (My own most vivid one concerns smelling American Family detergent in a grocery store and remembering a childhood experience at the house of a friend whose mother used that brand of soap.)

As students share their own smell stories, encourage them to remember more about the experience. You might say, "What other smells do you remember? What sounds were there? Who was there with you?" and so on. You might want to discuss studies indicating that smell experiences can evoke strong memory experiences.

## Activity 9

*Purpose:* To become aware of how all our senses can be used to experience even a simple thing much more completely.

*Process:* For this activity, you will need enough lemons for all group members. (If lemons are unavailable, use oranges or potatoes.) Begin the session by giving each student a lemon and instructing him to get to know his lemon as well as he can. (Allow no talking while students are getting to know their lemons.)

After three to five minutes, have each person say good-bye to his lemon and deposit it in the center of the group. (This part is more meaningful if it is done ritualistically. You know, *really* say good-bye.)

After all lemons have been deposited, tell group members to close their eyes. Each one should pick up a lemon at random and begin passing it around the circle with eyes closed. When a person thinks he has his lemon back, he should put it in front of him and keep passing the other lemons. Eventually everyone should have one lemon. At this point ask everyone to open his eyes and decide if he really has his own lemon. If he doesn't, he should find the person who does and negotiate for it.

After everyone is satisfied that he has his own lemon, tell each person to introduce his lemon. Tell him to introduce it by saying, "I'd like to introduce my lemon, he (she) is . . ." Encourage comprehensive descriptions of the lemon.

*Additional Process:* If this activity goes well, it will probably take two sessions to complete. Playing strength bombardment (see page 88) with the lemons and being the lemon and talking to the group as a lemon are both effective additional activities. Discuss whether lemons have feelings. To really set the idea, have students discuss "a time I felt like a lemon," or "somebody I know whom I used to ignore."

**Activity 10**
*Purpose:* To culminate the unit on sensory awareness by putting it all together; to experience staying in the here and now.
*Process:* Begin the session by reading the paragraphs below. Then discuss the meaning with the group for five minutes.

In our culture, all of us are preoccupied most of the time with anticipating the future and worrying about it or with daydreaming about the past and remembering how it was. We are always trying to be happier right now, and yet much of what we do prevents us from achieving that happiness.

To be in the here and now means to be in touch with your senses, to be aware of what you are seeing, hearing, smelling, and so on. Young children find it very easy to be in the here and now, and if you watch them play you notice that they seldom worry about what is going to happen even an hour or two hours from now and that they spend little time reminiscing. They are concerned with the present situation and with getting the most from it.

If, as teen-agers and adults, we could be more like young children, many of the problems that bother us would disappear.

Think about how many nights you weren't able to get to sleep because you were thinking about the future or the past, how many hours of the day you have wasted, and how many opportunities you have missed by not allowing your mind and body to experience what is happening now.

There is a saying that goes: "The future is only a dream and the past no longer exists. The present moment is the only reality."

Ask for four volunteers to sit in a "fish bowl," with the other students serving as observers. The task for the people in the fish bowl is to have a conversation without leaving the here and now. By necessity they will have to limit themselves to what they are seeing, hearing, smelling, tasting, touching, and feeling (inside), plus what they are thinking about right now. They probably won't get far. Be prepared to deal with awkward silences. After a few minutes, ask if some observers want to join the group. Eventually get everyone in one group and, going around the circle, have each one say, "Right now I feel . . ." or "Right now I hear . . ."

Discuss the experience. Emphasize how many problems we have that would be eliminated if we could learn to be in the here and now. Discuss times when it is hard to be in the here and now and times when it is easy.

Introduce the concept of stage fright. Have the students discuss it in the context of the lesson on being in the here and now. I heard a record once on which the kids and the teacher were singing a here-and-now song. It went "What's happening now ———, what's happening now?"* A name goes in the blank. The person named must sing the response, something like "Right now I smell Susie's perfume. That's what's happening now." Sounds like a good campfire song.

---

*The song is on an album of affective songs available from Community Psychological Consultants, Delmar Blvd., St. Louis, Missouri.

# TRUST

## Objectives

Students will:

a. Become aware of how trusting they feel they can be in this group.
b. Experience trusting or not trusting other group members.
c. Identify the kinds of people they trust and what other people think of them as trusting people.

## Activity 1

*Purpose:* To examine the present level of trust in this group; to experience trusting the group members.

*Process:* Begin the session by asking members whether they trust one another. Get them to discuss what degrees of trust they feel for different group members. After five minutes, say, "Today we are going to actually see how much we trust each other. Please pick a partner." After all partners are picked, tell them to spread out in the room and stand facing their partner. Then give these directions:

1. Decide who is A and who is B in your group.
2. A, turn around so your back is to B.
3. A, close your eyes and keep them closed.
4. When B says ready, A, you are going to fall backward with your legs stiff and B is going to catch you before you fall.
5. B, you must catch your partner. Whatever happens don't let him fall.

(You should act as spotter for anyone you're not sure of or for a dyad in which one person is much larger than the other.) After A has tried falling two or three times, have partners switch roles, with B falling and A catching. After a few minutes, tell students to trade partners and to repeat the process again. Make sure they do the process with at least three different partners. Bring them back to the circle and discuss their feelings about falling and about different partners. Discuss: Was it easy or hard to trust? Did you trust one partner more than another? Did you find your body resisting? How could you become more trusting?

*Additional Process:* If the students are receptive to the *trust fall,* you might want to try the *trust circle.* In the trust circle, one person stands in the center

and makes his body very stiff. When he is ready, he closes his eyes and falls backward. The *group* moves in close and passes him from person to person around the circle. This activity builds a high level of group trust very quickly. Make sure that everyone who wants to try gets a chance, including the leader. (Don't force anyone to do it who is reluctant. In fact, students should all have the option of being observers in this activity.)

## Activity 2

*Purpose:* To enhance feelings of trust through anonymous sharing of secrets.
*Process:* Today you are going to continue to build trust in the group but in a different way. Begin the session by giving each person a 3 × 5 card. Tell the group members to turn around so their backs are to the circle and tell them to write a secret on the card. They are not to put their name on the card. The secret should be something no one, or almost no one, knows about but them. After they have completed their secrets, pass a paper bag around and have each student drop his card into it. After all cards have been collected, shake the bag and pass it to the person on your left. He should take one card out and read it aloud as if it were his own. Then give the bag to the next person and have him remove one card and read it as if it were his own. Complete this process around the circle until all cards are read. Discuss the feelings they had as the secrets were shared. (This activity builds trust very quickly.)

## Activity 3

*Purpose:* To become aware of what kind of people each of us trusts.
*Process:* Begin the session by asking group members to remember a few high-lights from the last two sessions. Then say, "Today I want you to think about someone you really trust and someone you don't trust. I also want you to think about why you do or don't trust them." As kids share, collect the statements they made about what behaviors are trusting or nontrusting. It might help to have someone write down what is said about trust behaviors.

Focus on the different perceptions group members have of what consti-tutes a trustworthy person. Near the end of the discussion, ask if anyone has any questions for other group members who have shared. Encourage this type of cross-communication. Make sure contributors are remembered.

## Activity 4

*Purpose:* To take a public stand on trustworthiness.
*Process:* Begin by remembering two or three comments from yesterday. Then draw a continuum on the board and say, "This represents how most other people who know you see you in terms of being trustworthy. One end means they never trust you—0 percent; the other end means they trust you all the time—100 percent." Encourage students to put their names up where they think others would put them. Then ask why they put their names where they did.

If time remains, ask them to put their names up where they perceive *themselves* as trustworthy people. Discuss the differences in their perceptions with the perceptions of others. Before the time is up, ask people to summarize the unit on trust—what did they learn?

*Additional Process:* If time permits, or at another meeting, have the students brainstorm ways to get people to be more trusting.

## Objectives

Students will:

a. Become aware that wanting attention is normal and important to all people.
b. Be able to identify how they get people to pay attention to them.
c. Consider and evaluate good and bad ways for getting attention.
d. Confirm publicly how they feel about themselves as attention-getters.
e. Experience attention-getting behavior in the group.

## Activity 1

*Purpose:* To introduce the idea of the importance of attention-getting; to practice an adaptation of the interview technique.

*Process:* Today you are going to begin a new unit with the students. Begin the session by telling them so. Then ask them if they know how to do interviews. If all do, fine; if some don't, explain how interviewing works.

You are going to ask someone a question, and if he answers it, he gets to ask the next question. This process then continues until it dies out. If the process does not seem to be going well, jump in and ask another question. (It will be helpful if you ditto off ten to fifteen questions for interviews and distribute them to the students.)

After fifteen minutes have gone by, end the interviews and bring up the word "attention." Ask students for statements about what the word means to them. Definitions or personal references are O.K. Let the discussion about attention meander along until the session is over. You might ask them to look for a connection between what you did during the interviews and what you are saying about attention. Tell them that, until the next session, they should be aware of how they get attention from other people. Today emphasize that attention is a basic human need.

## Activity 2
*Purpose:* To increase awareness of ways we get attention.
*Process:* Begin today's session by saying, "At the end of the last session I asked you to be aware of some of the ways you get attention. Today we are going to talk about that. Think of at least one way that you get attention from others." (Let them know, if they're stuck, that home, school, and neighborhood examples are all O.K.)

As students share their ways of getting attention, accept and reflect their answers and ask each one whether the method usually works. Use your turn to guide the discussion into an area they are avoiding. For instance, if most of their examples are from home, bring up one from school or from a party or from a bus.

Before the session is ended, see to it that everyone gets remembered. Ask for generalizations about how people get attention.

## Activity 3
*Purpose:* To increase awareness of attention-getting behavior, focusing on negative behavior.
*Process:* Begin the session by reminding students of the topic in the last discussion. Have some people remember what was said yesterday.

Tell them that you are going to continue examining ways people get attention but that you are going to do it a little differently. Ask them to tell about a way they got attention that made someone else mad or angry. During the discussion, switch the topic to "something someone else does to get my attention." In all cases, accept the contribution, reflect it, and ask the person how that method works. What you want is for each person to begin to evaluate how he gets attention. Hopefully, students can begin to give up negative or counterproductive attention-getting strategies in favor of effective strategies. See that all contributors are remembered before you end the session.

### Activity 4

*Purpose:* To examine who we need attention from most; to reintroduce priority lists as a technique for examining ourselves.

*Process:* Begin by putting a large piece of paper (newsprint or butcher paper) in the center of the circle. Put "effective" and "ineffective" at the top of the paper in two columns. Tell students, "Today we are going to pool our knowledge of how to get attention. If you can think of a way of getting someone's attention that is effective, that is, that works without having a negative side effect, we'll list it in the 'effective' column. If it works but produces negative side effects, like getting in trouble, we'll list it in the 'ineffective' column." Continue this exercise until there are ten minutes left. Then introduce the following choices: "Who, of the following three people, do you need attention from most? That is, who would you hate to have ignore you most? Your mother, your best friend, or your father?" Have different students rank these choices and explain why they feel that way.

At the end of the session, roll up the effective-ineffective list and keep it until a later time. Bring it out at a future meeting when you are discussing classroom behavior.

### Activity 5

*Purpose:* To evaluate ourselves as attention-getters; to publicly affirm how much attention we need; to reintroduce the technique of putting ourselves on a line between two extreme points.

*Process:* Begin this session by putting a line on the board. Before you put the end points up, say, "Who can tell me what this line is going to be about?" Eventually, someone will say, "Attention." Then ask for a volunteer to describe one of the extremes. If students don't get the idea, do one end and let them do the other.

Attention-Lover Alfie _____ Unseeable Izzy

Alfie loves attention, he'll do anything to get it. He goes to church just so he can scream and get everyone to look at him. (Make up your own examples of Alfie's behavior.) Izzy is at the other extreme. He lives in a closet where he won't be noticed. At his wedding they forgot to have him stand in the receiving line to be congratulated. (Add your own further description.)

After the students have identified the end points, ask them to place their names on the line in the appropriate place based on how much attention they get. Use the same process you have used on previous occasions for discussing the "in between" technique.

*Additional Process:* If time remains after the "in between" game, tell the group to line up in a straight line *without any talking.* The first person in line should be the one who gets the most attention in the group, and everyone else should line up according to who gets the next most, on down to the one who gets the least. Remember, they must do this without talking. After they have done so, talk about how they decided who gets the most attention and who gets the least. In the next session consciously attempt to give more attention to the students who were placed at the low end of the line. If time remains, discuss group members get attention from others in the group. Actually list the specific behaviors that students use, like "Bill crosses his eyes," "teacher claps her hands," "Mary talks softly," and so on.

**Additional Discussion Topics**

How I feel when I don't get attention.
Somebody who can always get my attention.
One thing I do to draw attention to myself.
How my pets gets my attention.
A way I get kids in school to pay attention to me.
First impressions: How I come on when I don't know somebody.
How I use clothes to get attention.
A time when I didn't want attention.
How I know when people are paying attention to me.
A time I gave someone else attention because he needed it.
Ways to get attention from teachers.

# SELF-CONTROL

**Objectives**

Students will:

a. Accept their share of responsibility for controlling themselves.
b. See the connection between growing up physically and growing in self-control.
c. Be aware of different kinds of self-control.
d. Publicly affirm how they feel about themselves as self-controlling people.
e. Identify at least two times when they used self-control to help themselves or others.

**Activity 1**

*Purpose:* To introduce the subject of self-control as worthy of discussion; to help students become aware of a time they didn't lose control.

*Process:* Begin the session by asking the group members to think about a time they couldn't control their emotions. (But don't let them talk about it.) After a couple of minutes, pick someone to role-play, in pantomime, someone who has just stubbed his toe and is flipping out. After he does so, ask for someone else to pantomime one of the following situations, but don't tell the others which it is—they have to guess. Do three or four of these situations.

1. A student gets his report card and it says F in a subject in which he thought he was getting an A.
2. A boy or girl is in class trying to be serious but something terribly funny just happened and the student is trying not to crack up.
3. An eighth grade boy has just found out that the girl of his dreams wants to go with him. He is walking home alone.
4. A kid on the street has just called a boy's mother a dirty name in front of ten of his friends.

After the students have role-played these situations, tell them they are going to role-play a different kind of situation. First you need someone to tell the group about a time he almost lost control but didn't. After someone shares his story of almost losing control, pick people to role-play it with or without talking.

Continue this process of telling a story and then role-playing until the end of the period.

## Activity 2

*Purpose:* To experience different kinds of control (other vs. self).
*Process:* Begin the session by saying, "What happened the last time we met?" Encourage specific descriptions from as many people as are willing. Then say, "Today we're going to experience different degrees of control and freedom, and then we will talk about it." Then give them the following commands in this order.

1. "You are robots and I am your master. You can only do what I say and nothing else. Your body movements are mechanical and slow." (Now give them about three minutes of robot commands.) "Freeze."
2. "For the next few minutes you are free to do anything you want with one catch. You must lock arms with three other people and keep your arms latched." (Give them three minutes.) "Freeze."
3. "For the next three minutes you are free to do anything you want as long as you don't hurt anyone and don't leave the room." (Give them three minutes.) "Freeze."
4. "You are robots again. Stand straight and still. There is a fly on your nose but you may not touch it. Pretend it is really there and you want to brush it off but I won't let you—really get into that." (Give them two minutes.) "O.K., brush it off. Freeze."

5.  "Pick a partner. For three minutes one of you is the dictator and the other is the slave. Give the slave commands as cruelly and bluntly as you can. The slaves must not rebel." (After three minutes, say, "Switch.")

If any time remains, discuss feelings of different amounts of control. Have students rank the different degrees of freedom from the one they liked most to the one they liked least. Discuss: "a time I felt like a slave."

## Activity 3
*Purpose:* To have students evaluate where they are right now as self-controlling persons.
*Process:* Begin by remembering the last discussion. Go over any key statements that people made. Spend ten minutes discussing times you kept control or lost control. When ten minutes are left, put the following line on the board:

Blow-up Betty ———————————————————— Dud Debbie

Describe the extremes for them: Betty is always out of control—Debbie would rather die than lose control. Have students place themselves on the line. After several have put themselves up, put up a second line called the "Ideal-Me Line." Ask them to put themselves up on this one, too.

## Activity 4
*Purpose:* To help students see the connection between having self-control and having responsibility; to build positive feelings of self.
*Process:* Ask for definitions of the words "responsible" and "responsibility." Don't judge the different definitions—accept them and reflect them. Then introduce the following topic: "a time when I acted responsibly." Really push them to find at least one time when they accepted responsibility for their actions or for those of another person. It doesn't matter how trivial the incident is—accept all contributions equally. If possible, encourage group members to see the connection between acting responsibly and using self-control. Some of these stories will be examples of self-control.

Leave three minutes at the end of the session for these sentence stubs: "Being responsible is when . . ." and "I used self-control when . . ."

## Activity 5
*Purpose:* To identify times when we were able to control ourselves.
*Process:* Begin by remembering what you discussed at the last meeting. After a few minutes, introduce the following topic: "a time I wanted to blow up but didn't." As students share their stories about almost blowing up at brothers, teachers, parents, and others, encourage them to describe how it feels to control one's temper. Ask them whether they think little kids can

control their tempers as well as older kids. Ask them why they think as they do. Encourage them to discuss what they do when they feel like blowing up. (I used to throw rocks at bottles that I had lined up on the railroad tracks or smash orange crates with a hammer.)

## Additional Activities

Have the class sit absolutely still—no talking, moving, or blinking. The last person to move is the winner.

Build a card house while other students are harassing you (but are not touching the cards).

Sacrificing. Pick things you like to do and don't do them. How long can you hold out?

Role-play: employer-employee; teacher-student; someone about to lose control-someone with great self-control.

Have a nonverbal quarrel: two students argue; a third breaks it up—all nonverbally.

Brainstorm ways to avoid losing control.

## Additional Discussion Topics

A time I felt responsible.
A time I was proud that I controlled myself.
A time I didn't do something when it would have been easier to do it.
A time I stopped myself from hurting someone.
A time I kept myself out of trouble by keeping my mouth shut.
A responsibility I have at home.
A time I had to decide my own punishment.
A time I saved money for something instead of spending it.
A time I spent my lunch money for something else.
A time I controlled my anger.
A time I did my work while others goofed off.
A time I had to be on my best behavior in front of adults.
How I didn't do something and it helped someone else.

**Objectives**
Students will:

a.   Increase awareness of what tolerance is.
b.   Increase awareness of intolerant behavior.
c.   Identify strategies for becoming more tolerant.
d.   Experience intolerant behavior.
e.   Become aware of their individual levels of tolerance.

**Activity 1**
*Purpose:* To experience many possible ways of being included or excluded from groups.

*Process:* Begin the session by telling the students, "Today we are going to do something pretty different. You have to listen to me to get the directions down pat. I want everyone with blue eyes to go stand over there (point to some corner separate from the group). Everyone with nonblue eyes, stay here." Then make the following statement to the nonblue eyed people: "Boy, if there is one thing I can't stand, it's people with blue eyes. They think they're so cool." (Encourage three or four statements from others as they get the idea.)

Next, have everyone come back together. Say, "Will everyone with hair that covers their eyes go over in the corner." Then repeat the process, making remarks about the long-haired people. Repeat this process several more times using height, sex, hair color, and shoe size.

After several rounds, enthusiasm will be very high and you should calm the students down. Use the last five or ten minutes to talk about what happened. Questions that are good are: "What did I do? Does anybody see any reason for doing what we did? What words come to your mind following our game?"

## Activity 2

*Purpose:* To relate the grouping experience to the concept of tolerance; to become aware of how first impressions affect our opinions of others.
*Process:* Begin by asking several people to remember what they did at the last meeting. Then ask the following questions:

1. How many of you think first impressions are important?
2. How many of you think you made a good first impression on a teacher?
3. How many of you have had a good first impression of a teacher and have changed your mind after you got to know him?
4. How about the reverse of that?
5. How many of you have a very good friend you didn't like at first?

After they have responded to your questions by raising their hands, introduce the topic "my first impression and how it changed," or "somebody I didn't like when I first met him," or "how I feel about first impressions." Encourage sharing of experiences, with you guiding the discussion. By reflecting what individuals say, make sure everyone is remembered before you finish.

## Activity 3

*Purpose:* To become aware of how tolerance relates to groups in society.
*Process:* Begin by having individuals remember what happened at the last meeting. Then say, "I want you to think about the following: If you had to be a member of one of these groups, which would you choose first, which second and which third? Why?"

1.  American Indians.
2.  Black persons living in Chicago.
3.  Black persons living in a black African country.

As students explain their ranking, have them defend why they believe as they do. If the discussion wanes, ask them what it would be like to be an Indian or a black person. The idea is to rank types of people. Feel free to use other groups instead of the ones listed. Finish the session by whipping around the following stub: "Tolerance is . . ."

### Activity 4

*Purpose:* To identify things hard to tolerate in other people; to become aware of what we do that others can't tolerate.

*Process:* Begin the session by asking group members to recall what was discussed on the previous day, then say, "Today I want you to think about things people do that are hard for you to tolerate. You know, things that others say or do that really bug you." Then give your own example of something like that—something that you can't stand in another person.

Allow group members to discuss anything that seems appropriate. You should reflect what they say. If the discussion wanes, switch the topic to "something others can't stand in me." (Try to save this part for the next session, though.) Make sure you remember what has been said before you end the session.

### Activity 5

*Purpose:* To bring together and process all the experiences from the unit on tolerance.

*Process:* Begin the session by having students remember things from all the previous tolerance sessions. After they have exhausted their memories, ask the following questions.

1.  Why have we been doing all this?
2.  Has anyone learned anything?
3.  What does "tolerance" mean?
4.  Do you think you are more tolerant or less tolerant than you were a year ago?
5.  Are you more tolerant or less tolerant than your parents, brothers, or sisters?

Feel free to make up and use any other questions that seem appropriate. For an additional activity, have the class members brainstorm ways they could change themselves to become more tolerant of one another.

Other questions on tolerance. How many of you:

1.  Like the color orange?
2.  Like shoulder-length hair on boys?

3. Like long hair on girls?
4. Think it's O.K. to smoke?
5. Think it's O.K. for women to spoke pipes?
6. Would vote for a woman president?
7. Think it's O.K. for men to cry?
8. Think it's O.K. for women to cry?
9. Would share your lunch with a black person?
10. Think black people dance better than white people?
11. Think that Japanese know karate best?
12. Think Italians make the best pizzas?
13. Think that most Italians are gangsters?
14. Think Catholic schools are stricter than public schools?
15. Think long-haired people are hippies?
16. Think it's O.K. for a woman to be a truck driver?
17. Think women should be drafted?
18. Would marry someone of a different race or religion?
19. Think fat people have a better sense of humor?
20. Think people with Southern accents are hillbillies?
21. Think women are worse drivers than men?

## Additional Discussion Topics

Because of one or two people, I hated the whole group.
A time my prejudice or intolerance got in the way.
Something I just cannot tolerate.
Someone I would not vote for because of age, religion, sex, or race.
How I deal with intolerance or prejudice in an older person.
A time an adult was more prejudiced than me.
A time I became friends with someone everyone else was against.
How I deal with intolerance or prejudice against me.
A time I helped a friend become less prejudiced.
A time someone was different but it didn't matter.
A time I was tolerant of someone's ideas.
A time I exercised extreme tolerance.
A time I became a little less intolerant.
A time I accepted an idea offered by someone I didn't like.
How I am uniquely different from others.

**Objectives**

Students will:

a. Become sensitive to the effect their behavior has on others.
b. Be able to identify times when their behavior was both positive and negative.
c. Understand the difference between feeling or thinking something and actually doing it.
d. Gain practice in evaluating other people's behavior as good or bad.

## Activity 1

*Purpose:* To increase student awareness of the effect their behavior has on others; to encourage self-evaluation of good behavior.

*Process:* It should be obvious that we are now moving from the abstract notion about right and wrong behavior to a more personal concept. Today's task is simple enough to describe, but be prepared to deal with resistance from the group in talking about it. Ask the group members to think about "something I did that was a good thing to do." As different examples are shared, ask students how they knew that what they did was a good thing to do. Help them become aware that people usually find out whether an action is good or bad by the reactions of others.

If the discussion lags, broaden the topic by asking for examples of "something I thought was good but someone else thought was bad." Accept all contributions without judging and remember the contributors before the end of the session.

## Activity 2

*Purpose:* To sensitize students to the fact that all of us have done things we think are wrong.

*Process:* Begin today's session by remembering some of the comments from yesterday. Then introduce the topic "something I did that was a bad thing to do." There is much more at stake here than just a superficial discussion. If these students can begin to own the fact that they do some things that they think are bad, they will be moving toward maturity. Your main message to them is that doing a bad thing doesn't mean you're a bad person.

As they are able to tell their stories about negative behavior, ask them how they felt when they had done a bad thing. Let them know that all people do bad things sometimes and that the important thing is to be able to admit that you did something bad and to learn from the experience. Make sure that you share an experience from your life. By doing so, you show them what you are preaching: that you can do a bad thing and still be a good person. Remember what people said before you end the session.

## Activity 3

*Purpose:* To help students develop awareness of ambivalent behavior and of different perceptions of behavior.

*Process:* Today you are going to have the students take a stand on what they consider good behavior and bad behavior. You are going to do a physical continuum with them.

Get some construction paper and, with a magic marker, make the following posters:

1. I think that was a very good thing to do.
2. I'm not sure whether it was good or bad.
3. I think that was a very bad thing to do.

Tape the posters along one wall of the room, one at one end, one in the middle, and one at the other end. When the group is seated in the circle say, "For the last two days we have been talking about behavior. What is good and what is bad. Today I am going to describe people who did different things in certain situations and I want you to go and stand in the place that shows whether you think it was good or bad behavior."

After they understand what to do, describe each situation in the following list. After each round, ask students for explanations of why they stood where they did. A good way to elicit comments is to pretend you have a microphone and go up to someone and say, "Why are you here?"

### The Situations

1.  In the Old West a wagon train was stopped because Indians were nearby. In one wagon a woman was holding her sick baby. She believed that if the Indians heard the baby cry they would know the location of the wagon train and kill everybody in it. So when the baby started to cry, she smothered it until it died. What do you think about the woman's behavior? Would you say it was all good, all bad, or somewhere in between?

2.  On Halloween, a third-grade boy, to get even with the neighborhood grouch, threw rotten eggs all over her house.

3.  In an attempt to get even, this woman put a razor blade in an apple and gave it to the boy who she believed threw eggs at her house.

4.  After being told he could go to Disneyworld if he got an A in math, a junior-high boy got a copy of the final exam answers and copied them before taking the test.

5.  When the principal asked him whether he saw who started the fight on the playground, the boy lied because he knew it was his best friend.

6.  When the principal asked whether she knew the person who was selling LSD on the schoolground, the high-school girl said, "No," because she was secretly married to the seller.

7.  The teacher gave an F to an eighth-grade girl who had done the work but who had called the teacher an "old bag" to her face.

After you have completed this activity, sit down with the class and discuss the problem of knowing what is right and wrong. Ask them for their personal definitions of right and wrong. (You should play the devil's advocate to get them to see all sides of the problem.) Following the discussion, have them write about right and wrong in their diaries.

### Activity 4

*Purpose:* To increase student awareness of the fact that having a bad feeling or a bad thought is not the same as doing a bad thing.

*Process:* Begin by remembering what has been discussed so far. Then ask these questions.

1. How many of you ever felt like killing somebody?
2. How many of you ever thought you would like to tattle on someone and get them in trouble?
3. How many of you ever thought about cheating on a test?
4. How many of you ever thought about running away?
5. How many of you ever wanted to beat up your brother or sister?
6. How many of you ever wanted to beat up your parents?

Then ask if anyone ever felt like doing a bad thing but didn't do it.

Encourage students to share their stories. Tell them as they share their stories that what they are talking about is growing up. Little kids think feeling and doing are the same. They often feel guilty about having bad feelings. Everyone has bad feelings and thoughts—even terrible ones. But that doesn't mean everyone is a bad person. It is important that a person can be honest about his bad feelings—only then can he overcome them. Try to get them to make this generalization, but if they don't, then do it for them.

Finally, ask them to write thought papers on what it means to be a good person. Read them.

### Objectives
Students will:

a.    Identify things they like to do.
b.    See the contradictions between what they do and what they say they like to do.
c.    Practice setting small meaningful goals.
d.    Help each other evaluate appropriate goals.
e.    Set goals to improve at something.
f.    Publicly affirm how they see themselves as goal-oriented people.
g.    Identify from a list of goals which ones are poorly stated.
h.    Be able to explain the five conditions of a successful goal.

### Activity 1
*Purpose:* To increase students' awareness of how their favorite things to do reflect their values; to confront students with the degree of congruency between what they say they like and what they actually do.

*Process:* Begin the session by having each person number from one to twenty on the left side of a piece of notebook paper, leaving the right half blank. Tell students to list at least ten things (twenty would be better) they like to do—activities they enjoy being engaged in. If they have difficulty getting started, give them examples of the kinds of things that they can write: things they do on vacation, games and sports, activities around the house, things in school, little idiosyncrasies like cleaning their ears, favorite foods to eat, and so forth. You should make your list at the same time they make theirs. Give them five to ten minutes to complete their lists. After their lists are completed, explain that now you are going to give them a code for their lists. Several possible codes are listed here.*

20 Things I like to do:

| | | Alone or others A others | Costs $ $ | Did last month | Rank |
|---|---|---|---|---|---|
| 1 | Eat popcorn | | | | |
| 2 | Babysit | o | | m | |
| 3 | Go to circus | o | $ | | |
| 4 | Watch TV | A | | m | |
| 5 | Swim | A | | | 2 |
| 6 | Go to Wisconsin | o | $ | m | |
| 7 | Play football | o | | m | |
| 8 | Play basketball | o | | | |
| 9 | Eat ice cream | A | $ | m | |
| 10 | Sleep late | A | | m | |
| 11 | Tell spook stories | o | | m | |
| 12 | Go to camp | o | $ | | 1 |
| 13 | Visit Kerry | c | | m | |
| 14 | Wear jeans | A | | m | |
| 15 | Climb hills | A | | m | |
| 16 | Lie in Sun | A | | | |
| 17 | Sing | A | | | |
| 18 | Tell jokes | o | | m | |
| 19 | Be with Joey | o | | m | |
| 20 | Hug Mom | o | | m | 3 |

---

*This activity, called "Twenty Things You Like To Do," is one of the best values activities around. I first experienced it at an affective education conference with Sid Simon.

Put a P next to an activity if you like to do it best with other people, whether one other person or a whole group. If you like to do it best alone, put an A next to it. If you think no one else in this room has it on his list, put N next to it. If you think you would not want your parents to see it, put SEE next to it. If it costs money everytime you do it, put $ next to it. If you like it best in winter, put W by it. If it is a risky thing to do but you still like it, put R by it. If you could only keep five things, put * by the five you would keep. If you don't think you will be doing this in five years, put −5 next to it. If you wish you did it more, put √ by it. Put the date (approximately) when you last did each thing on the list.

You are encouraged to make up other codes that fit your situation. Don't use more than seven or eight codes in any one activity. After the students and you have coded the lists, carry on a discussion about the activity. Ask the following questions:

1. Would anyone like to make an "I learned" statement about this activity?
2. Was anyone surprised by how his list came out?
3. Was it hard to choose a top five?
4. Did anyone discover something about himself he didn't know?
5. Could we share some of the things we listed?

Asking questions that are related to a particular code is also good—for example, "Did anyone have several things on his list that involved taking a big risk?" Finish by having each student complete this sentence on the back of his list: "What I learned from this activity is . . ." (Make sure they file their completed lists.)

**Activity 2**

*Purpose:* To relate what students learned yesterday to the idea that goal setting can help you do things you like to do better and more often.

*Process:* Begin by asking several group members to remember what happened at the last session. Have them take out their lists from the previous session and ask them to find one activity on the list that they would like to set a goal about. Give them a few minutes to identify the activity and the proposed goal. Make copies of the Goal-Setting Worksheet and have students write their goals on it. After each student has stated his goal, you and the group should analyze it to see if it meets the five conditions at the top of the worksheet. If it doesn't meet the conditions, have the group evaluate it and help the student restate it until the goal meets the conditions established for an effective goal. Emphasize the fact that goals can be big or little. It's probably better for them to set small goals at this point.

Repeat this same process of goal statement, group evaluation, and goal restatement for each student. This process will take the entire session. It is important that part of a goal-setting session be devoted to remembering

## GOAL-SETTING WORKSHEET

A good goal is one that meets the following five conditions:

1. It must be conceivable—that is, capable of being put into words.

2. It must be within the realm of possibility for the person setting it.

3. It must be controllable. If it involves another person, you need his or her permission.

4. It must be measurable. It must be so stated that, at some point in time, you can say, "I did," or "I didn't."

5. It must be stated with no alternative (no "either-or").

A goal to be accomplished by _____ (date)_____

I will _____

_____

_____

_____

_____

_____

_____

_____

_____

_____

_____

_____

_____

_____

_____

Signed _____

what goals were set at the previous session and having those people who were to accomplish their goal by this session report on whether they did accomplish it. Accept no excuses from students who failed to accomplish their goals.

### Activity 3

*Purpose:* To gain practice at identifying goals that are poorly stated.

*Process:* This is a fairly cognitive activity, so some kids will think you are playing regular teacher on them. Tell them that it is important to do so if they are going to really understand how to set good goals.

Begin by having those who set goals at the last session report to the group. Did they accomplish their goals? NO EXCUSES.

Then discuss again "the five conditions of a good goal." Give them some examples of goals that don't meet the conditions. Here are some:

- *Not conceivable:* "I'm going to really make something of myself." (Not clear—what is "something?")
- *Not possible:* "I'm going to be an Olympic wrestler when I'm fourteen." (Impossible.)
- *Not controllable:* "I'm going to get Miss Jones to like me." (You don't control Miss Jones.)
- *Not measurable:* "I'm going to take out the garbage." (When?)
- *Has alternatives:* "I'm going to read a book or watch TV tonight." (Pick only one, please.)

When you think the students understand the conditions, give them copies of "Ten Goals" (page 78). Working in dyads, they should complete the worksheet while you facilitate. Encourage them to argue about which goals meet which conditions. Here are the answers:

Goal one: 4; Goal two: 2, 3; Goal three: 5, maybe 4; Goal four: 1, 3; Goal five: 3; Goal six: 3; Goal seven: yes; Goal eight: 1, 2, 3, 4, 5; Goal nine: yes; Goal ten: 1, 3, 4, 5.

### Activity 4

*Purpose:* To help students identify significant goals in their lives; to begin taking action toward accomplishing their goals.

*Process:* Begin by remembering what happened at the last session. Ask someone to recapitulate the five conditions of a good goal. Distribute the "Goal Distillation" form (page 79) and fill it out in the group. Take them carefully through the whole process. Make the last thing they do a ritual commitment to accomplish one of the goals. (Having them raise their hands, one at a time, and swear that they will do it is one example of a ritual. Another is to have all group members chant their goal out loud after they state it.) Make certain they file their completed forms for later reference.

**Activity 5**

*Purpose:* To increase students' confidence that they can improve their skills if they want to.

*Process:* Begin by having a few students remember what they did two sessions ago. Ask them to remember whether they coded anything that they wanted to do better. After a short discussion, encourage any group member to share "something I would like to do better." After six or seven people have shared what they want to do better, begin to have the group suggest ways that each person could improve at something. As students share what they would like to do better, and as others offer suggestions, make it clear to all that you think all the students could accomplish their goals and learn to do things better. If interest in this activity is high, continue it for a second session.

*Additional Process:* After talking about this subject for a while, a continuum dealing with this idea would be appropriate. Use the extremes of Always-Improving Inga and Never-Tries Tim. Allow students to put themselves up where they think they belong.

Always-
Improving ———————————————————————————— Tries
Inga                                                                          Tim

Never-

Have them state goals again that meet the criteria for good goals stated earlier. As a final experience in this unit, you might have them use the form "Goals to Accomplish" (page 80) to list several goals they want to accomplish during the coming few weeks. Following this unit, it is recommended that you have the students set goals each week for the remainder of the year.

# TEN GOALS

Read over each stated goal and code it in the following way: If it lacks condition 1 (conceivable), put a 1 next to it. If it fails condition 2 (possible), put a 2 by it. If it fails condition 3 (controllable), put a 3 by it. If it fails condition 4 (measurable), put a 4 by it. If it fails condition 5 (no alternative), put a 5 by it. If it meets all five conditions, put "yes" next to it.

1.  I will do my homework tonight.

2.  I will win the U.S. Open Golf Tournament by June 30th, 1976.

3.  Tonight, I will either take out the garbage or watch TV before 10 P.M.

4.  By the time I am twenty-one, I will discover something that will revolutionize the world.

5.  I will take Cathy out to a show Friday night.

6.  I will get an A on my science test Friday.

7.  I will get up in time to get to school by 8:15 Monday morning.

8.  I will buy my mother the neatest gift ever for Mother's Day.

9.  By 3:00 this afternoon, I will invite Cathy to go to my party.

10.  I will be picked to be captain of something this year.

---

Make up two goals that are poorly stated, for sharing with the class.

1. _____

_____

_____

_____

2. _____

_____

_____

_____

# GOAL DISTILLATION

1.  Write down three goals you would really like to accomplish in the next three months.

    a.  _____

    b.  _____

    c.  _____

2.  Rank order them from most important to least important.

    1.  _____

    2.  _____

    3.  _____

3.  List five things you *could* do to make number 1 come about.

    1.  _____

    2.  _____

    3.  _____

    4.  _____

    5.  _____

4.  Circle any of the five that you will do. If you aren't sure, don't circle.

5.  Set goals indicating what you will do.

    1.  _____

    2.  _____

    3.  _____

    4.  _____

    5.  _____

# GOALS TO ACCOMPLISH

1. This coming week, I want to accomplish the following goals

|  In School  |  At Home  |
| --- | --- |
| a. _____ | f. _____ |
| _____ | _____ |
| b. _____ | g. _____ |
| _____ | _____ |
| c. _____ | h. _____ |
| _____ | _____ |
| d. _____ | i. _____ |
| _____ | _____ |
| e. _____ | j. _____ |

With Friends

k. _____

_____

l. _____

_____

m. _____

_____

n. _____

_____

o. _____

_____

2. The three most important goals stated above are _____, _____, and _____.

3. What might prevent me from accomplishing my goals?

1. _____
2. _____
3. _____
4. _____
5. _____

4. State each goal you will accomplish and indicate the date by which it will be accomplished.

_____

_____

_____

_____

_____

_____

_____

_____

_____

_____

_____

## Objectives

Students will:

a. Take risks in the group by sharing data about themselves.
b. Discover new things about other students.
c. Identify what levels of risks they are comfortable with in a group.
d. Identify how private or public they are about revealing themselves.

## Activity 1

*Purpose:* To reintroduce interviews.

*Process:* Begin the lesson by saying, "Earlier this year we did some interviewing. Today we are going to do some interviews again. At the beginning I will be asking most of the questions, but later you will be asking each other questions. I would like to start by conducting an interview with a volunteer. Who wishes to volunteer?" After someone has volunteered, tell him the rules for being interviewed.* They are:

---

*Interviewing has been around for a long time but Sid Simon and his associates have developed the technique of the public interview into a powerful value-clarifying strategy.

1. If you answer, you must answer honestly.
2. If you don't want to answer a particular question, say, "Pass."
3. After the interview, you can ask me any questions that I asked you.

Begin the interview by asking the following questions:

1. What is your name?
2. Do you like your name?
3. How many places have you lived?
4. Which place did you like best? Which did you like least?
5. If you could be any age, what age would you choose and why?
6. Tell me something you like and dislike about your brothers and sisters.
7. If you could change your school, how would you do it?
8. Have you ever had a shot?
9. What two things are you good at?
10. What would be the perfect meal?

After you complete the interview, tell him he can ask you two or three questions. Then say, "I want to get the rest of you involved a little, so let's go around and answer the following question." Use number 7. If time permits, do another interview. Feel free to use any questions that you think are appropriate.

## Activity 2
*Purpose:* To encourage self-disclosure in response to interview questions; to get to know each other better; to build positive group feeling.
*Process:* Begin the session by asking group members to remember some of the answers to interview questions at the last meeting. After a few have been remembered, introduce the concept of the shotgun interview. To do a shotgun interview, pick one provocative question and ask several students randomly for their answers. Do it quickly, skipping around the circle. Follow this procedure twice, then ask for two more volunteers to be interviewed in depth. After the interviews, ask group members to remember some of the interview answers from the session.

## Activity 3
*Purpose:* To introduce another interview strategy; to involve students in the development of interview questions.
*Process:* Begin by explaining what the person-to-person interview is. In this process, you begin by asking one student an interview question. If the student answers it, he is allowed to ask any person in the circle the next question. If his question is answered, the person answering it becomes the next questioner, and so on. After following this process for five to ten minutes, have each student take out a piece of scratch paper and make up a few interview questions of his own for five minutes. After everyone has made up some questions, begin the interview by having one of the students ask a question from

his own list. Let the game continue until the class is over. You may have to coach the question askers to get them to use a variety of questions.

### Activity 4

*Purpose:* To experience intimacy by interviewing someone in private; to build trust in dyadic groups.

*Process:* Begin the session by telling students, "Today we're going to do a special kind of interview. First, look around the group and think about the kinds of questions you would like to ask different people in this group. By yourself, come up with a list of five to ten questions." Give them five minutes, then have them form dyads. (If there are, say, fourteen students in the group, count them off: "1, 2, 3, 4, 5, 6, 7, 1, 2, 3, 4, 5, 6, 7." The two 1's will be a dyad, the two 2's, another dyad, and so on.) Each group of two should find a quiet place where they can interview each other. Give them ten minutes to interview each other. During the last five minutes, each member should introduce his partner to the whole group and relate one thing he has learned about his partner.

### Activity 5

*Purpose:* To culminate the interview phase of this unit; to introduce the concept of group interview.

*Process:* Begin today's lesson by saying, "Today we are going to do some group interviewing. Who wants to be interviewed by the whole group?" After a volunteer is chosen, begin by asking a couple of questions yourself. Then tell him to call on people to ask him questions. Stop the interview after ten minutes and use one of the questions that was asked as a sentence stub. Then do another group interview. Continue like this until the period ends.

### Activity 6

*Purpose:* To examine the level of self-disclosure we are comfortable with.

*Process:* Tell students, "We have been interviewing each other for the last five sessions and we have been telling each other things about our personal lives. You may think you shouldn't have said some of the things you did. All of us have a certain level of sharing that we are comfortable with. If someone asks us to share something beyond that, depending on the person, we may not want to tell. This activity will give you a chance to think about your own personal feelings about this."

Have each student put five columns on a piece of paper and label the columns "Strangers," "Know a Little," "Know Well," "Best Friends," "Me Only." After everyone has finished the columns, begin reading off the list of situations below. As you read each item, each person will decide how private it is. If he thinks he would tell it to strangers, he writes the key word in the "Strangers" column, and so on. After you have suggested about ten things, encourage students to put three or four more of their own in the columns.

To whom would you tell

1. Something you're ashamed of?
2. That you got an F?
3. Your nickname?
4. Where your father works?
5. Your phone number?
6. Your address?
7. How much money your father or mother makes?
8. That you cheated on a test?
9. Whom you love?
10. What you are really afraid of?
11. How you feel about yourself?

After the activity, discuss in general how you decide whom to share different things with.

# PERSONAL STRENGTHS

**Objectives**

Students will:

a.  Increase their vocabulary for naming strengths.
b.  Identify strengths that help them in their own lives.
c.  Experience being bombarded with strength words from fellow group members.
d.  Become aware of strengths they would like to have by the time they are twenty-one.

**Activity 1**

*Purpose:* To increase awareness of personal strengths; to identify words that name strengths.

*Process:* Today begins a four-session activity that will enhance the feeling of trust developed so far in the group. Today's activity is designed to get the students ready for the upcoming strength bombardment.

Use newsprint or butcher paper for this activity. Explain to the students that there are many words that name strengths—good things about people that you like or that you think help make them successful. Today the group is going to make a list of as many of those kinds of words as they can think of.

Then spend the rest of the session brainstorming words (strength words). If they are limiting their words to certain areas, suggest other words to broaden their concepts. At the end of the session, roll up the list and save it for the next session.

**Activity 2**

*Purpose:* To prepare for the strength bombardment activity.

*Process:* Begin the session by taking out the strength list and posting it on a wall or in the middle of the group. Give each child enough gummed stickers

for each other person in the circle. Tell the group members to write the initials or first name of every other person in the group on the stickers. Then tell them they are to think of a strength for each person and write it on the sticker that has that person's initials. (This process will probably take the whole period. There will be questions and some confusion about how to do it. You will probably need to explain what to do several times.)

If they finish writing and there is time left, collect the stickers, making sure you know whose is whose, and finish the period with a sentence stub, "I Feel good about myself when . . ." (Make sure you don't lose or damage the stickers.)

### Activities 3 and 4

*Purpose:* To receive strengths from class members (strength bombardment).
*Process:* For the next two sessions you are going to play strength bombardment. Give each person a blank piece of paper and have him put his name at the top. Begin with the person on your left and have him pass his paper to you. You are going to model the proper response. You should take the sticker you have written previously for him and put it on his sheet. After you put his sticker on, look at him and say, "Bill, the strength I see in you is . . ." It is important that you use the personal approach. Avoid saying "his" or "her" strength.

After you have given him a strength, pass along his paper to your right and have each person in turn place a sticker on his paper. Each person should look at him and say, "Bill, the strength I see in you is . . ." The person receiving strengths is not allowed to respond to or question what is being said. He can only accept strengths. Repeat this process for every person in the circle. You will be the last one to receive strengths.

If people want to give additional strengths to someone, they should be encouraged to do so. They can just write them on the paper. This activity will take two days to complete.

Encourage the group to save their strength sheets for a later session. They can tape or glue them on notebooks or put them in lockers. If you have the time, complete this activity in one session.

### Activity 5.

*Purpose:* To examine our own areas of growth in the light of our own strengths.
*Process:* Begin by asking each member to tell the group what he thinks is his greatest strength, based on what people said at the last two sessions. When all have done so, pass out copies of the Strength Worksheet. This form should be filled out by each class member in the circle.

After everyone has filled out the form, ask if anyone would like to share the skill he wants to improve and what he will do to improve it. (See if you can get every student to state some goal before he leaves the class.)

If the form doesn't seem appropriate, ask them to write a brief thought paper called "The Me I Want to Be and How I Can Get There."

## STRENGTH WORKSHEET

1.  Name one strength that you wish you had or wish you had to a greater degree. _____
    _____

2.  What is the thing you do or say that is keeping you from using the strength mentioned in number 1? _____
    _____

3.  What are you doing when the thing you do or say in number 2 occurs?
    _____
    _____

    a. When does it occur? _____
    b. With whom? _____
    c. In what situation? _____

4.  List three steps you can take to change the situation described above.
    _____
    _____
    _____

5.  Rank the three steps in order of importance. _____
    _____
    _____
    _____

6.  Do them.

MAKING PROMISES

## Objectives
Students will:

a.  Become aware of when they have broken promises.
b.  Become more sensitive to the feelings of others when promises are broken.
c.  Publicly affirm how they see themselves as promise keepers.
d.  Compare their self-evaluations with others' evaluations of them as promise keepers.

## Activity 1
*Purpose:* To increase students' awareness of when they have broken promises; to become sensitive to the feelings of others when promises are not kept.

*Process:* Today you are beginning a short unit on promises. Begin the session by asking students the following questions: "How many of you have made a promise today, this week, during the last month? How many of you have ever broken a promise? How many of you have ever had someone else break a promise they made to you?"

Today you are going to ask them to think of "a time I made a promise and kept it." As group members share their promises kept, encourage them to evaluate how the other person felt when the promise was kept. Draw from them the generalization that usually when you are able to keep a promise, both you and the other person have a good feeling. (If the discussion wanes, switch the topic to "a time someone made a promise to me and kept it."

Spend the last few minutes remembering what people have said.

## Activity 2

*Purpose:* To increase students' understanding of how people feel when promises are not kept; to increase awareness that all of us have broken promises.
*Process:* Begin by remembering some of the comments from yesterday. Then tell students that it takes courage to tell about a broken promise but that it is important that one be honest with oneself. Introduce the topic "the time I made a promise and broke it."

Elicit experiences concerning broken promises and, as you did yesterday, encourage students to describe the feelings that were associated with the broken-promise incident. You will facilitate the discussion by going first today, showing them that you have broken promises in your life.

Spend the last five minutes reflecting what they have said. Ask for them to write in their diaries about the problem of promising.

## Activity 3

*Purpose:* To increase sensitivity to making promises by making here-and-now commitments to group members.
*Process:* Tell them that today they're going to play the game "What Can I Do for YOU?" To play the game, someone raises his hand to get permission to ask another student what he can do for that person. The person asked can either say "No, thank you," or can actually suggest something.

The purpose of today's game is to give the students an opportunity to learn how to offer someone a favor without being afraid of being rejected. In a way this is a practice in etiquette—but it is more, too. In the first place, no child is pressured into offering a favor. Rather, he is offered the opportunity to do so if he wishes. Next, the favor that is accepted must be both *conceivable,* and *reasonable.* Finally, when the student offering the favor learns what another person would like him to do, he must state that it is something that he wants to do, that it is possible, and that it is reasonable. Then he decides (a) whether he can do it and (b) when he will do it. (The favor need not be carried out during the regular group discussion.)

The teacher should be emphasizing these main points as the lesson progresses. Emphasis should be placed on the nice feelings associated with offering and receiving kind behavior and on how important it is to keep commitments. Tell the children they will spend the next session finding out how well the commitments were kept.

**Activity 4**

*Purpose:* To increase sensitivity to making promises by making here-and-now commitments to group members.

*Process:* Continue the promises unit by checking on promises made in the previous session. Use your own judgment as to how long to stay with this task. If the group is really beginning to respond to the task, encourage them to ask for favors and make commitments.

After you have concluded the remembering of commitments from yesterday, introduce the game "What You Could Do For Me." The purpose of this game is to provide the students with a chance to learn how to ask for favors (a very hard thing for most of us). As on the previous day, requests must be conceivable and reasonable.

As soon as a child asks for such a favor and another child shows his willingness—and agrees to its possibility and reasonableness—the second child must make a commitment about when the promise will be fulfilled.

Remind the children about the nice feelings that are associated with giving kind behavior and about the fact that when a commitment is made but not kept, bad feelings are aroused. Some discussion should be held on this point.

Tell the children that, in the next class discussion, they will be reviewing which commitments were kept.

*Additional Process:* Depending on the mood of the group, an additional activity to reinforce the feelings generated by offering kind behavior is the head-tapping, body-slapping activity. Divide the group into threes. Each triad should engage in the following process, with all triad members getting a turn.

One person bends at the waist and tries to relax. The other two begin by gently slapping the back of the bent person, gradually increasing the vigor of the slaps. They continue slapping down the back, sides, haunches, thighs, and calves of the slapee and then back up again. When they get to the person's head, they gently tap his scalp with the tips of their fingers, then tap it vigorously. Finally they relax and gently rub the head, neck, and back of the focus person. After this process, they rotate and another triad member becomes the focus. This activity is very relaxing and pleasurable and quickly builds strong group feeling. (It would be wise for you to model this activity first with two other group members.) Don't do this exercise if your community is uptight about "touchy-feelie" activities.

# TAKING TESTS

**Objectives**

Students will:

a.  Understand the need for tests.
b.  Know how to use test results.
c.  Take tests seriously and try their best on them.
d.  Learn new techniques for taking tests.
e.  Learn how to prepare for tests.
f.  Take a public stand on cheating.

**Activity 1**

*Purpose:* To experience a testing situation that will demonstrate the importance of following directions.

*Process:* Make sure you have a very serious face. Tell students that today they are going to take a test and that some important decisions about their lives will be based on this test. (This is a lie.) Give them a dittoed sheet called "Following Directions." (See the form below.)

When all students have the test paper in front of them, separate them so they have to work alone and then say, "Please read the directions carefully and follow them exactly. O.K., begin." Allow no talking during the test.

## FOLLOWING DIRECTIONS

Read all the questions on the page and then go back to number 1 and begin answering them.

1. What is your full name?
2. What is your address?
3. When was the last time you ate chicken?
4. Look at the person on your right and write down the color of his or her eyes.
5. Say your name *out loud* three times.
6. Put your finger in your ear and say, "Woo Woo Woo!"
7. Stand up and stretch.
8. List three records that you think are neat.
9. Say the Pledge of Allegiance out loud.
10. Ignore all the above directions. Sign your name and be quiet so no one catches on to the joke.

Give the group fifteen minutes at most to catch on. Spend the last ten minutes discussing what happened. Ask them how they felt when they discovered they had been tricked. Have they ever done the same thing in a real situation? What is the lesson in this activity? Continue discussion until the period ends.

**Activity 2**
*Purpose:* To increase student awareness about the reasons for tests; to identify the different kinds of tests we take.
*Process:* Begin the session by saying, "What did we talk about yesterday? What was the point of the discussion and test?" After they have rehashed yesterday's lesson, tell them that today they are just going to have an open-ended discussion about tests. Use the following questions to get a lively discussion going. Limit your responses to accepting their statements and asking clarifying questions.

1. How do you feel about tests in general?
2. What happens to you before and during a test?
3. How do you get ready for a test?

4. Why do teachers give tests?

5. What are the kinds of tests that you have taken in your life?

Brief them by telling them that tomorrow they will be taking another kind of test.

### Activity 3

*Purpose:* To experience taking another kind of test; to reinforce the idea that you have to read tests carefully for important information.

*Process:* As soon as everyone is ready, have them all take out a sheet of paper and number it from 1 to 10. You will read the following common-sense questions to them and they will answer them on their paper.

1. A scientist found a coin in the desert dated 750 B.C. Many scientists thought he was lying. Why? (A coin could never have been dated B.C.)
2. Two men played chess. They played five games and each won three. How do you explain this? (They had different opponents.)
3. A man boasted: "In my bedroom the nearest lamp is ten feet from my bed. Alone in the room, without wires, strings, or anything, I can turn out the light and get into bed before the room is dark." Is it possible? How? (He does it in the daytime.)
4. What weighs more, a ton of feathers or a ton of bricks? (They weigh the same.)
5. What is Smokey the Bear's middle name? (His middle name is "the.")
6. If one field has three haystacks and another field has two and a half haystacks and you combine them, how many haystacks do you have? (You have one haystack.)
7. How many two-cent stamps in a dozen? (There are twelve.)
8. How many animals of each kind did Moses bring on the Ark? (None. Noah built the Ark.)
9. How far can a dog run into the woods? (He can only run half-way into the woods; after that, he's running out.)
10. If a plane crashed on the Canadian-American border, where would the survivors be buried? (The survivors would not be buried—they would be alive.)

After students have completed the test, go over the answers together. Discuss what assumptions they made about each question. Example: Did they assume all questions would contain accurate information? What was their reaction to this test experience? What is the best attitude to have when you take a test?

### Activity 4

*Purpose:* To help students increase awareness of different kinds of tests.

*Process:* Begin by telling the students that they have taken more tests than they imagine, and that, just to get an idea of how many, they are going to make a list of all the tests they have taken in school.

Begin having them list tests. Add any of your own that they don't think of. After a large list is developed, work together to group them into different categories. Examples include: physical tests, intelligence tests, achievement tests, aptitude tests, diagnostic tests, projective tests, and self-concept tests.

Discuss the different purposes of tests, what teachers do with them, and so forth. Your goal is to get the students to have a mature respect for tests, even though they are usually no fun to take.

## Activity 5

*Purpose:* To examine the moral question of cheating on tests.

*Process:* Begin by having people remember what happened at the last session. Ask what the major points were, then draw a continuum line on the board and describe the end points. At one end is Cheating Charlie. He cheats all the time—he even cheats when he knows the right answer. At the other end is Honest Ollie. He would rather die than cheat on a test. You couldn't pay him to cheat.

After the students and you have placed yourselves on the continuum, engage them in a general discussion about the rightness or wrongness of cheating. Use the topics "a time I cheated and it was O.K." and "a time I cheated and it was wrong." Discuss when it is O.K. to cheat and when it is wrong.

## Activity 6

*Purpose:* To identify strategies for studying for tests that will help school achievement.

*Process:* Start right out by giving students a hypothetical situation. Say, "Tomorrow you are going to take a test in science of everything you have studied this year. How will you study tonight for the test?" Let each person tell his own personal style of studying. Ask appropriate questions to get them to examine better ways to study. Have the kids who usually get A's tell how they study and compare their methods to those of the kids who get C's, D's and F's.

Reemphasize everything you have already discussed about taking tests. If you have any pet theories, share them.

*Additional Process:* Have each student make up a short test on taking tests (to be turned in at the next meeting), or take an additional session and prepare a handbook on taking tests. Reproduce and distribute the handbook to other classes.

# ROLES

## Objectives
Students will:

a. Understand the difference between societal roles and interpersonal roles.
b. Be able to identify role behavior in others.
c. Value facilitating roles over destructive roles.
d. Become more aware of their own role tendencies.

## Activity 1
*Purpose:* To experience how different roles affect group progress; to become aware of what typical roles people take on in groups.

*Process:* Begin the session by asking the students what the difference is between an actor and a person in real life. Elicit responses from several group members. Tell them, "Today we are going to do some acting. There is a very good reason for us to do acting, and hopefully, we can learn something about ourselves. I have copies here of a script for all of you and I would like some volunteers to act out the scene." At this point distribute copies of the following script.

(Pick volunteers to play the roles. After the group has gone through the script, ask for others to play it again. Go through the script twice and then do a group role-play without a script, having people adapt the roles to your own group. At some point stop role-playing and have students discuss why different people play certain roles. Do people play the same role in every group? Are some roles automatically bad? What would happen if a group had all leaders or all clowns? Continue discussion until class ends.)

## Script for Group Roles Activity

There are a number of roles that group members play at different times within the group. The role that a person plays requires both his own willingness to assume the role and the group's willingness to accept him in that role. For example, if he chooses to assume the role of clown, the group may allow him to continue his clown role or may stop him by expressing their irritation with this role, thus trying to force him to play a different role in the group.

Some of these group roles are:

1. *Mother:* sees to it that "needs" are met; takes care of one person at a time.
2. *Leader:* sees that tasks get done.
3. *Caring Helper:* sees that everyone's needs are met; sees that all the cards are on the table; moves towards all persons in the group.
4. *Pusher:* wants to move ahead as quickly as possible.
5. *Clown:* tries to get attention—to make others laugh.
6. *Sad Sack:* may at times be used as victim by others.
7. *Dominator:* dominates group discussion.
8. *Isolate:* remains an observer, or may resist group involvement by critizing what's going on, either verbally or nonverbally.
9. *Preacher:* keeps telling the group what it should or should not do.

Group members may be asked to choose a specific role and to play that role within the group. Members may later exchange roles and discuss how comfortable or uncomfortable they felt in their role and may also discuss reasons why people choose to play these roles at different times within the group. They may also discuss whether or not the group accepted them in their roles or attempted to question or challenge their role.

The Roles:

Motherly Mary
Leader Larry
Helping Fred
Pushy Paul
Clowning Clem
Sad Sack Sandy
Dominating Debbie
Lonely Lou
Preacher Perry

*Leader Larry:* Today, I would like the discussion to be about the group, what we like to get out of our circle, and what we must do to have a good time and learn something.

*Helping Fred:* It sounds like you mentioned a couple of things, like: "what do we want to happen," and "what kinds of rules do we need in this group." Maybe we should decide what to discuss first. What do you think, Lou?

*Lonely Lou:* [Shrugs]

*Helping Fred:* Debbie?

*Dominating Debbie:* I think we should begin by deciding what we want to do. First of all, we should do important things . . . well, I mean, we shouldn't goof off. Everybody knows that a circle group is intended to be a significant experience. Just the other day, I was reading an article which . . . oh, that reminds me of something. Do you know that you can't believe half the things that you read? Newsmen are so prejudiced.

*Leader Larry:* You have a point, Debbie. However, it seems like we are avoiding the original problem.

*Pushy Paul:* Yeah, come on. Let's decide what we're going to do. Better yet, let's talk about rules—like participation.

*Preacher Perry:* Everybody should talk and participate.

*Clowning Clem:* Sandy has to talk. She always has to talk . . . Ha ha ha.

*Sad Sack Sandy:* I'll quit if you keep mouthing off like that.

*Motherly Mary:* Don't quit, Sandy. I'm for you. Quit pickin' on her, Clem!

*Clowning Clem:* I don't have to pick on her. She's dumb enough that I don't have to point out her faults . . . Ha ha ha.

[Some of the group giggles. Sandy pretends she doesn't hear. Lou yawns.]

*Helping Fred:* Well, what should we do about participation?

*Preacher Perry:* As I said, everybody talks.

*Pushy Paul:* Okay, Perry says everybody talks. How about it? Lou? Debbie? Sandy? Mary? Let's get this issue settled so we can move on!

*Dominating Debbie:* We should all talk because we all have voices and we all have ideas. Why, the best idea we have is to have an enjoyable and rewarding experience. Like this issue about newspaper reporting. That is communicating. Even if some of the things are wrong, they are reported. When a person reads the paper, he is involved in communicating. That is what is important . . . communication. From the earliest of times, we know of people communicating. Adam and Eve and the serpent. Moses and the burning bush.

*Leader Larry:* It may be difficult for some people to speak in a group.

*Motherly Mary:* If we don't pick on Sandy, it would be better.

*Helping Fred:* Perhaps with more trust, some people will feel more comfortable in sharing their ideas.

*Preacher Perry:* Everybody should trust and be trusted.

[Lou yawns and looks around for something to read. Clem jumps up and fiendishly dances around. He makes a quick move toward Sandy, trying to scare her. Sandy giggles a little.]

*Clowning Clem* [singing] : Trust me, trust me, trust me . . .

*Pushy Paul:* Well, that's settled. We all try to trust and be trusted. Let's move on to the next thing!

## Activity 2

*Purpose:* To increase awareness of how each of us plays different roles in our own lives; to relate the role skit to our own lives.

*Process:* Begin the session by asking a few group members to remember what happened at the last meeting. As people recall what happened, encourage them to say what the point was—why the skit was done. Once it seems that they understand the point, tell them that today they are going to make a list of the roles they play in life. Get them started by saying, "All of you play the role of son or daughter and student; what other roles do you play?" Make a list of the roles they say they play. (Use the blackboard, newsprint, butcher paper, or just have someone record on notebook paper.)

After a large list is generated, use the following list of questions to get a discussion going about roles:

1. Which roles are your favorite?
2. Which roles do you wish you didn't play?
3. Which roles do you play that you didn't used to play?
4. Which roles will you not play when you're an adult?
5. Which role would you like to play?
6. Have you ever played a role that was really phony—that wasn't you?

Let the discussion continue till the end of the period.

## Activity 3

*Purpose:* To increase student understanding of why people play phony roles; to encourage value judgments from students regarding how they want to be.

*Process:* Begin the session by remembering what happened at the previous session. Then say, "Have any of you ever met someone who always acted superior,—who thought he was better than you?" (Watch their faces, and as they begin nodding, you will know they want to talk.) Have students tell their stories about someone who acts superior. Encourage them to think about why the person acts superior and what he needs. Move them into other common role behavior: somebody who lies all the time, sombody who is always putting himself down, and so forth. Try to get students to say something like, "People who act in these ways usually don't like themselves very much and are trying to cover it up. You can help such people by accepting them for what they really are and by ignoring their phony behavior." Ask each person to tell what the ideal person would be like. What roles would he play and not play? Let the discussion go until the end of the session.

### Activity 4

*Purpose:* To help students make personal commitments about their own role behavior.

*Process:* Begin by remembering the previous discussion. Encourage specific remembering of group members. Then put a long line on the board and describe the end points. At one end is Academy-Award Andie. He is an actor—always playing roles. No one knows what he is really like because he never is just himself. At the other extreme is Roleless Roland. Roland doesn't play any roles. In fact, people don't know how to react around him. They don't know if he is a boy or girl, father or son, student or teacher, or anything. Students are then invited to have their names placed on the board next to their own opinion about how many roles they play. Ask each person who puts his name up to give some reason why he feels he belongs there. Stop after half or more have put their names on the line.

Draw a second line, having the same end points, and tell them this is the "Ideal Me" line. Say, "If you could be just the way you wanted, where would you place yourself on this line?" Ask how often they would play roles, and what kind of roles they would play. Finish the session by asking for "I learned" statements about the unit on role behavior.

### Additional Activities

Prepare an "Is" book ("Happiness is," "Misery is," and so on).
Try selling yourself through a mock newspaper ad.
Choose a student for the day to receive strength bombardment. Focus on pictures of him, his favorite things, and his accomplishments. Change students each day.
Role-play situations in which people cop-out by making excuses. ("Let's go to a movie tonight!" Excuse: "I can't, I have to wash my hair.")
Show the film *The Hunter and the Forest.*
Have kids make a mask for each different role they play. (Student, son, paperboy, athlete, and so on.)

Have students role-play becoming the teacher; becoming parents; becoming the principal; becoming other kids; pretending to be a friend; having a substitute teacher for a day; being a substitute teacher for a day; being the teacher's pet; and so on.

Study a famous person (for example, the President, or an actress). Make a poster, collage, or booklet showing all the roles this person has played.

Play roles on TV.

Use qualification cards—cards containing various qualifications. Read them and tell what job each depicts.

Simulate TV talk shows. Let the emcee interview students with appropriate questions.

Make a list of all roles you play. Decide which ones you would rather not play.

List twenty roles you play and code them. For example, put a P by one if it is phony; put a B or G if it is a role boys or girls play; put a 3 if you think you'll be playing this role in three years.

**Additional Discussion Topics**

A time I wished I wasn't a student.
A time I wanted to babysit and couldn't.
A time I wished I was an only child.
A time my brother (sister) got me into trouble.
A time I acted cool to impress someone.
A time I pretended I didn't need any friends.
A time I wanted to leave the movie and was afraid to.
A time I was afraid I would get caught.
A time I didn't know whether or not to tell.
A time I couldn't participate because of being a boy (girl).
A time I wished I didn't —— so well.
A time I wished I wasn't the baby (oldest) of the family.
A time someone pretended to be my friend but wasn't.
A time someone liked me because I could help him.
A time someone acted like a hard guy but wasn't.
A time I misbehaved to get attention.
A time someone said he didn't like me.
A time I had to pretend so that I could be accepted.
How I am different at school and away from school.
A role that is fun to play.
The most important role I am in now.
The kind of role I would most like to play.
The role I play in my daydreams.
The different roles I play depend on who I'm with.

My role in the world seems to be . . .
A time I felt bad after I had been role-playing.
Because of my parents, I feel I have to play the role of . . .
Just because I am a boy (girl) I feel I have to . . .
A phony role I am sometimes forced to play.
I think someone is phony when . . .
I know when someone is phony by . . .
A time when I misunderstood someone.
A time when someone really misunderstood me.
When I am —— I can really be myself. [place or time]
The real self I would like to be.
I can (cannot) be my real self at school because . . .
I have to act differently when . . .
Nobody but me does . . .

Sometimes topics can be reworded into yes-or-no questions as a warm-up for a session on that topic.

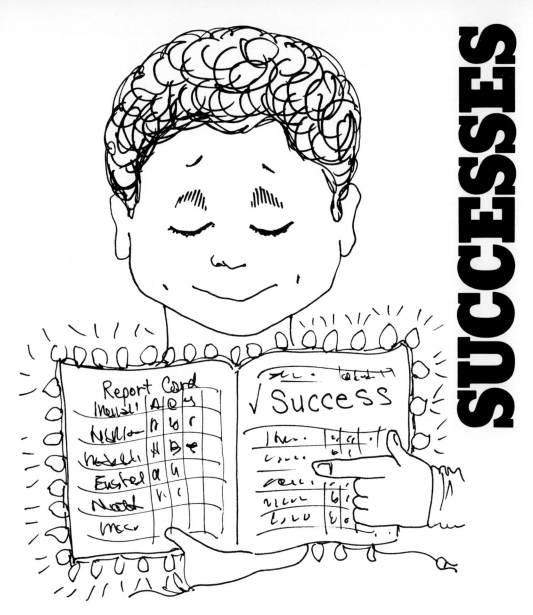

## Objectives

Students will:

a.  Identify key success experiences during their lives.
b.  Discover what is necessary for them to be successful.
c.  Decide on a symbol for success.
d.  Feel confident that they can be successful.

## Activity 1

*Purpose:* To increase student sensitivity to the concept of success; to identify small success experiences.

*Process:* Begin the session by asking the students what "success" means. Encourage several different definitions. You may ask someone to look up the word in the dictionary. After several students have tried to describe what success means, introduce one of the following topics: "something I have at home that is a personal success symbol" or "a success I have had in life."

As students discuss the topic, accept and reflect their contributions. Don't go into much detail today since you will have plenty of time to explore the idea of success with the group. Before the session ends, have each contribution remembered by someone in the group.

### Activities 2 and 3

*Purpose:* To help students increase their awareness of past successes.

*Process:* Begin by asking a few students to remember what was done at the last session, then ask the group if they know what a "time line" is. After a few have suggested definitions say, "For the next few days we are going to be using a very special kind of time line to examine our past successes." Have all students draw a long line on a piece of paper and mark it off with one space for each year of his life. When all have done so, explain that what they are to do today is think about their lives in terms of as many success experiences or high points—happy peaks—that they can remember. Say "Begin with your birth and make marks along the line at approximate places where you had a successful experience. Write a few words by each mark to explain what the event was. You will have an opportunity to tell us all about it at a later time."

At this point you will have to answer some questions about what is expected. Give them examples of what successes are, but let them know that anything they think of is a success to them—others don't have to agree. Help them get started filling in their time lines. It is important that they work alone on this part of the activity. You should complete your time line as well. They may finish filling in their time lines within the period. If so, begin having the individuals share them with the group.

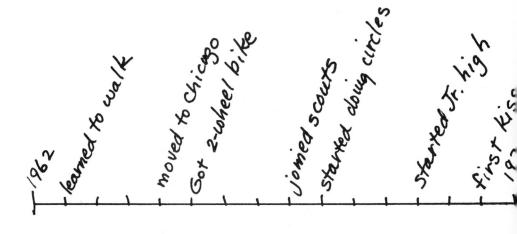

When an individual is sharing his time line, have him hold it up and point to different events as he discusses them. If you see some pattern or a few key events, refer to them in a clarifying way. (For example, It seems many of your successes involve pets.")

Encourage other students to ask questions of the sharing person. Expect this exercise to move slowly at first—most people feel they are bragging if they tell about their successes. If someone mentions this, go with it. Spend some time talking about what bragging is.

## Activity 4

*Purpose:* To continue to reinforce the awareness of positive past experiences.
*Process:* Begin by having people remember some of the peak experiences other people gave as part of their time-line sharing. After at least one thing about each person has been remembered, give the following statement: "Think of something that you would consider to be your greatest accomplishment as a student, your greatest accomplishment as a son or daughter, and your greatest accomplishment as a friend."

Spend ten to fifteen minutes eliciting responses from students about these areas. You might have to really pull it out of them or else they'll feel like they're bragging about their accomplishments. You should probably go first to give them an idea about what is appropriate to talk about. As people share accomplishments, reflect each one and emphasize that you heard it: "This is your accomplishment . . ." or ". . . is what you did." This constant reiterating of what they have done will help build self-confidence in the students.

Before the session is over, have the students write out the answers to the following questions on 3 × 5 cards. (Each student should be given six cards—one for each question.)

1. What personal accomplishment are you proudest of?
2. What was your biggest failure during the past year?
3. Name two things you believe in.
4. What adult would you like to be like when you grow up?
5. If you could spend the next year working on a goal, what would it be?
6. Name three adjectives you would like your friends to use to describe you.

Collect the cards for each student and save them for the next session.

## Activity 5

*Purpose:* To aid students' identification of successes, failures, and goals.
*Process:* Begin by reminding the group of the 3 × 5 cards activity. Tell them to pick a partner in the group whom they don't know very well and to find a quiet place where they can share their six cards. Let them spend five to ten minutes with their partner, sharing the six categories. Call them back to-

gether and have each child introduce his partner to the group. He can say anything he wants, but he must also describe his partner using three words that end in "ing." Spend the remainder of the session introducing partners. Ask, "Were you surprised by your friend's cards?"

### Activity 6

*Purpose:* To help students identify what conditions they need in order to be successful.

*Process:* Say, "As people shared their time lines and greatest accomplishments, we noticed patterns—certain similar conditions that were necessary for you to be successful. Today we are going to analyze our own success pattern." On the left side of a piece of paper, each student should make a list of ten to twenty success experiences he has had in his life. When everyone has at least ten, say, "Now we are going to code these to learn some things about our success patterns. Put P by the success if it involved learning something new. Put R by it if other people recognized you for it. Put M by it if you received a medal or other award. Put 5 next to those successes that happened more than five years ago. Put 1 next to those that occurred during the last year. Put * by the five most important ones. Rank order the top five from most important to least important." (Add other codes that seem appropriate.) After they have been coded, discuss them using "I learned" statements and "I wish" statements. Also have them discuss, "What are some successes you hope to have during the next two years?" and "Overall, what kinds of experiences make you feel successful?" Finish with this sentence stub: "I feel successful when . . ."

### Activity 7

*Purpose:* To reinforce students' success concepts.

*Process:* Begin by saying, "We have been trying to identify all the ways we have been successful in the past. Hopefully, from this you have gotten the feeling that you, all of you, have the potential to be successful in the future. Today we are going to go around and tell each person all the good things we think they can do or all the successes we think they will have during the next ten years."

Start with the person on your left. Encourage everyone to raise his hand and tell this person what successes each expects him to accomplish, what predictions each makes for him, and what strengths each sees in him. (This is really an informal strength bombardment.)

### Additional Activities

Show the film *Second Effort* (Lombardi).
Play the match-up game: List things students do well and things students would like to do. Make up matching groups (those who can play chess,

with those who would like to) and suggest they get together and share. Follow up at later date.

Play the fortunetelling game: "I see you in five years . . ."

Make a poster or collage titled "We Can."

Make a poster on which students place their names at the top, followed by various activities (reading, sleeping, swimming, playing with a pet) rank ordered according to value. Instead of ranking with numbers, print the most valued activity in large letters, the next most valued in somewhat smaller letters, and so on.

Make a hope-for-the-future tree, with branches for various vocations with students' names. Students may subscribe to more than one branch.

Have each student list twenty of his own skills and then rank and code them. (Let the students choose their own codes.)


## Additional Discussion Topics

Something I can do well.

Something I can't do well.

Something I'd like to do well.

Something everyone else can do that I wish I could do.

Something I can do that I don't like.

Something I can do but I'd like to do better.

Something I'd like to teach someone.

Something I didn't think I could do but did.

Something new I did this year.

Something I bragged about and couldn't do.

Something I bragged about and didn't have to prove.

A time I had to prove myself.

Something people wanted me to prove and I didn't think I had to.

A time I was called "chicken" and I knew I was.

A time it mattered that I tried to do something.

A time I helped the team win.

A time I was a leader.

A time I was afraid I'd fail the team.

How I felt the first time I learned how to do something.

Something I would like to try that I never have.

Something I would like to be able to do by the time I am twenty.

Something I can do today that I couldn't do a year ago.

The things I do best.

Someone who seems to do everything well.

A time I felt I couldn't do anything right.

A time I realized I could do something if I tried.

If I had to give up one skill I possess, it would be . . .

Something I do because I was encouraged.

Something I taught someone.
A time I learned by watching.
The most important thing someone taught me.
I felt successful when . . .
I'm very good at . . .
When I am successful, I feel . . .
A time when success went to my head.
A success I would most like to achieve.
I will feel successful when . . .
A time when it was difficult to accept winning.
I consider it a failure to . . .
A time I failed and it was hard to admit.
A time I failed and someone made me feel better.
A time someone helped me overcome a failure.
A time I tried something and wasn't afraid of failure.
A time I learned from a mistake.
When I succeed or fail, my friends . . .
A time when I felt better after I had talked to someone.
Something I'm always making excuses for doing or not doing.
A time I didn't bother to make excuses.
What I do when I fail.
The greatest failure in the past year.
My greatest success in the past year.

**MORAL JUDGMENT**

## Objectives
Students will:

a. Become aware of what they believe is right and wrong.
b. Identify different methods for evaluating right and wrong behavior.
c. Identify the conflict in each of us about doing the "right" thing.
d. Identify times when they think they did the right thing.

## Activity 1

*Purpose:* To gain student interest regarding the moral judgment unit; to increase awareness of different opinions about what is right and what is wrong.

*Process:* Begin the session by giving each child a 3 × 5 card. Then tell the following story to the students:

> A group of students are in a discount store. One of them, Mary, notices that her best friend, Sue, has slipped away from the group and is putting some earrings in her purse. Mary notices a man watching Sue and sees him point to the group in an angry way. What would you do in that situation if you were Mary?

First have each person write a short answer on the 3 × 5 card. Collect them and read them anonymously. After you have read all the cards, open the discussion to everyone. Encourage disagreement about what would be the right thing to do. As the discussion progresses, bring up the issue of right and wrong behavior. Get people to take a stand on the right thing to do. The group will probably break into the loyalty versus honesty issue. Before the group ends, get them to vote on what action seems the most right or the most wrong.

### Activity 2

*Purpose:* To continue examination of right and wrong behavior.

*Process:* Begin the session by remembering what you discussed at the previous session. Then tell the students another story about someone who had to decide between right and wrong. (Several story possibilities are included at the end of this section.) You may want them to write down their responses on 3 × 5 cards first, or you might want to discuss it right away. Regardless, see that you encourage them to look at the situation from different ways. Get students to make statements about the rightness or wrongness of a given behavior. Once again, allow everyone to vote on which course of action they think would be best.

After they have discussed different opinions, ask for volunteers to role-play the characters in the story. Let two sets of actors role-play and then continue discussing it.

### Additional Decision Stories

1. You are going over to your friend's apartment building and, as you walk into the courtyard, you see your friend and another person climbing out of the basement window with an electric drill. The janitor comes running around from the back and stops all three of you. He asks you whether you saw the others climb out of the windows. What would you say?

2. You and a friend go to a party, at which most of the kids are two years older than you. When you get there, some of the other kids start teasing your friend, but they don't know you're with him. What do you do?

3. You are taking a test and you notice that a cute boy (girl), whom you have been trying to get to notice you, sitting next to you. You notice that he (she) is copying your test answers and that the teacher is walking up and down the aisle. What do you do?

4. You are babysitting and you have been told not to let anyone in. Two very good friends come by and want to come in. You know nothing bad could possibly happen. What do you do?

5. You are eating dinner at a friend's house and his mother serves you this horrible-looking, smelly stuff. Everyone is sitting around the table enjoying it. What do you do?

**Activity 3**

*Purpose:* To increase student awareness of the conflict that goes on in each of us concerning doing the right thing.

*Process:* Begin by saying, "I was thinking that sometimes I'm not sure what is the right thing to do in a certain situation." Tell them your experience of a time when you weren't sure what was the right thing to do. After your story, invite others to tell about their experience along those same lines. After three or four have shared their experiences, explain to the group that whenever a person is unsure of himself there are two voices in his head arguing about what to do. Tell them you would like to play a game to demonstrate how this happens. Pick someone who has already told a story or who has a story involving a choice situation between right and wrong behavior.

Put two chairs in the center of the circle and have the student sit in one. Tell him that when he sits in that chair he feels one way about the situation and when he sits in the other chair he feels the opposite way. Tell him to carry on a conversation between the two voices. When he changes voices, he must change chairs. Coach him by standing next to him and whispering in his ear about different things to say to the other person. Let him work on it for a few minutes and then stop him. Ask for another volunteer. By now you will probably have several people who want to try it. Continue playing the chairs game till the session is over.

*Additional Process:* You may take an entire second session to play the chairs game or you may want students to discuss it as a group after a few have done it. Once again, when you discuss it, encourage them to make flat-out statements about the right thing to do in a particular situation. Ask them, "How do you decide what is the right thing to do?"

**Activity 4**

*Purpose:* To help students discover that they have the ability to do the right thing.

*Process:* Begin the session by having several group members recall what they have been doing so far in this unit. Then introduce the topic for the day: "a time when I did the right thing." Listen to the children's stories of when they did the right thing. Accept and reflect their contributions. Help them see that all of them have the ability to do the right thing. Make sure that all contributions are remembered.

*Additional Process:* Do a physical continuum with the students to get them to publicly state what they believe about doing the right thing. Put a smiling face, a neutral face, and a sad face up on the wall. Tell them to stand where they feel they are, from "I always do the right thing" to "I sometimes do the right thing" to "I almost never do the right thing." Use the following sentence whip: "I was proud I did the right thing when I . . ."

**IDENTIFYING CONCERNS**

*This unit is good for developing interest in self-examination. It relies mainly on written responses, which are later talked about and shared voluntarily in the group.*

*It is also useful for increasing students' awareness of their attitudes toward family members and others as well as toward themselves.*

**Objectives**
Students will:

a. Learn a new technique for generating data about themselves.
b. Discover that they all have similar concerns about other people.
c. See the relationship between resentments, demands, and appreciations.
d. Experience low-risk self-disclosure that builds group cohesiveness.

**Activity 1**
*Purpose:* To introduce the students to the concept of the fantasy telegram; to begin to build a desire for self-disclosure in a nonthreatening environment.

*Process:* Begin today's session by saying something like, "Today we're going to begin a unit in which we are going to be using some make-believe telegrams, and we're going to be writing some things out on paper and maybe read them and talk about them together."

After the children are situated in the circle, give each one a 3 X 5 card, then say, "Think about someone who is very important to you—a member of your family, a friend, someone at school, someone who is far away—and imagine that you are sending him or her a telegram. This telegram has to begin with the words, "I urge you," followed by whatever you urge the person to do. Don't put your own name on it because it's not important that we know who wrote which telegram."

Give the children three to four minutes to think about whom they will send the telegram to and to write it. If you see some children who are not writing, encourage them, in as gentle a way as possible, to write the telegram. You might want to give them more examples so they can think of something. At this point it's really not important how deeply they get into the idea as long as they understand the process and do it the first time. You'll be using this technique again later when it will be more meaningful to the students.

When the telegrams are completed, collect them and mix them up. Without any comment, read each one aloud.

After you've read the telegrams, try to involve the students in an informal discussion for about ten minutes, using some of the following questions: "Did any of you hear an 'I urge' telegram other than your own that you really felt was interesting or that really could have been written by you?" (To go into it, you might ask them to give their example of such a telegram.) "What if you received [*put in one of the particular telegram messages*]—what do you think your response would be? If someone really sent you a telegram like that, how do you think you would react?"

Allow this discussion to go on. Ask any other questions that seem to come out of it or just ask children to react to the experience. Say something like, "Does anybody have a reaction to what we've done so far?" With five minutes left, give the cards back (it doesn't matter whether they get their original card) and tell them to think of someone else they would like to send a really important telegram to. Tell them to think of something they really would like to urge someone to do and then to write it out on the back of the card. Let them write out the telegram until the end of the period. Make sure you collect the telegrams before they leave.

### Activity 2

*Purpose:* To develop the ability of the students to openly share "I urge" telegrams without writing them first; to help diagnose the kinds of things the students are concerned about through the kinds of telegrams that they would send to different people.

*Process:* Begin the session by asking three or four participants to remember what happened at the last session. Encourage them to remember specifically what some of the telegrams were. After several have been remembered, say something like, "Today we're going to continue thinking about things we might urge other people to do—people who are important to us and who we care about. So I'd like you to just close your eyes for a minute and try to picture in your mind someone important to you—someone you didn't send an 'I urge' telegram to yesterday—and think about what you'd like to urge them to do." See to it that the people in the circle close their eyes, and give them twenty to thirty seconds to try to get into the experience.

After enough time has passed, have them open their eyes, and ask whether anyone would like to share the kind of telegram he'd like to send to someone. Allow the students to share the different telegrams they would send for about fifteen minutes of the circle.

At the end of that time, cut them off (even if there are people who still have telegrams that they want to share) and say, "I'd like to remember now what some of the people have said—what kind of telegrams they would send." Then do a remembering session in which primarily, the people who haven't shared do the remembering of what the others have said.

Save three or four minutes at the end of the period to read the telegrams from yesterday that were written but that didn't get shared. This session will end with you reading, without comment, the "I urge" telegrams that were written in the last five minutes yesterday.

### Activity 3

*Purpose:* To use the "I urge" telegram approach to force the participants to examine what they are dissatisfied with in their own lives.

*Process:* Begin the session by encouraging several members to remember what happened yesterday, and allow the remembering of what happened yesterday to go on for three or four minutes. At some point say, "Today I'm going to ask you to do something that might be a little harder than what we've been doing cause it requires that you really be honest with yourself." At this point, hand them all 3 X 5 cards and say, "Think about some area of your own life that is not the way you want it to be. It can be anything at all in your own personal life that you're not satisfied with. I want you to write yourself an "I urge' telegram about this. Start by saying 'Self, I urge you to . . .' and then write about the problem. You don't have to put your name on it."

Give the participants a minute or two to think about what they would like to urge themselves to do. After all the cards have been completed, collect them, mix them up, and give them back to the participants. Tell the students, "If you get your own card back, pretend that it's someone else's. I'm not interested in finding out who said what, but I would like each of you to read one of the others' telegrams, and we'll all just listen quietly as they are read."

Then have each member read the card that he has in his hand and let everyone else listen. After all the telegrams are read, use the following questions to get the children into a discussion about how you can go about changing yourself into the kind of person you want to be: "Are some of the things people urge themselves to do easier than others? Which ones are easier and why do you say that? How would you go about fulfilling or answering one of the telegrams that someone read here today?"

Bring up the question of resolutions—why most resolutions don't work. Encourage the students to tell about a time when they actually urged themselves to do something and to tell whether or not they were successful doing it. Let this discussion continue until the period ends.

## Activity 4

*Purpose:* To use telegrams to become aware of wishes.

*Process:* Have the students close their eyes and think about the following. "If someone came in the room with a 'best news' telegram for you—the best news you could get right now—what would your telegram say?" Encourage group members to share their fantasy telegrams in the group. As people share, encourage them to get into the telegrams by asking the appropriate questions. Make sure everyone is remembered before the session is completed.

## Activity 5

*Purpose:* To increase the students' awareness of which of their peers are the most important to them; to become aware that there are things they resent about, and related demands they make on, all people they care about; to become aware that there are also things they appreciate about the people they care about.

*Process:* For this activity each person will need a piece of scratch paper and something to write with.

Tell each member of the circle that he is to make a list of ten people whom he comes in contact with in his everyday life and who is less than 18 years of age. This list can include his best friend, people that he sees on the way to school every day, brothers and sisters, nieces, nephews, aunts, uncles, and others as long as they are under 18 years of age. Be sure to tell students to leave space after each name.

After they have made their lists, tell them to rank the ten names in the following way: "Put a 1 next to the person you would miss the most if he were to move away or die or just weren't around anymore. Put a 2 next to the name of the person whose leaving would make you feel next saddest, and so on, down to a 10 next to the person whose leaving really wouldn't matter very much. If you're a girl, put a G next to every girl on the list. If you're a boy, put a B next to every boy. Put a 3 next to the name of those people you don't think you'll know or see very much within three years from today. Put an F next to the name of any person on your list with whom you have had an argument or a fight in the last month. Put a P next to the name of any person on your list whom you would invite to a party on your birthday."

If you can think of any other codes that you would like to have the children use, introduce them, but at some point have them stop and have a brief discussion about what they have been doing. Some of the questions you might ask are:

1. Was anybody surprised by some of the things they found out from doing this?
2. Would anybody like to make any kind of an "I learned" statement?
3. Would someone be willing to share some of the things you discovered as you coded your list?
4. If we were to do this again, would you change your list and have different people on it?
5. Was it easy or hard to decide how to rank the people on your list?
6. Were there some people it was hard to choose between, and were there others that were easy to rank?

Encourage any reactions you can get to any of these questions and make up your own questions if these aren't appropriate. Make sure that you leave five to eight minutes at the end of the session, because the next thing you're going to say is, "Pick one of the top three people on your list. On the back of the list, or on another piece of paper, write the name of that person and below it write a sentence that starts with the words 'I resent,' and then fill in somethat you resent that they have done." (You may have to explain what "resent" means.)

After they have written what they resent, tell them to continue the statement by writing "I demand," and putting in the demand that goes with the resentment. Explain to the students that, whether they know it or not, implied in every resentment is some demand that they would make on a person. You may have to give them an example, such as "Mother, I resent that you always make me take out the garbage and I demand that my brothers and sisters share the job equally with me from now on."

After they have written their resentment and demand statement, tell them to write "but I appreciate," and then encourage them to finish the sentence with a statement of appreciation showing that, even though they have a resentment and they want to make a demand on this person, there is something about him that they appreciate very much.

The final statement, then, should have a resentment part, a demand part, and an appreciation part. If time is left, collect the papers and read the resentment, demand, and appreciation statements. If no time remains, collect the papers and, at the next session, begin by reading all statements.

### Activity 6
*Purpose:* To encourage the children to openly share resentment, demands, and appreciation; to elicit from them things they are concerned with about the way school is run.

*Process:* Begin today's session by reading the statements from the previous session. If you've already read them, begin by having the children remember what they did at the past session.

After you have done so, tell them, "Today I want you to think about school and I want you to think about something you resent about the way the school is operated, about the way you're treated in school, or about anything you want. Then think of some demand that could go with your resentment that you would like to make on the school. But you have to think about something you appreciate about school, too. So your statement, if you're going to make one, has to have all three parts: something you resent, something you demand, and something you appreciate. Think about that, and anybody who wants to make their resentment, demand, and appreciation statements can do so."

You can spend the rest of this session eliciting statements from the children. It might be helpful to list the statements as they are made. If the kids get hung up thinking about the appreciation statements, you might just want to stop there and have a brainstorming session in which you say, "O.K., for the next five minutes we're going to make a list of all the possible things that we appreciate about school—anything that is worth appreciating. There are no wrong answers. Just shout it out and pick someone in the circle to write it down."

You might want to end this session, if there is time, by whipping this sentence stub around the circle: "If I could change the school in one way, I'd . . ."

## Objectives

Students will:

a. Experience working as a group to solve a common problem.
b. Become aware of the importance of good question asking for solving problems.
c. Practice giving advice to others.
d. Evaluate and classify advice into categories.
e. Become aware of what clarifying questions are.
f. Practice asking clarifying questions.
g. Identify times when different problem-solving strategies are beneficial.
h. See the relationships between problem-solving strategies and decision making.

## Activity 1

*Purpose:* To experience working as a group to solve a common problem; to increase awareness that question asking is an important skill; to develop a feeling of self-confidence as a group.

*Process:* Introduce the idea that, for this activity, you will act as a computer. The students can ask you questions, but you can only answer them yes or no. (You can also say, "You're on the wrong track" and "Important question.") They are to figure out the answers to these riddles:

1. A woman gave a piece of food to the man she lived with. His eating of the food resulted in his death. Even though this event became world famous, she was never brought to trial. (The man and woman were Adan and Eve.)

2. A man enters a bar in Chicago during the noon hour ans asks the bartender for a drink of water. The bartender reaches under the counter, draws out a gun and points it at the man, who then says, "Thank you," turns around, and walks out. (The man had the hiccups; the bartender scared him)

3. In a room is a table, some broken glass on the floor, and some water on the floor. Mary is dead. John is standing beside her. How did Mary die? (John is a cat; Mary, a goldfish. John pushed the bowl off the table.)

4. A man lives on the twenty-fifth floor in an apartment house. Each day he gets in the elevator, goes down to the lobby, and goes to work. Each evening he returns to the building, gets in the elevator, goes up to the fourteenth floor, gets out of the elevator, and walks up the last ten flights. Why? (The man is a midget. He can't reach above the fourteenth floor button.)

5. A man who worked in a circus was found in his room—dead. Next to his bed was a gun and his cane, which had been sawed off at the bottom. What happened? (He was a blind midget clown. He thought he was growing taller because someone was cutting his cane shorter and shorter, so he committed suicide.)

6. Two men were bound and put into their car trunk following a robbery. In the morning a passing person heard noises coming from the trunk, and the two were found. One man had died and one was quite alive and unharmed. Why? (There was a spare tire in the trunk. One man had breathed the air.)

7. A woman, Mrs. Jones was killed in a "skiing accident" in Switzerland. When Mr. Smith in Chicago read of her death, he called the police and said, "It was murder, and Mr. Jones is the culprit." How did he know? (Mr. Smith is a ticket agent and he sold Mr. Jones one round-trip and one one-way ticket to Switzerland.)

8. There is a car accident. A man is killed in the crash and his son is critically injured. The boy is rushed to the hospital and is prepared for surgery. When the doctor comes in to operate and sees the boy, the doctor says, "I can't operate, that's my son!" (The doctor is the boy's mother.)

## Activity 2

*Purpose:* To continue building awareness about the importance of asking the right questions.

*Process:* Begin by reminding the students of what they did yesterday. Ask who can remember some of the key questions that were asked during the questioning game. Tell them that today you have with you a crystal ball that can answer one, and only one, question from each person. They have to decide how they want to use their precious question. It will be more effective if you have some object resembling a crystal ball. An old glass globe (possibly a dining-room fixture) will serve this purpose.

One at a time, let each person approach the crystal ball and ask it his question. Appoint someone to record the questions asked and the names of the persons who asked them. After all students have asked their questions, discuss the experience. Ask them:

1. Which of your questions could have been answered without using the crystal ball?
2. What are the things you are obviously concerned about from your questions?
3. What question would the following people ask the crystal ball:
   your mother, the principal, the President, your best friend, your father?
4. When you were five years old, what question would you have asked?
5. What question might you ask when you are twenty-one?

Summarize by remembering the original questions before you leave.

## Activity 3

*Purpose:* To relate students' increasing skill as problem solvers to solving other people's interpersonal problems.

*Process:* Begin the session by bringing in an *Ann Landers* or *Dear Abby* column that has appropriate content, and read the problem, but not the answer, to the class. These questions will serve as examples for questions you will ask the students to invent.

Give each person a 4 X 6 index card and tell him to invent a typical kind of problem that someone of his age might have. (Give students ten minutes to complete this.) It is important that they don't put their names on the cards. Have them begin all the letters with "Dear Group," and sign them with made-up names. Collect all the completed problem cards and rubber-band them together for the next session.

## Activities 4-6

*Purpose:* To act as a problem-solving group for semifictitious problems; to gain practice in offering solutions.

*Process:* For each of these three sessions, the process should be the same: Read a problem from one of the cards and discuss it as a group. You should act as a facilitator and bring up all the possibilities that the students might miss. Try to keep your opinions out of the discussion. When you think a problem has been examined as much as possible, ask your group secretary to write an answer on the back of the card; then go on to the next problem. (The group will love this activity and will invent wilder and wilder problems to talk about.)

*Additional Process:* This activity could become a whole program by itself. The next step, after answering pseudoproblems, is to have people submit *real* problems to the group anonymously. The group discusses each problem, finally agrees on an answer, and then writes the answer to the person submitting the problem. You might want to advertise in the school paper and spend one session a week on problem solving. (This activity is a good way to begin developing the concept of *consensus* in your group. If you require that all group members agree on a solution before you write it, you will be encouraging consensus.)

**Activity 7**

*Purpose:* To practice a new skill for helping people solve their own problems; to be able to compare advice-giving to clarifying responses.

*Process:* Ask for four volunteers to join you in a "fish bowl," with the rest of the group being observers. Explain to the people in the fish bowl that today they are going to try to help someone make a decision in an entirely different way than they have been doing up till now. Instruct the members to think of a decision that they have to make that they haven't yet decided on. Get one person to volunteer to be the central person. It will be his job to describe the decision that is to be made and to tell the rest of the participants what conditions exist regarding the decision. The helpers may ask any questions of the person to help him look at the decision from different vantage points, but they may not make statements of any kind. The observers are watchdogs. They should shout out if someone takes the spotlight away from the central person by giving advice, sharing his own problem, or even empathizing. Focus-helpers can only ask questions. The following questions are useful in helping the person think about his decision:

1. Have you considered the consequences of the different choices? What are they?
2. Where could you get help in making this decision?
3. Have you been concerned about this for a long time?
4. What assumptions must you make to decide one way or another?
5. Are there other alternatives to the ones you have mentioned?
6. Have you discussed this with parents, teachers, friends, and others?
7. If you were older (younger), richer (poorer), a boy (a girl), would the decision be easier to make?
8. Have you examined the risks involved in your decision? What are they?

9. What's the worst thing that can happen?
10. What's the best thing that can happen?

After you have demonstrated the game for fifteen minutes, stop and let the observers tell what they've noticed. If time permits before the end of the period, have each person write out a decision he has to make in the near future. If no time is left for that, assign it as homework.

### Activity 8

*Purpose:* To gain practice in asking clarifying questions.

*Process:* Remind the group members of the decision activity that was assigned last session. If some don't have one written out, give them a few minutes to do so. Break up the group into triads and have each group decide on a central person and on two helpers. They should repeat the process they used in the fish bowl yesterday. You should act as the watchdog, going from group to group. Make sure the helpers understand that they are not to make statements, give advice, or empathize. The central person is in complete control and can end the discussion at any time. When one person is through, another should play that role. (Try to get all three in each group to experience being the central person.)

### Activity 9

*Purpose:* To draw conclusions about the appropriateness of different strategies for helping people solve problems and make decisions.

*Process:* Begin by asking group members to contrast the different methods for solving problems that they have been practicing during the last five sessions. The basic strategies they mention should include clarifying questions, advising, sharing personal experiences, preaching, and moralizing. Discuss which strategies are effective at which times and for what kinds of problems.

Discuss one or both of the following topics: "a decision I made all by myself" and "a time I couldn't decide between two things."

# SELF-CONCEPT

**Objectives**

Students will:

a. Become sensitive to the many dimensions of the self-concept.

b. Become more aware of the ways in which each of them is unique.

c. Experience checking out their own perceptions of themselves against others' perceptions of them.

d. Publicly affirm some aspect of their own physical selves that they are happy about.

e. Become more sensitive to how their self-concept changes over time.

f. Write their own self-evaluation following the unit.

## Activity 1

*Purpose:* To introduce the students to the concept of "self;" to encourage students to look at themselves; to introduce the Q-sort technique.

*Process:* Today is the first session in a series on self-concept. Give each group member five 3 × 5 index cards. Tell him to make a pile of the five blank cards and to write his answers to the question "Who am I?" on the first card. Tell him to put the completed card on the bottom of the pile so that a blank card is on top. Repeat this process five times—until all students have answered the question five times.

Ask the students to rank their answers from the "I am" they like best to the one they like least. Give them rubber bands and have them band their cards. Collect the packs of cards and mix them up, then redistribute them randomly. Tell students that if they get their own cards back, they are to pretend they belong to someone else. Have each child read the cards he has. Discuss cards in any way you wish for the rest of the session. (Encourage students to talk about all the different people each person is.) Discuss how one's view of himself compares to how others think of him.

## Activity 2

*Purpose:* To identify ways in which each student is unique; to help students begin to feel comfortable with differences.

*Process:* Begin by asking five or six members to remember something that happened at the last session. Then ask the following questions in a general way: "How many of you have never eaten liver? How many of you have never gone bowling? How many of you have never been to Chicago (or New York or Los Angeles)?

Then say, "Today we're going to play a game called 'something I've never done that everyone else has done.' The way you get points (tokens) is to raise your hand and tell us something you have never done. I will ask the rest of the class how many have done it. You get one token from everyone who *has* done it. After you have one turn, you must wait until everyone else who has a hand up gets his turn. If no one who hasn't had a turn has his hand up, you may have a second turn, and so on. The idea is to think of things you have never done that you think everybody, or almost everybody, has done. It is important that you say real things." (It is helpful if you cut 3 × 5 cards into 3 × 1 strips and give twenty strips to each person. These become the tokens. People hand them out after each turn.)

Play this game for the entire session, leaving a couple of minutes at the end to comment on the experience. Questions for discussion may include: "Were any of you surprised at what was said? Did you find someone else who hasn't done the same things you haven't done? Are we more alike or different from each other?"

## Activity 3

*Purpose:* To continue emphasis on the uniqueness of each person; to understand that each person is "one of a kind."

*Process:* Begin today's lession by asking four or five students to remember the last session. Then give each person a blank piece of paper and have him write the following sentence: "One way I am unique compared to everyone in this circle is . . ." After students copy the sentence stub and you explain what "unique" means, tell them to finish the sentence in three different ways. Then help each person put his thumb print at the bottom of his paper. (For this part you will need an ink pad. Use your own resourcefulness to obtain one.)

After each student has completed his uniqueness statement and his thumb print, have him tear off the piece of paper containing the thumb print. Now collect the uniqueness statements and read them out loud. While the students listen, have them get to know their thumb prints. Collect the thumb prints at the end of the session.

*Additional Process:* On 3 X 5 cards, have each student write the same name. Put all the name cards in the center and mix them up. Then have each person find his own handwriting. Discuss other ways in which each individual is unique.

### Activity 4

*Purpose:* To continue emphasis on students' unique self-concepts.

*Process:* Ask three or four members to remember what happened last time, then bring out the thumb prints and put them in the middle of the group. Tell each person to find his thumb print. Give them three minutes and then say, "Now we will fingerprint your thumb again to see whether you were right." Discuss how they found their thumb prints.

State the following: "You are unique. There has never been anyone like you and there never will be again." Discuss: "Is that good or bad?" Do you agree? What are some implications of the statement?" Ask three or four people to summarize the sessions on uniqueness.

### Activity 5

*Purpose:* To help students find something attractive in their own faces; to encourage, on the part of each student, public disclosure that they like themselves.

*Process:* When everyone is seated, take out a hand mirror—the larger the better—and give it to the person on your right. Tell the person that he is to look in the mirror and see something that he likes about his face. You might begin by explaining that people are all very critical of themselves. Today's activity is to give everyone a chance to focus on what it is a person likes about the way he looks. The first person should look in the mirror, notice what he likes, and say, "I like my . . ." He should then give the mirror to the next person, who will repeat the process. The mirror should go around the circle in this way, with each person telling something he likes about his face.

If a person receives the mirror and says he can't find anything he likes, or if he only says bad things, ask if anyone else in the group can see something in his face that they like. After two or three have responded, ask him to look again. Gently encourage him to say something, but accept it if he can't find anything right now.

After all group members have passed the mirror around, ask if anyone can see something they like in the face of another person. (This is a kind of physical strength bombardment.) Encourage people to use the personal approach again, saying, "I like your nose," rather than "He has a nice nose." If people broaden the strokes to include personality traits or other body parts, accept it and let them continue. (See to it that each person gets at least one other person to say something nice about him.)

(CAUTION: *If there is someone in your group who has an unusually severe physical problem or deformity,* don't *use this activity!*)

### Activity 6

*Purpose:* To help students experience making self-evaluations; to help them give and get feedback on how others see them.

*Process:* As soon as the students are ready, give each a blank piece of paper and ask them to tear it into ten pieces. Next, have them write a word that describes them in some way on each piece of paper. (You can give examples to get them started, but don't give them actual words.) Next, tell them to make a pile with the word they like most on top and the one they like least on the bottom. Tell them no one has to share his list if he doesn't want to. Ask for a volunteer to share four words from his list without saying how the four were ranked. Ask other students to suggest how this person would probably rank the words. After three different people have given their opinions, ask the person how he really ranked them. Do this with two people this session and continue it in the next session. (Collect the lists to safeguard them.)

### Activity 7

*Purpose:* To continue helping students give and get feedback on self-concept.

*Process:* Begin the lesson by having three or four people remember what was done last time. Return the lists and continue the guessing activity. If five minutes are left at the end of the session, have students complete this sentence stub: "Most people think I am . . ." Another excellent stub is "I used to be —— but now I'm ——."

### Activity 8

*Purpose:* To examine how our personalities have changed since we were little.

*Process:* Begin the session by asking the group, "What have we learned about ourselves during the past two weeks?" (You might want to limit the interaction to "I learned" statements—like, "I learned I am the only one who has never gotten in trouble at school.") Next, say, "Today I want you to think about how your personality has changed since you were in first grade. Think about things you used to believe, things you used to do, ways you used to act, and so on."

As students share ways in which they have changed, encourage them to evaluate the changes by asking them, "Are you glad about that?" and, "Do you wish that hadn't happened?" Leave at least five minutes at the end to remember what everyone said.

## Activity 9

*Purpose:* To allow students the opportunity to express their opinions about the kind of person they are.

*Process:* When they are ready, have students take out a sheet of notebook paper and tell them you want them to write a thought paper titled: "This is Me," based on everything they have thought about during this unit. Tell students, "If anyone doesn't want me to read his paper out loud, write "don't read" on the top," then collect the papers. Read any that are completed, but don't name the writers.

*Alternate Process:* Bring paper bags and crayolas for all members. Have them decorate the outside of their bags with facts about themselves that everyone knows, and inside put pieces of paper that contain more private statements, words, or pictures that they don't share with everyone. Encourage people to bring things out of their bags and share them with the group, or have them pick partners and share privately with that one other person.

## Activity 10

*Purpose:* To increase the student's understanding that his self-concept comes from other people.

*Process:* Get a piece of construction paper and print IALAC on it in very large letters (This stands for I am lovable and capable.") Tape the sign to your chest so that when the group members sit down, they notice your sign. Then tell them your own hammed-up version of the following story (Making sure that you tear a piece of your sign off after each negative statement):

> Once upon a time there was a fourth-grade boy. One morning, he woke up and started to think about what a good day this was going to be. While he was thinking of that, his sister walked by his room and said, "Good morning, creep." [Tear a piece of your sign off.] He ignored his sister's comment and went into the bathroom to get ready for school.
>
> His mother came into the bathroom as he was finishing up and, noticing the water on the floor, screamed, "How many times have I told you not to spill water on the floor when you wash? And besides, you didn't comb your hair."
>
> Recovering from these wounds he went down to the breakfast table and ate his oatmeal, which was cold because no one cared enough to wake him early when it was going to be hot.

Off he went to school, still optimistic about the day. Halfway to school, two of his friends ran by him, and as they did so they chanted, "Hi woman, beat you to school!" He started to run, mainly because he was mad and partly because he didn't like being called "woman." But he wasn't able to catch up to them. As he got to the schoolyard the same two kids were saying, "Na na na na na na, you're a slow runner!" He started to get into a fight with one of the kids, but just then a strong arm grabbed his shoulder and the principal hollered at him for starting fights on the schoolgrounds.

After he found out that he would have to stay after school for two afternoons (for fighting on school property), he hurried along to his classroom, where at least he knew people liked him. Because of the play-ground incident, he was five minutes late, and as he snuck in the door Mrs. Brown said, "Billy, why are you late?" and, without letting him answer, followed up, "If there is one thing I can't stand, it's someone who is late all the time." She said this, even though Billy knew he had only been late two times all year.

The first business of the day was to pass back the science test from yesterday. Billy had studied hard for this test but his grade on it was a D; not only that, the teacher had also drawn a face with a frown on it. Billy felt hurt by that because he wasn't smart but he had tried awfully hard on the test.

Anyway, things went along, and about 10:30 it was time for art. The teacher passed out the construction paper and the paints and, as Billy began to put down his exciting idea on the construction paper, the girl behind him looked at it and said, "What's that ugly thing?"

[Begin picking up pieces of the sign as nice things happen.]

Someway or another, he made it to lunchtime. At lunch, he was sitting alone, eating his bologna sandwich, when a fourth-grade girl sat down next to him and asked him if he would like some potato chips. He felt real good that she cared enough about him to offer him some potato chips. He spent the entire lunch hour talking with her about the rotten morning he had had. It seemed that she, too, had had a bad morning.

Reinforced by his lunch experience, Billy went back to class and worked hard through the afternoon. Twice the teacher complimented him on his writing and his questions in a discussion. Before he left at the end of the day, the class had picked him to be the milk boy for next week. As he left school, two of his classmates congratulated him and offered to walk him home.

When he got home, his mother was waiting for him at the door with some chocolate milk and some chocolate cookies. She apologized for being in a bad mood that morning and said, "I really love you children, but some-times I have a headache. I try not to take it out on you, but I can't help it."

Billy's dad came home at 6:00 and brought a neat new gift—a Tonka truck for Billy. However, his father had forgotten to buy a gift for his sister and her feelings were hurt.

So as we leave the story of Billy and his family, we hear his sister say, as she walks by his room, "Good night, creep."

### The End

[By now you should have all the pieces of the sign in your hands. Ask the students, "What happened?"]

After the students understand the story, help them make a list of the kinds of verbal and nonverbal statements they hear each day, and help group them into "sign building" and "sign destroying."

Before you leave, give each a 3 X 5 card with IALAC written on it. Have them wear it for the rest of the day, tearing off little pieces each time they feel put down by someone else. At the next session, have them begin by reporting on how they fared.

For a homework assignment, have each student fill out a copy of the form on page 132 ("Today is the First Day of the Rest of Your Life"). Tell them they are to complete it and bring it back to circle at the next meeting. Begin the next session by having volunteers report on how they completed the form.

*Additional Process:* At the end of this unit, a good brainstorming activity would be to have students list ways they could make the classroom a sign-building place, and then implement some of the suggestions.

## TODAY IS THE FIRST DAY OF
## THE REST OF YOUR LIFE

1.    Explain the above statement in your own words.

_____

_____

_____

_____

2.    List three words you wish described you.

_____

_____

_____

3.    Now, you will really have to think. Write down some of the exact things you will have to do to become more like the person described by each word you have listed. Be as clear as you can.

_____

_____

_____

_____

_____

_____

_____

_____

_____

_____

_____

_____

# STUDY SKILLS

*The overall purpose of this unit is to increase the awareness of students about what good study habits are and about how their habits help or hinder them from doing well in school. The unit is six sessions in length, so it can only be a beginning. If you and your students feel that this topic should have a larger emphasis in your program, go to it.*

**Objectives**
Students will:

a.   Know what skills are called study skills.
b.   Improve at least one study skill.
c.   Take a public stand on their own concept of themselves as students.
d.   Discuss good and bad ways to review for an exam.
e.   Identify effective studying strategies for improved school achievement.

**Activity 1**
Begin the session with the following questions:

How many of you

1. Do pretty well on tests?
2. Have ever failed a test?
3. Think you could get better grades?
4. Can study with the TV on?
5. Wish you were more organized in school?
6. Know how to make an outline?
7. Actually take notes in class on what the teacher says?
8. Ever reread your notes?
9. Think only smart kids can get A's?
10. Have a system for studying before an important exam?
    (Add others, if you think of any.)

After the questioning session is done, ask the group for a definition of "studying." Encourage several different definitions and write them down on paper or on the board. At this point have all students take out paper and pencils. Tell them that you are going to give them a short lecture on how to study and that they are to take notes on it.

After you deliver your lecture (it is outlined below), the students will read samples of their notes. After a few students have read their notes, get them to discuss good and bad note-taking methods. Some points to bring out are:

1. Listen attentively—don't let your mind wander.
2. Ask questions when you don't understand something.
3. Make your handwriting legible.
4. Only write key ideas—not every word.
5. Organize or reread your notes later.

*Minilecture on Studying*

I. Improving Your Reading Ability
   A. Different kinds of reading
      1. Skimming
      2. Reflective reading
      3. Pleasure reading
      4. Other kinds
   B. Learning how to read different subjects
      1. Math
      2. Science
      3. Social studies
      4. Reading and language arts
   C. Reading Comprehensions
      1. Main ideas
      2. Reading for detail

II. Preparing an Outline
   A.   Outline form
   B.   Consistency

III. Note Taking
   A.   Listening
   B.   Note-taking form
   C.   Rereading notes
   D.   Other hints

IV. Home Study
   A.   Physical setup
        1.   Distractions
        2.   Trivial tasks
        3.   Lighting
   B.   Organization
   C.   Goal setting

V. Review
   A.   Organization
   B.   Evaluation of subject matter
   C.   Helpful hints

Design your lecture around this outline. Add strategies that you think are important. Make the lecture short—five to ten minutes. Finish the session by having everyone finish this sentence stub: "I can study best when . . ."

## Activity 2

Have each student take out a piece of paper and divide it as shown in the form on page 136.

Be sure they leave three or four lines after each number. You are going to have them fill in the paper for the following activities:

1.   Reviewing for a test?
2.   Listening to a lecture?
3.   Watching a movie in school?
4.   Doing homework?
5.   Getting a good grade?
6.   Doing a report?

Encourage them to list a few things they do for each activity—whether they are good study practices or not.

After they fill out the paper, discuss their patterns for the remainder of the session. When someone shares a particular pattern for one activity, ask him whether he likes the pattern and whether he has done it that way for long. Finish the session with the following sentence stub: "Studying is . . ."

**What procedures do you follow for:**

1. _____
_____
_____

2. _____
_____
_____

3. _____
_____

4. _____
_____

5. _____
_____

6. _____
_____

**Activity 3**
Begin by reviewing the last two sessions, then introduce the topic for discussion: "Little things I do to avoid work" (or "ways that I put off getting down to work," or "how I procrastinate," or "my personal trivia"). You may have to give a few personal examples to get them started. Discuss the topic for the entire period. Finish the session with the following stub: "About studying, I'm proudest of . . ."

**Activity 4**
Before the session, make up a ditto master that says the following:

*Unscramble the Outline*
Reorganize these outline symbols in proper form:

III., I., A., b., B., a., II., C., 2., D., IV., 1., A., B., 1., A., B., 2.

Let the students work in twos to unscramble the outline and to get it in proper form. Give them ten minutes to work on it, then bring them back together and do it as a whole group. Now is the time to give them information on proper outline form. Discuss how good outlining can be helpful for them.

Answer key for scrambled outline:

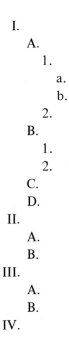

I.
    A.
        1.
            a.
            b.
        2.
    B.
        1.
        2.
    C.
    D.
II.
    A.
    B.
III.
    A.
    B.
IV.

### Activity 5

Begin by having several students remember what you have been discussing for the past four sessions. Encourage the remembering of several specific skills, then put a line on the board. Say, "This line represents a continuum from the world's worst studier to the world's best. I want you to tell me what would be going on in the home of a student at each end—the worst and the best." There should be quite a bit of humor as students describe the extremes. Then ask them to describe the quarter points and the midpoint. Spend ten to fifteen minutes describing different study habits and then ask students to put their names on the line where they think they belong. As each person puts his name up, have him describe something he does that makes him think he belongs at that particular point.

Before the period ends, have each student state a goal—to be accomplished within a week—about improving his study habits in some way.

### Activity 6

Today will be spent discussing how to handle hypothetical situations about studying. One example that you could spend the whole session on is provided here, but feel free to come up with your own or to have the students make some up:

A typical grade-school student has just received word that tomorrow there will be a test in science—a test on which his second trimester grade will depend. He has worked hard in the class and feels he should do O.K. on the exam. He has an appointment to play Monopoly at his friend's house in the evening. It is now 3:15 P.M. What should he do?

Consider the following questions as you discuss the situation with the students:

1. Should he play Monopoly?
2. Does he need to review?
3. How should he review?
4. Should he study alone, with a friend, or with a group?
5. What specific steps for reviewing should he take?
6. What material should he study and what should he ignore?
7. How should he decide what to study?

It might be helpful to break the circle up into groups and have them find alternatives about this situation or about another study-related situation. To do so, students brainstorm all the possible things that the boy could do to solve or handle the situation. They then pick two or three possibilities and list all the good consequences of doing each and all the bad consequences of doing each*

The point of this entire unit is to get the students thinking about the importance of having good study skills. If the students are interested in pursuing it further, you can have them discuss different hypothetical or real study situations for several more sessions. Have one person bring up a real problem related to using good study habits and allow the others to react by saying what they would do or what they think is right to do.

---

*I first did this activity at an education convention, in a group led by Lee Howe of Temple University.

**BOYS AND GIRLS**

**Objectives**

Students will:

a.  Become sensitive to personality differences between boys and girls.
b.  Become aware of boy and girl roles in our society.
c.  Identify ways of coping with boy-girl disagreements.

**Activity 1**

*Purpose:* To increase group awareness of the differences between boys and girls. (Personality differences, difference in likes and dislikes, and so on—not so much physical differences.)

*Process:* Begin the session by telling the group that for the first part of the period they are to divide into pairs, with two girls or two boys in each pair. If you have an even number of boys and girls you will have no problem. However, you might have to have three girls in one group or three boys in one group (or it might be fun to have one boy-girl group if you have an odd number). Tell each dyad that they are to make a list of all the things that they think are different about boys and girls. When the giggling stops, tell them to forget physical differences—they're already aware of those. Tell them you want them to make a list of all the things they can think of that girls like to do (that they think are girl things) or that boys like to do (that they think are boy things)—habits, personality traits, ways of acting, anything they can think of.

Give them ten to fifteen minutes to complete their lists, and then, for the last part of the discussion, bring them back into the group and allow each couple to share its list. If time remains in this session, compile one group list. You might appoint a secretary to list, on large pieces of construction paper or butcher paper, the consensus of this group—eliminating statements that are the same for both boys and girls, and including only those statements that the group agrees are specifically "boy statements" or specifically "girl statements."

### Activity 2

*Purpose:* To analyze yesterday's experience in terms of how our culture has affected our ideas of what boys are like and what girls are like.

*Process:* Begin the session by asking several people to remember what they did yesterday. After some statements have been made, bring out the list of boy and girl differences that they made yesterday and ask them what they think about it. Encourage discussion of the things that are on the list. Do they agree with them? Do they have second thoughts? Do they like it that way? Do they wish it were different? Just get them to ask some different questions and talk about the subject a little bit.

Now, play the following song for them: "When We Grow Up," from the album *Free To Be You and Me* by Marlo Thomas and Friends. The song is about the typical roles that people are expected to follow in our society. The song deals with a boy and girl who wonder if they will still be able to be friends when they grow up and have to act like "men" and "women."

After the students listen to the record, spend the rest of the session discussing how it relates to what they did the day before. Begin to get them to make commitments, one way or another, about whether they think boys should do certain things and girls should do certain other things, or whether they think boys and girls should be allowed to have more opportunity to do the kinds of things the other sex usually is allowed to do. (Have them brainstorm ways that our society limits what boys and girls can do.)

### Activity 3

*Purpose:* To help students relate the discussion of boy and girl differences to the way boys and girls react to each other.

*Process:* Once again, you'll start the session remembering what you've been doing so far in the area of boy-girl differences. After a few people have re-stated what happened so far, say, "Today I want you to be thinking about the main problems that boys have in getting along with girls, and the main problems girls have in getting along with boys. Let's really get it out in the open and be honest about it today. You can tell us about a problem you have in getting along with a boy or a girl, or you can tell us about problems in general that you think kids your age have in getting along with boys or girls. Then we'll talk about them and see if we can come up with any possible answers for handling those situations."

After you've said that, encourage the children to offer experiences about communication difficulties with the opposite sex and look for similarities in responses. For example, if someone says, "Boys are always teasing me and calling me names, and I don't know what to do about that," you might say (after you've reflected what she said), "Does anyone else have that problem?" Get five or six girls to say that that's their problem, and then have them analyze why they think that happens. Just let this process carry on until the end of the discussion. This activity could expand into several sessions.

**Activity 4**

*Purpose:* To bring to a conclusion the series of discussions about boys and girls; to increase students' awareness of all the strategies used to get a positive response from someone else without taking too big a risk.

*Process:* Begin by asking some members who haven't been too involved in the discussions to remember what has happened up till now. After they have remembered, say, "Today we're going to talk about the positive-response game." Explain that the positive-response game is played by everyone but that it primarily involves the area of boy-girl relationships. Tell them that it's just a fact of life that all boys and all girls are involved in trying to get members of the opposite sex to respond positively—to say they like you or to go with you or just to smile and respond positively in some way. Tell them, "We all need that, and yet, it would really be scary to go up to someone and say, 'I like you, do you like me?' for fear of being told, 'No, I don't like you.' Most of us could not handle being told that directly, so we come up with all kinds of clever ways to get people to give us a positive response without our taking a big risk by coming right out and asking.

"Today I'd like you to think of all the ways you know that people do this. Maybe this is the way you get a positive response from a boy or a girl, or a way that you have noticed that a boy or girl tries to get you to respond in a nice way, or some way that a friend of yours does it. Let's make a list of as many ways as we can that boys and girls try to get positive responses from each other."

Following this introduction, they should really be ready to talk honestly about the response game. Encourage them to tell their stories. You might go first—telling of a way in which you have gotten members of the opposite sex to respond positively to you.

After the students have shared their stories, explain to them that there is nothing wrong with beating around the bush instead of coming right out with whatever they want to say or do. Sometimes it's much smarter, because the risk involved in coming right out and asking for affection is really too great. An excellent discussion topic to follow this up is "one way I draw attention to myself."

## Additional Activities

Make up nicknames based on good points of students.

Write the history of some part of you, such as your hair.

Make a composite person of the group (using some attribute from each group member).

Have each person fill out a card with names of five people he or she would like to talk with. Every five minutes, have partners switch. Give possible discussion topics (such as "my favorite things").

## Additional Discussion Topics

(Some of these extra topics and activities relate directly to the study of boy-girl relationships. Others refer to the concept of appearance, which is so important to boys and girls of all ages.)

How to get attention from the opposite sex.

A time when someone had a crush on me.

A time when I had a crush on someone.

A boy (girl) I would like to speak to but am afraid to.

A time I revealed my feelings for another.

A time I was with a member of the opposite sex and didn't know what to say.

A time a boy (girl) said something to me and I was embarrassed.

A time I wish I hadn't told a boy (girl) something.

A time when I was the only boy (girl).

A time I was embarrassed when I was with my boyfriend (girl friend).

A time I wanted to date, but my parents wouldn't let me.

How my parents react to my boyfriend (girl friend).

A time I was supposed to act like a "man" ("lady") because I was a boy or girl.

A time I acted tough to impress my boyfriend (girl freind).

My best feature is . . .

My worst feature is . . .

What I think people notice first about me.

A time when I felt all eyes were on me.

How I react when people are looking at me.

A time I thought I looked nice and someone told me I didn't.

A time I really looked bad and something important happened.

A time I didn't want my picture taken.

A time that I was very self-conscious about my appearance.

A time someone's physical appearance influenced my opinion of them.

Why physical appearance is or isn't important to me.

Why I wish I was taller, shorter, thinner.

If I could change one thing about the way I look.

One thing I have improved about my appearance.

One thing about me I could improve and haven't.

Something I want to change about myself but can't.
How I react to a person's severe physical handicap.
Something about the way I look that used to bother me but doesn't now.

# SURVIVAL

**Objectives**

Students will:

a.  Know the resources in the school that are for helping them with their problems.
b.  Gain experience in handling awkward situations through role-playing.
c.  Learn several ways to handle common hallway, locker, and lunchroom problems.
d.  Understand the reasoning behind school organization.
e.  Discuss effective ways for coping with common student-teacher problems.
f.  Be aware of both the opportunities and responsibilities that are theirs as students.
g.  Discuss the best ways for handling older students.

**Activity 1**

*Purpose:* To help students begin to identify what they are concerned about in the school.

*Process:* Introduce the unit by asking students for some comparisons between their school and any other schools they know about. As they list comparisons, put them on paper or on the board. Spend about ten minutes getting the comparisons, then announce "For the next couple of weeks we are going to be discussing life in this school and how you can make it a good place to be for you."

For the rest of the session encourage students to talk about the biggest problems they have encountered in the school. Broaden the discussion to get them to state, generally, what children in their grade are most concerned about in the school. (The whole direction of this unit might come out of this discussion.) You are really trying to identify student concerns for future lessons.

Before they leave, tell them to be looking around and thinking about the problems of children in their grade.

## Activity 2

*Purpose:* To give students practice in handling awkward situations.

*Process:* Begin by asking students to remember what was discussed at the last session. Then introduce them to the concept of role-playing. Tell them that role-playing is a way to look at typical situations by acting them out and then discussing different ways to handle them. Pick the hammiest kids, at first, to role-play the following situations:

1. You are trying to pass someone in the hall who keeps moving the same way you do, so you can't get by each other.
2. Your locker won't open and you're going to be late for class. A teacher is in the hall saying, "Let's get to class!"
3. A kid calls you a name in class and says, "After class, you're in for it!"
4. You are standing in the lunch line and a bigger kid butts in front of you.
5. You rip your pants (or dress) in class and it is time to leave.
6. You come up to a group of kids at lunch who are talking about someone you like and they are really knocking him or her.

This activity will be a noisy, active one. Let the students get into it within reasonable limits. After the six situations have been acted out (each may be acted out in several different ways), calm the students down. After they are calm, go back to the first situation and have them discuss different ways to handle it. Elicit as many different ways as possible. Spend the rest of the period going through the different role-plays, discussing different ways for handling each situation. Tell students that wherever they see a place to make a good point about how a situation should be handled, they should jump in and make it.

## Activity 3

*Purpose:* To help students become aware of what school resources are available and how to use them.

*Process:* Begin by remembering the main points that were made at the last session, then introduce one of the resources in the following list and ask, "What is this for?" Collect different concepts of what the resource is for. Next, ask, "What is the best way to use this school resource?" Once again, collect different opinions of the best way to use the resource. If you finish the list with time remaining, encourage people to tell about a time when they made use of a particular resource.

School Resources for Students:

1.  School nurse.
2.  Principal.
3.  Learning center and director.
4.  All teachers (especially teachers with special talents).
5.  Knowledgeable students.
6.  Handbooks.
7.  School psychologist.
8.  School library.
9.  Janitor.
10. Secretary.
11. Yourself.
12. Cafeteria staff.
13. Bus driver.
14. Public telephone.

After different resources have been discussed, encourage students to look upon themselves as the most valuable resource in the school. Have them tell how they can use their own potential as a resource.

### Activity 4

*Purpose:* To help students understand why schools are organized in a certain way.

*Process:* Begin by having several students remember what happened at the last meeting. Ask the group whether they can explain why the school is set up the way it is. Children will indicate by their responses what they understand about the school organization. Spend some time explaining the ideas behind the organization, such as class scheduling, special classes, and so on. If this discussion "bombs," and there is plenty of time left, open up the discussion to "how I solved a problem with a teacher." Encourage students to discuss the topic without mentioning the teacher's name. Reinforce those who share by remembering what they said.

### Activity 5

*Purpose:* To increase students' general awareness of their likes and dislikes about school.

*Process:* After remembering what has been discussed so far, tell the students that you'd like them to think of something they *like* and something they *dislike* about school. They must give examples of both. Reflect all responses without judging them. Near the end of the session, make sure each person who contributed is remembered. Let them know that it is O.K. to like some things and dislike others and that it is also O.K. to try and change things but that it isn't O.K. to just criticize what you don't like without doing something constructive about it.

### Activity 6

*Purpose:* To help students summarize all the learning from the unit into a useful product.

*Process:* Today is the final session on survival. Begin the session by saying, "Today we're going to pretend that you have been given the responsibility of developing an underground handbook for incoming students—a handbook that will really help them get along in this school." Spend the entire session having different students write down suggestions about the handbook. If time remains, ask students to make "I learned" statements about the entire unit.

*Additional Process:* Assign the class to work on committees to actually prepare the handbook. This project could become a super way to help your class gain a feeling of control over their lives. When the handbook is complete, make copies and have groups of students go to other classrooms explaining what is in the book.

**Objectives**
Students will:

a.  Become aware of the conditions under which people are likely to lie.
b.  Identify how lying and maturity are related.
c.  Identify certain methods for knowing when someone is lying.
d.  Take a public stand on lying as an appropriate behavior.

**Activity 1**
*Purpose:* To help students become aware of conditions under which they are likely to lie; to see the connection between lying and maturity.
*Process:* Begin by asking, "How many of you have ever lied? Have lied today? Lie more than you used to? Think lying is always bad? Have a friend who lies a lot? Think there's a difference between lying and exaggerating?" After the students have responded, have them whip the following sentence stub around the circle: "I would lie if . . ."

Now introduce the topic "something I used to lie about that I don't lie about now." As students tell their particular stories, ask them whether they think most little children would tell the same lies. Also ask them whether they think age is the big reason they have changed.

Before the session is over, remember what each person has said. Draw out, from the group, the generalization that excessive lying is usually a sign of immaturity—that people who lie all the time probably feel they won't be accepted if they are just themselves. Deal with the different reasons for lying. Ask, "Why do adults lie? What is a value conflict?"

## Activity 2

*Purpose:* To help students become sensitive to when someone is lying; to experience lying and being lied to.

*Process:* Tell the group that today they're going to play a lying game. Each person will have three minutes to think of a story to tell about himself. It can be true or it can be a lie. After everyone has thought of a story, each person will tell his own, and the group will try to decide who is lying. After listening to each particular story, those who think it was a lie will raise their hands. The storyteller gets one point for each person he fools. (The storyteller must tell the truth at the end.)

Before game time, you may want to catch two or three people and tell them to be sure to tell the truth—most students will relish the chance to lie so you have to set it up a little. Also, be prepared for deep self-disclosure, as students share really "heavy" stuff to win points.

After the game is over, discuss the activity. How did you know when someone was lying or telling the truth? Have you ever been tricked?

*Additional Process:* The TV game *To Tell the Truth* can be modeled pretty closely to make this activity even more fun.\* Pick three contestants. All will tell the same story, but only one will be telling the truth. The class can ask questions for a few minutes and then you can play the emcee and say, "Now, will the real truth teller please stand up?" The group can then discuss how people gave themselves away or didn't give themselves away.

## Activity 3

*Purpose:* To aid students in publicly affirming their opinion on lying.

*Process:* Do a physical continuum on lying. First, describe the two end points, "Liar Larry" and Truthful Tom." Ask each group member, one at a time, to go stand along the wall in the position where he thinks he belongs. As each person goes to the wall, he must tell the others why he chose his particular spot. Accept all explanations, but if someone says, "I don't know," don't accept it. He must give some reason, even if it is, "Because I don't want to tell you what I really think."

If time remains, have the students stand where they would like to be. This might require bunching up at or near one end. (You'll be surprised.)

---

\*In fact, every TV game show can be made into a humanistic class activity. Elaborate!

Discuss how students could move from where they are to where they want to be. Relate this to the goal setting you have done, and have each student set a goal. Have them line up again as they think other kids see them.

**Activity 4**

*Purpose:* To identify problems students have that involve lying; to discuss possible solutions.

*Process:* Begin by asking for volunteers to rehash what they have been discussing during this unit. Get as many different comments as possible. Don't evaluate the comments—just accept them. Then encourage participants to bring up some of the problems they have regarding lying or being lied to. Examples are: "someone who lies all the time," "lying and getting in deeper: how to get out," "the boy who cries wolf: when to believe him," and "lying to protect a friend."

As each student discusses a problem, let the group offer suggestions, ask questions, and share experiences until something positive has evolved. Deal with as many situations as you have time for. Reintroduce the idea of focusing on one child at a time.

# DECISIONS

**Objectives**

Students will:

a. Become sensitive to the importance of wise decision making and the number of decisions they have to make.
b. Identify the components of a critical decision.
c. Identify available resources for help in making important decisions.
d. Become aware of how risk is involved in decision making.
e. Take a public stand on how they see themselves as decision makers.
f. Begin to think about their futures as being controlled by decisions they make now.

**Activity 1**

*Purpose:* To enable students to gain experiences at making forced choices and in publicly defending their choices.

*Process:* Explain that today one corner of the room will represent one choice and another corner will represent an opposite, or different, choice. Begin the activity by saying, "In that corner is McDonald's, and in that corner is Mr. Steak. Go to the corner of your choice." When they have all gone to their chosen spot, approach one group and, pretending to be a reporter, ask some-one, "Why are you here?" Elicit responses in this manner from three people in each group, then ask them to regroup in the center of the room. Repeat this process for at least six or seven different choice pairs. Follow each choice episode by asking some why they are where they are.

Select your choice pairs from this list (or make up some of your own):

1. Are you more of a leader or a follower?
2. Are you a grouper or an aloner?
3. Are you spring or autumn?
4. Are you more yes or more no?
5. Are you more like, "Two heads are better than one," or "Too many cooks spoil the broth"?
6. Are you more like "A stitch in time saves nine," or "Better late than never"?
7. Are you more like a question or an answer?
8. Are you more like a teacher or a student?
9. If you needed advice would you go to your mother or your father?
10. Are you more parent or child?

After you have gone through the forced-choice process several times, ask the class to come up with other choices. The more involved they get now, the better.

Take at least ten minutes to discuss, as a whole group, the problem of choosing between two opposite choices. At this point, you are making students aware of their choices. Later they will examine strategies for choosing more wisely.

**Activity 2**
*Purpose:* To increase student awareness of the number of decisions made each day and of the interrelationship of different decisions (how one decision affect many others).
*Process:* For today's activity, make copies of "Which Decision Is Important?" (page 154) for all students.

Read the story "To Decide or Not to Decide" (next page) to them, then let them work on the worksheet. When they complete the worksheet, discuss how they voted on the important decisions, encouraging different views as to which decision was most important. Make a grid of their responses and dis-cuss the experience in any way that seems appropriate. The grid should look like this:

| DECISION | MOST IMPORTANT | 2ND MOST IMPORTANT | 3RD MOST IMPORTANT | LEAST IMPORTANT |
|---|---|---|---|---|
| 1. | | | | |
| 2. | | | | |
| 3. | | | | |
| 4. | | | | |
| 5. | | | | |
| 6. | | | | |

*To Decide or Not to Decide*
(A day in the life of Tommy)

The sound of the newsman announcing the expressway traffic backup is the first sound Tommy hears this very average Tuesday morning. As he slams the top of the clock radio to get a few more minutes sleep, the thought pops into his head that if he doesn't get up he won't have to face the snow, the teachers, and the whining of his sister. He gets up anyway.

By some miracle, young Tom makes it to the bathroom in the dark, finds the light, and stares at the sleepy-looking but rather handsome lad in the mirror. After a brief conversation with his attractive friend, the real Tommy reaches automatically for his toothbrush. It occurs to him that if he skips the brushing and face-washing bit he can avoid having to touch water at least until supper. (He hates water!) "I mean, who would know? Mom would know! She'd probably smell my breath and guess the awful truth— and what about those two cute rah rahs in my science class?" Needless to say, he performs the washing rituals, and we next pick him up staring into his closet. Another decision! If he wears his good old "wear-it-forever" flannel shirt, he'll be ready for the lunchtime football game, but the queen of the house wouldn't approve. And if Miss Breznahan (old "clothes-make-the man" Breznahan) asks him to debate the causes of the energy crisis, he'll be through. The flannel shirt stays in the closet and we catch up to our hero on the way to the kitchen buttoning his "Mr. Straight" normal sixth-grade boy's shirt. (He is, of course, attired in other appropriate middle-school clothing, including wrinkled Levis, worn-out Earth shoes, and socks that don't match.)

All this choosing has taken valuable time, and stopping to eat now would eliminate the possibility of picking on his friend Morris before first period. A tangerine will have to do, and zoom, our hero is off to another day at the place (Kurt Vonnegut Middle School—an open-design school with a French provincial faculty).

The bell announces the beginning of first period. The science teacher announces a test covering last week's stuff and our hero is in trouble. Had he not watched the test pattern on TV til 2 A.M. he would have studied. Ah, well, yesterday's bad decisions are today's depressions. Our hero is in luck, though, one of the cute rah rahs is sitting across the aisle, with her obviously perfect paper in plain view. What will our eleven-and-three-quarter year-old hero do? Her answers must be right. "If I fail this test, I'm sure to be grounded." The penalty pales in comparison. He cheats. Our hero has become an anti-hero (or has he?).

Second period finds Tommy filling out a form for next year's schedule and having to choose between continuing with band or taking Spanish. Maybe he is feeling guilty from the science incident, but the choise is made: leave band and take Spanish.

Between second period and 3:30, Tommy has to decide whether to play the "soap-dish game" in the bathroom instead of going to the Learning Center, whether to play hockey or chase the girls at lunch, and whether to debate the energy crisis today or to wait until tomorrow. (Old Brezzy liked the shirt.) As a bell began the day, so does a bell end the day, and our anti-hero rushes home to practice his trombone after declining an invitation to play "guts" frisbee with the second-best frisbee player in the sixth grade. (You will pardon our hero if he prefers to see himself as number one.)

After dinner, Ernie, the brother of one of the cute rah rahs, called and invited Tommy to attend a hockey game Saturday night and, of course, this conflicts with Dad's invitation to go ice fishing overnight. Tommy leaves this decision hanging and turns on the TV as *Kung Fu* comes into focus, and just before Tommy's brain is totally absorbed, the thought comes into his head that if he studies math instead, he might survive tomorrow's math test.

Finally, as the test pattern sinks slowly into the TV Tommy decides enough is enough and goes to bed.

### Which Decision is Important?

Tommy had a pretty typical day in the story. Here is a list of the decisions he faced that day:

1. Whether to get out of bed.
2. Whether to brush his teeth and wash his face.
3. What shirt to wear.
4. Whether to eat anything for breakfast.
5. Whether to cheat on his science test.
6. Whether to take Spanish or band next year.
7. Whether to play the "soap-dish game" in the bathroom.
8. Whether to back out of the debate on the energy crisis.
9. Whether to go to the park or play ball during lunch.

10. Whether to play "guts" frisbee after school or clean his room and practice the trombone.
11. Whether to go to the baseball game with Ernie or fishing with his father.
12. Whether to watch *Kung Fu* or study for his math test.
13. Whether to go to bed.

(See if you can find other decisions that Tommy made.)

From this list, pick out the five most important decisions Tommy made. List them in order of importance and, after each, indicate why you think this was an important decision for him.

After you have made your list, compare it with those of others in the class. From this comparison, see if you and the class can come up with an explanation of what makes a decision an important one to a person.

## Activity 3

*Purpose:* To help students become aware of the fact that there are decision helpers all around.

*Process:* Begin the session by asking, "How did Tommy decide what to wear to school in the story?" As students share different answers, guide them into a minidiscussion of the questions: How does one decide? What factors are considered?

Make copies of the following test, and have the students work in small groups to complete the matching. As you discuss this quiz, encourage group members to share the decisions they have made and the processes they went through before they decided.

### TEST: WHERE TO FIND HELP IN MAKING DECISIONS

Match the particular decisions to be made with the best place to get help in making them.

*Decision To Be Made*

1. What to order in a restaurant.
2. Whether to watch TV.
3. Where to buy a bike.
4. Whether to buy a pair of socks.
5. When to buy someone a birthday present.
6. When to leave for home from your friend's house.
7. Whether to plan on going swimming tomorrow.
8. Whether to buy a particular record.
9. Which way is shortest from your house to a hospital.
10. How to find out whether you are sick.
11. Whether to do your homework.

*Where to Get Help*

a. Price tag.
b. Map.
c. Weather forecast.
d. Thermometer.
e. Newspaper ads.
f. Last report card.
g. *TV Guide.*
h. Radio.
i. Calendar.
j. Menu.
k. Clock.

(Answers: 1. j; 2. g; 3. e; 4. a; 5. i; 6. k; 7. c; 8. h; 9. b; 10. d; 11. f.)

Encourage students to discuss other possible sources of help in making these (and other) decisions.

### Activity 4

*Purpose:* To help students examine the level of risk involved in every decision.

*Process:* Remind the group of the activity they did several days ago concerning Tommy's important decisions. Either read, or state in your own words, the following: "Every student is faced with a number of important decisions every day. Some are more important than others and some are easier to make than others, but most have something in common. For example, five of Tommy's decisions were what shirt to wear, whether to go to school, whether to cheat on a science test, whether to take Spanish or band in junior high, and whether to go to a hockey game or to go fishing. Each of his decisions had a common element of *risk* or *chance*. Something is unknown in each case. No matter how much information he gets, there will be something unknown. In every decision you make, some risk is involved."

Spend fifteen minutes discussing the risks involved in Tommy's decisions. For the last fifteen minutes, ask whether anyone will share a personal decision he made and tell what risk was involved. Also ask: "Can anyone think of a decision he made that didn't involve any risk?" Encourage group members to question the storyteller about his decision.

### Activity 5

*Purpose:* To sensitize the group members to their own decisions.

*Process:* Begin by telling students, "We have been talking mostly about other people's decisions lately. Today I'd like to discuss what decisions *you* had to make these last few weeks." Spend the next fifteen minutes eliciting responses about decisions that they have made. When ten minutes are left, give out copies of the Decision Diary worksheet.

Tell them to record all the decisions they can identify on Saturday and Sunday and to bring in their Decision Diaries on Monday to discuss them together. (Obviously, you can do this on any day.)

*Additional Process:* If possible, you might try to get a person from the community who has to make many important decisions to come in and talk about how he goes about making them.

### Activity 6

*Purpose:* To provide students with continued awareness of risk-taking strategies for making personal decisions.

*Process:* Ask for a definition of risk. Collect several different definitions, then say, "Sometimes the risk involved in a certain decision is worth the outcome and sometimes it isn't. Today we're going to look at some decisions and discuss the risks involved in making different choices." Give them each a copy of the following activity sheet (to which other decisions can easily be added):

# DECISION DIARY

Every moment of your day, you are making decisions. When you elect to spend your time one way rather than another, you are making a decision. Keep track of the main decisions you make this Saturday and Sunday and bring your completed diary to the group on Monday. (Write your decision in column one, the time in column two, and "yes" or "no" in the appropriate boxes.)

| | DECISION | TIME | Was this a free choice? | Does it affect others? | Were there several alternatives to choose from? | Are you glad you chose this way? | Did you think about your choice? |
|---|---|---|---|---|---|---|---|
| **SATURDAY** | 1. | | | | | | |
| | 2. | | | | | | |
| | 3. | | | | | | |
| | 4. | | | | | | |
| | 5. | | | | | | |
| | 6. | | | | | | |
| **SUNDAY** | 1. | | | | | | |
| | 2. | | | | | | |
| | 3. | | | | | | |
| | 4. | | | | | | |
| | 5. | | | | | | |
| | 6. | | | | | | |

Every time we make a decision, we take a risk. So before we make that decision, we should *weigh,* or consider, the risk involved. Look at the decisions to be made; then write what you think the risks involved are.

| *Decision to Be Made* | *Risks Involved* |
|---|---|
| 1.  Whether to cheat on a test. | *If I don't cheat, I may flunk. If I do cheat, I may get caught.* |
| 2.  Whether to go swimming or to play baseball. | _____ |
| 3.  What kind of shoes to buy. | _____ |
| 4.  Whether to take art or a foreign language next year. | _____ |
| 5.  Whether to ask a girl for a date. | _____ |
| 6.  Whether to fight someone. | _____ |

After the students complete the activity sheet, ask for volunteers to discuss "a time when I made a bad decision." Accept the contributions that are made and reflect the stories back. Help each storyteller to examine his reasons for making that particular decision.

**Activity 7**
*Purpose:* To enable students to examine how decisions about spending money are made at home.
*Process:* Tell the class to think about things they have in their homes that were purchased. Have everyone make a list of ten to twenty "things in my house." These can be food products, toys, cosmetics, drugs, appliances, and so forth. After everyone has finished, have students go over their lists using these codes: Put the initials of the person who was responsible for bringing it into the house next to each item. Put a happy face by it if you like having it in your house. Put LUX by it if you think it is a luxury. Put NEC by it if you think it is a necessity. If it is mainly designed for children, put CH by it. Put K by five things you would keep if you had to throw out everything else on your list. If you think you will have this product in your house when you are an adult, put ADULT by it.

Encourage the children to make up other codes. (They should be very good at this sort of thing by now.) Encourage the class to make "I learned" statements about the activity. Ask them, "How are decisions made at your house? Are you glad about it?"

*Additional Process:* This unit could easily expand into a month-long study. Students could interview people who have made big decisions, could examine alternatives involved in decisions, and so forth. Here are some discussion topics on decisions that you might want to have students consider:

1. A time I made a good decision.
2. A time I made a bad decision.
3. A time when I couldn't make a decision.
4. A time I made a decision too late.
5. A time I made a decision too early.
6. A decision my parents were proud of.
7. A decision my parents weren't proud of.
8. A decision I made to please my friends.
9. A decision I made that didn't please my friends.
10. A time I made a decision that hurt somebody.
11. A time I made a decision that helped somebody.

The following activity sheets, on considering the feelings of others and on considering alternatives, are self-explanatory. They should be helpful in your class.

# CONSIDERING THE FEELINGS OF OTHERS
## WHEN MAKING A DECISION

Before we make a decision, we should consider how that choice will affect others and their feelings. In the following situations, tell whose feelings should be considered in each case and why. (You may need to consider more than one person's feelings in a given case.)

1. Walking home from school, Pam and Cindy find a kitten. Both girls want to take it home with them.

   _____

   _____

2. Jan asks Carol to go swimming with her. Carol agrees to go, then she calls her cousin and invites her, without discussing it with Jan.

   _____

   _____

3. Sheryl wants to bring her guinea pig (which doesn't have a cage) to science class.

   _____

   _____

4. Jim offers to give you some permanent decals (which he doesn't think his big sister wants anymore) to put on your bedroom wall.

   _____

   _____

5. A friend's dog has just had puppies; you can have one free.

   _____

   _____

(This exercise can either be done individually or in small groups and can be discussed later as a class.)

# CONSIDERING ALTERNATIVES

Today is Monday. Mike needs $2.00 to go to the show with the guys on Saturday.

Ways that Mike can get $2.00:

1. Not buy a lunch ticket.
2. Borrow from his friends.
3. Ask his folks for money.
4. Earn the money.
5. Steal the money.

Here are the things Mike considered about each of the ways to get $2.00:

1. If I don't buy a lunch ticket, I'll go all week without lunch.
2. If I borrow from my friends, I'll have to pay them back.
3. My folks don't like it when I ask them for money.
4. If I earn the money, I'll have to work one night.
5. It's not right to steal, and it would be bad to get caught.

Has Mike left out important considerations about any of the ways he has thought of to get $2.00? In what other ways can Mike get $2.00? What things should Mike consider about these other ways?

_____

_____

_____

_____

_____

_____

_____

A good final activity might be to have everyone complete the following "Good or Bad Decisions Test" and then discuss it as a total group. After students have discussed the test, have them stand in a line, with the ones who think they are good decision makers at one end and the ones who think they are poor decision makers at the other end. Ask different ones, "Why are you here?" Collect statements from several students.

## GOOD OR BAD DECISIONS TEST

Number a sheet of paper from 1 to 10; read the following statements. If the underlined decision is a good one, write G after the number and explain why; if it is a bad one, write a B and explain why.

1. In a baseball game, with one man on and two men out, the coach gave the man on base the sign to run on the hit.
2. Jim met a boy that he had never seen before. The boy asked Jim to loan him $1.00, and promised that he would pay Jim back $2.00 the next day. Jim loaned the strange boy $1.00.
3. Jan picked up a stray cat on her way home from school. Jan's mother is allergic to cats and dogs, but Jan thought that she could keep the cat in her room. Jan brought the cat home.
4. You have just stepped on a nail; you might need a tetanus shot. You decide to wait until your sore bothers you before you tell someone.
5. You want to have your friend stay overnight Friday. Before you ask your friend, you ask your parents.
6. Duane wants to ride his bike to school instead of taking the bus as usual, but there are black clouds in the sky. Duane decides to ride his bike anyway.
7. Tom's dad saw an ad for a used TV. Without turning the set on, Tom's dad bought it for $25.00.
8. While Sue was babysitting for her three-year-old baby brother, a girl friend drove up in her new car. The girl friend told Sue to leave her little brother and ride around the block in the car. Sue thought a minute and then decided to bring her little brother with her.
9. Sheila's mom gave her $6.00 to buy a new pair of shoes. Sheila found a pair of shoes on sale for $2.00 that were just a little tight. If she bought them, she'd have enough money left over to buy a record she's been wanting. She decided not to buy them.
10. In one week, Jeff's family will be moving from their house into an apartment. Jeff's parents tell him that he must sell his minibike before they move, as there's no place to store it at the apartment. Jeff gets an offer of $85.00, but he wants $100.00. He decides to accept the offer.

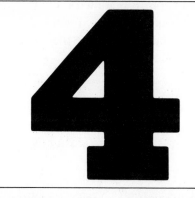

# 4

# DEVELOPING YOUR OWN LESSON PLANS

In this section I want to share with you the process I go through when designing or planning awareness units. I will take you step by step through the development of a unit and then devote the rest of the section to the listing of data that could be developed into units.

## LONELINESS

Let's begin with the idea of loneliness. Suppose you would like your class to spend a couple of weeks looking at loneliness: what it is; how it feels; why it exists; how to get rid of it; when it is O.K.; and so on.

### Activity 1

You can begin the unit by asking ten to fifteen questions of the "How many of you" variety, to begin to focus everyone's attention on the concept of loneliness.

How many of you

1. Have ever been lonely?
2. Have ever been lonely in a crowd?
3. Have ever been alone and not felt lonely?
4. Are often lonely?
5. Sometimes like to feel lonely?
6. Watch TV when you feel lonely?
7. Know somebody who is very lonely?
8. Ever consciously helped make a lonely person feel less lonely?
9. Have a special thing you do to stop being lonely?
10. Sometimes talk to yourself?

Following the questions, say, "Class, for the next several days we are going to be studying loneliness and finding out how we all feel about it and what we can do when we feel lonely to get out of it.

"Right now I would like you to find some place in the room where you can crouch down by yourself, away from everyone, with your eyes closed." Then go around and make sure everyone is getting into it. "O.K., now keep your eyes closed and imagine that you're really lonely—you're all alone, there is no one around—feel what that feels like." After about two minutes, bring them out of it and have them sit closely together in a circle. Begin the discussion by saying, "What was it like for you?" Then collect statements from the students concerning the experience. Allow the students to pursue a general discussion of the topic until the session is over.

### Activity 2

Begin this session by asking several students to remember key contributions from the previous day. After a sufficient time, introduce the following topic: "what I do when I'm lonely." Encourage the students to share times when they felt lonely. Encourage comprehensive descriptions of feelings of loneliness. When two students share a similar experience, draw attention to the similarities, letting them know that many of us feel lonely in similar situations. Continue the discussion until all who want a turn get one. See to it that each contribution is remembered by someone in the group. Before you finish, go around the group having everyone complete the sentence stub "I feel lonely when . . ."

## Activity 3
Begin, as always, by remembering a few contributions from the previous session. (By now, you will have put up some butcher paper on the wall and will have written "Loneliness Is" in very big letters at the top.) Point out that the latest graffiti paper is up, and encourage them to write sentence completions whenever they want to.

After some have scribbled, go to the board and draw a long line across it. At one end write "Lonely Lou" and then describe him to the group. Lonely Lou is the loneliest person in the world. At the other end is Never-Lonely Ned. Ned is always feeling like he is part of a group. He is always understood and listened to. In fact, there are five trained psychiatrists who stay with him twenty-four hours a day keeping him from ever feeling lonely.

Ask the class, "Where are you? Who would be willing to tell us where you think you are?" In the beginning, only a few will risk putting themselves up. When someone puts himself up, ask him gently to give you an example of when he feels lonely. Probably about ten will finally put themselves up. Before you finish, draw another line and say, "This is the 'Ideal Me' line. Who would like to be different than he is now?" At this point, encourage some to make decisions about whether they like themselves just as they are or would like to change.

## Activity 4
Gather the students in a circle and refer to the graffiti wall, mentioning how much longer it will be up. Then introduce the topic "situations where I feel lonely." Encourage them to share different situations when they get lonely. Accept and reflect all contributions. Either on this same day, or on the next, break the group into smaller groups of three or four. The idea is for one person to tell about certain situations in which he is lonely and for others to focus on him and to reflect his statements and ask questions to help the central person consider alternatives. During the small-groups time, you should observe all the groups in order to help them along.

To have the class experience being excluded play, "breaking in," in which one group member stands outside a tightly grouped circle and tries to force his way in while the class tries to keep him out. After several have tried this, discuss how it felt and then discuss "A time I wanted to be part of the group." Accept all contributions and make sure all are remembered.

### Activity 5

Without any introduction, put this on the board: "Where would you be lone-liest: on a camping trip alone, at a party where you didn't know anyone, or during your first day at a new school?"

When students begin to realize what you are doing, acknowledge that you would like them to make a priority list of lonely places. Use several dif-ferent priority lists before you get the discussion going. Some others might be: "Who's loneliest: old people, single people, or kids in orphanages? Which of these is least lonely: Christmas morning, family dinner, or an assembly at school?" If time permits, discuss "what I did when I didn't have a friend."

You could go on and on with this unit. You could set goals, discuss more topics, or do other activities (like picking teams or making lists of places). You could brainstorm ways to become less lonely. You could do something for people who are really lonely, like write letters to people in veterans' hospitals, and so on. You could role-play different situations. You could use fantasy to go to different places—lonely, not lonely—and so on. Depending on the class, this unit could "bomb out" in three days, or it could become the year's biggest project.

Finally, all the strategies, the topics, and the techniques become secon-dary to a group of people—some children and an adult who care about each other and about learning. Here, in a climate of trust, openness, interdepend-ence, and listening, these people are learning what it means to be human. Learning that its O.K. to admit you're scared or lonely or angry, that it's O.K. to be proud of your skills and your accomplishments, that it's O.K., and possible, to get better at anything you want to get better at, and that it's possible to understand other people mainly because they are pretty much like you are. It is most important to emphasize: "You may not be *super* per-son, but you are *you*—the only you that ever was or ever will be, and you really are O.K."

Following are some other concerns that might be developed, and some possible things that might be dealt with, in awareness units. These examples may give you some ideas for units you want to write.

### FEELINGS

As you develop this unit, keep in mind that feelings are learned behaviors; consequently, one can control them most of the time. Everyone has good and bad feelings, and that's all right. What is important is what one does with a feeling—that is, how one handles it. It is important to own one's feelings and not to deny or distort them. This can be accomplished by using appro-priate "I" messages. Emphasize to your students that almost everyone has had the same feelings at some time. Accept everything that is said nonjudg-mentally. If the students are reluctant to discuss certain kinds of feelings, let them know that it takes courage to talk about one's real feelings. Help them become aware that they all have had pretty much the same feelings. Talk about the differences between feeling something and actually doing it. Say, "Having a bad feeling is not the same as doing something bad." Emphasize that everyone has bad feelings sometime and that having bad feelings does not mean that one is a bad person.

## Possible Activities for a Feelings Unit

These activities are purposely left open ended so that you can adapt them to fit your situation:

Collages: Make pictures of good feelings and bad feelings.

Diary: Write down feelings for a week.

Reward someone for making someone else feel good.

Bad-feeling bag: Switch bags with someone and share.

Good-bad feelings chart.

Bad feelings: Everyone help solve bad feelings; make someone feel good.

Awareness calendar: All students begin the day by recording information about themselves: moods, quality of sleep, pains, and so forth.

Brainstorm: All the words you can think of between happy and sad or between good and bad.

"I" messages: In dyads, practice making "I" messages that tell your feelings. Use the form: "I feel _____ when you _____ because _____ ."

Continuum from Open Ollie to Closed Cathy: Put a mark by the place where you are between the two. Put a mark where you would like to be. Where do your friends think you are?

Pantomime moods and emotions: Play charades with feelings as tasks.

Facial expressions of feelings: Everybody look angry, sad, happy, and so forth.

Crayon scribble: Divide a large sheet of paper in half. Have students scribble on one side to classical music, on the other side to rock music. Compare the feelings the music creates.

Analyze feelings in pop songs.

Phrase tones: Take a phrase like "I don't believe it." Say it as many ways as possible and discuss various meanings.

Role-play: Receiving a present; being scolded; being rejected by a friend.

## Possible Discussion Topics for a Feelings Unit

When I was bored.

When I lost patience with someone.

When I felt bad and it felt good.

When I had a good feeling.

When I had a bad feeling.

When I made someone else make me feel good.

When I made someone else make me feel bad.

What someone could do to make me feel good today.

When I was lonely.

When I was afraid.

What someone could do to make me feel good.

## PERSONAL IDENTITY

As you begin this unit, keep in mind the fact that everyone is O.K. and worthy of respect. Having more skills or interests is a good thing, but it doesn't make one more worthy than someone else. Urge the students to be honest about themselves. As leader, your acceptance of what is shared is important. Risk telling them about yourself and accept nonjudgmentally what they say. Be careful not to praise certain contributions more than others. This practice tends to produce parroting of "teacher-approved" comments.

Every individual is unique—the only one that exists with his specific characteristics. We share many characteristics common to others. By communicating with others, we can gain insight into aspects of ourselves we hadn't thought about. It is important to be honest in assessing ourselves. We must be aware of both assets and limitations.

### Possible Activities for a Personal Identity Unit

Make a collage that expresses your personality.

Me in a Box: Put objects and symbols in a box that stands for you. Share in small groups or with the whole class.

Self-commercial: Write a commercial as if you were a product.

"Self fair": Each student or group sets up a booth celebrating their strengths, accomplishments, pride, hopes, and fears. Invite parents to come and be part of the fair.

Body Tracing: Friends trace each other's bodies on butcher paper and then glue pictures on the body to stand for likes and dislikes. Put the body tracings up in the room and add to them during the year.

Success object: Show and tell one that is important to you.

Write down ten adjectives that describe you and rank them from best to worst. Have the class guess how you ranked them.

Write short essays: "Who I Am." and "Who I Want To Be."

Make a list of twenty things about yourself you wouldn't share in this group. Code them: Next to each thing that you think people would laugh at put an L, next to any items that you think would get you in trouble put a T, and so on. Discuss what you learned about yourself.

Time line of my life: Each student draws a time line portraying significant events in his life. Groups then share their lines.

Life Picture Map: Student gets a large manila paper and crayolas and draws his life. Share the pictures in small groups.

Uniqueness cards: Students write answers to the question: "What is one

way you are unique when compared with everyone in this room?"
Collect them and read them aloud—anonymously.

I Am's: Each student makes a list of I Am's and then tapes it to his
chest. The class then mills around silently reading each other's I Am's.

Baby pictures: Bring them in and share them.

Public self vs. private self: Get a large bag, on the outside put picture
and words that people know about you, and inside put objects and
pictures that represent the part you don't share. Pick someone and
risk sharing from inside your bag.

Make a strengths collage or strengths tree.

Make a personality scrapbook, collage, or book packet.

Write a secret autobiography and have another student read it and try
to guess who it is.

Make your family tree (interview parents about their backgrounds).

Switch roles with a person in your group. Say, "Today, I'll try to be
you and you be me." Get in another person's shoes.

Make a travel brochure or advertisement for yourself or for a place you
enjoy.

Write the history of your hair.

## Possible Discussion Topics for a Personal Identity Unit

How am I like (unlike) the person sitting next to me?

What one thing am I wearing that I'd hate to give away?

What does my hair say about me?

Would I change my name if I could? To what?

How I greet people when I meet someone new.

What I do when I'm embarrassed.

What I say when I answer the phone.

What I do when I'm angry. Does it work?

What I see in my friend that reminds me of me.

What I dislike in my friend that I see in myself.

Things I like or dislike about myself.

Something my parents want me to do.

Things I like (my favorite things to see, hear, smell, and so forth).

A time I did something expected of me, rather than what I wanted to
do—and how it felt.

How I would describe myself on the phone to someone who's never seen me.

What habits I have.

What habits I have changed.

Little things that make me feel good (bad).

Pet peeves that I have.

Something I can do well (and why).

A way I am different from everyone else.

Something others can do better than I can.

Something I can't do but would like to do.

A way I am like my mother or father.

A way I am different from my mother or father.

Something I did because my friend wanted me to.

A time I tried to be what I wasn't and felt uncomfortable.

The one thing that makes me most like I am.

A time I felt bad because I was different.

Something I do that everybody does.

Certain characteristics or habits that I have because of my past.

A past experience or person who has influenced me most.

The kind of person I really am.

A time I did something just because someone else wanted me to.

A time when people expected too much of me.

Things about myself I want to change.

The kind of person I would like to be.

## Possible Sentence Stubs for a Personal Identity Unit

People dislike me because . . .

Something no one knows about me . . .

I would be successful ten years from now if . . .

I like friends because . . .

My parents would like me to be able to . . .

People like me because . . .

My teachers would like me to be able to . . .

I make others happy when I . . .

I like myself because . . .

When I do my best, I do it because . . .

## THE WAY IT IS AND SOME OF THE WAYS IT COULD BE

This unit would be spent looking at the world we live in and what the future will be like. It would deal with some of the following ideas:

1. As we grow up we become more aware of what is happening in the world.
2. Becoming an adult can be very scary and very exciting.
3. We have many different feelings about what goes on in the world.
4. Everybody has experienced personal tragedy of some kind.
5. It is hard to stand up for what you believe in when others don't.
6. Each of us has many ways to escape from reality for awhile.
7. There are many sad things and many happy things about the world.
8. Each of us has the power to make the world a better place.
9. Many things that happen give us very mixed feelings.
10. All of us have had problems that we have solved.
11. We can help each other solve problems by working together.
12. Solving a problem often means deciding what is most important at that moment.
13. Some problems are outside of our control.

14. The future can be both scary and exciting.
15. Each person has control over his own destiny.
16. There are things you can do now to bring about the future you want.
17. There are ways to handle the anxiety we often feel about the future.
18. It is hard to stay in the here and now and not anticipate the future.
19. Traditional roles and careers are breaking down—more and more you can be whatever you choose to be.

## Possible Activities for a "Way It Is" Unit

Masks: Put on someone else (a famous person or a friend). Play the role for an hour.

Role-play: Illustrating an emotion by showing how it can be both good and bad.

Read, or get a record of, "The Secret Life of Walter Mitty" (James Thurber).

Tape, play, and discuss "The Monsters Are Due on Maple Street" (Rod Serling).

Show the film: *Four Artists Paint a Tree*. After viewing, discuss different viewpoints. Look at a common object from different viewpoints.

Write science fiction stories, predictions, or possible futures for yourself.

Show the film: *Occurrence at Owl Creek Bridge*.

Pretend-interview: One student plays world-famous figure, and the class asks questions. The person answers as he things the famous person would.

Students and teacher make up common problems and everyone solves them together.

Show the film: *A Chairy Tale*.

Role-play problem situations: What should Johnny do?

Compare TV families and real-life families. How are they alike and different?

Ranking game: What problems are hardest to solve?

Time Capsule: List objects that you think would tell people one hundred years from now what you were like; what society was like.

Telegram of the future: "Best news" telegram.

Make predictions about the world, the nation, your family, and yourself. Support your predictions. Have a minicourse on forecasting.

Discuss what probability estimating is.

Bring in professional people for discussion of community problems.

Give a two-minute talk on a person you want to pattern your life after.

Discuss pros and cons of various professional careers.

TV show selection: Choose performers—whom are you most like? Sonny or Cher? Archie or Edith?

Make a poster-picture of yourself showing all the things you would like to do.

Have a "seer" draw the name of a student and predict what that student will do.

Show the film: *The Long Flight.*

Fantasy: "I see you in five years . . ."

Brainstorm: Cliches that people use.

List twenty gifts you'd give the world.

Make collages of the ideal world.

Cut out "before and after" pictures; paste them side by side.

Take field trips into the real world.

Invite real people to talk to the class.

**Possible Discussion Topics for a "Way It Is" Unit**

Something I know about this year that I didn't know about a year ago.

A worry I have about growing up.

Something I look forward to about growing up.

The most exciting thing about growing up.

How I could change what I don't like about me.

A time I thought I might die.

Something terrible that happened to me (or my parents, friends, and so forth).

A time I knew the answer but no one would listen.

A time my friend let me down.

How I get away from my problems.

A time I fixed something myself.

Something I learned how to do by myself.

A time I had a fight with a friend and solved it.

An enemy I now have for a friend.

An embarrassing predicament I solved.

How I earned the money I needed.

A time I said I was sorry but didn't mean it.

A time I was sorry but didn't say so.

A time my friend and I fixed something together.

How I would spend thirty free minutes after school.

A class problem we had and how we solved it.

A school problem we need to solve.

A problem I have at home.

A time I saw what happened and had two choices.

What clothes, songs, and dances will be popular ten years from now.

What I like and dislike about being an American.

What I like and dislike about television.

A part of my future that I'm afraid to think about.

A decision about the future that I'm afraid to make.

Something I can do this year to make the future better.

What I can do or am doing to meet future goals.

Times when I would rather be in the future than in the present.
How I helped someone overcome fears about the future.
How I influenced someone else's future.
How I see you (someone in the circle) in five years.
Something that would make my future exciting.
Plans I am making now that will help me in the future.
What I would like to be doing in ten years.

## Possible Sentence Stubs for a "Way It Is" Unit

The people of the world should worry about . . .
If I could change one thing in the world I would . . .
The worst thing in all the world is . . .
I wish everyone believed . . .
If I could change the world . . .
The best time of day for me is . . .
I feel the biggest problem the world is facing is . . .
I feel the most suppressed group in the world is . . .
In the world, the things that make me feel good (bad) are . . .
If I could change the world, one thing I would do is . . .
One way in which what I do with my life will affect the world is . . .
My perfect world would be . . .
If I could live anywhere else in the world it would be . . .
My feelings about newspapers are . . .
Movies are good (bad) because . . .
When a disaster happens in the world, I feel . . .
At the turn of the century, I feel that the world will be . . .
A time when the world was in the best shape was . . .
A person in history who I feel has changed the world is . . .
The reason I am on this particular spot in the world is . . .
My feelings about war are . . .
If I could control my future I would . . .
A perfect plan for my future would be . . .
One future goal I have for myself is . . .
My daydreams about the future are . . .
I like to pretend that I am . . .
To be what I want to be I must . . .
I am happy when I think of myself as . . .
The only way I will fail in what I want to be is . . .

## BEHAVIOR

Elsewhere in this book a unit dealing with behavior is outlined in great detail.
The topic of behavior—of understanding why people behave as they do, understanding your own behavior patterns, and learning how to cope with other
people—could be a whole year's work in awareness sessions. As you conduct

awareness sessions around this theme, try to develop the following insights in students:

1. Life is much easier when we can get along well with adults.
2. Parents and teachers are responsible for us and care about us.
3. We can dislike somebody and still get along with him.
4. Accepting and coping with authority are signs of maturity.
5. Every person must learn to cope with many difficult situations in life.
6. Personal effectiveness means meeting our own needs without preventing others from meeting theirs.
7. Each of us can learn how to avoid trouble.
8. There are many "good" ways to cope with angry feelings that avoid hurting others.
9. We can "unlearn" the ineffective things we do.
10. Sometimes it is harder to cope with success or good things than with bad things (success can go to our head).
11. Behavior is "how we act."
12. Being happy depends on our ability to get along with our peers.
13. Treating others the way we want to be treated is a good way to get along.
14. Name calling and killer statements (put-downs) make it difficult to get along with others.
15. Being honest about our feelings helps others understand us.
16. We should try to get into the other person's shoes to understand how he feels. Active listening is helpful.
17. There is a big difference between feelings and thoughts compared to behavior.
18. How we behave tells others more about us than what we say.
19. All of us have done things that were good things to do and all of us have done things that were bad things to do.
20. We all have the power to consider the consequences of our behavior and to try new and different behavior.
21. Sometimes one person sees a behavior as good and another person sees the same behavior as bad.
22. All people behave out of the same needs and feelings.
23. All people need to feel worthwhile and loved, and their behavior is an attempt to obtain those feelings.
24. Anger is usually fear that is turned around.
25. People usually lie or exaggerate to make themselves look better.
26. By observing people we can usually tell what is motivating them.
27. What we do has a significant effect on what others do.
28. Each of us must accept responsibility for how our behavior affects others.
29. All healthy relationships are sometimes negative in nature (best friends quarrel often).

## Possible Activities for a Behavior Unit

Rumor clinic: Start a phrase around the room. Each person whispers it to the next person. See how it ends up.

Reverse Debate: Argue the side you don't agree with.

Role-play: Being stuck in an elevator; taking a bus ride; losing a big game.

Everyone talks, no one listens: Discuss a problem in this manner.

Thumbs down: Tape your thumb down and try to do simple activities (tying your shoes, buttoning your shirt, and so forth).

Ranking game: Hardest thing for you to cope with (failures, anger, affection, and so on).

Killer statements (put-downs): Everyone shout out killer statements at the same time. Talk about why we use killer statements. When someone makes a killer statement have them turn it around.

Role-play: Fighting on the playground; not inviting someone to a party.

Name Chant: Chant one student's name over and over.

Write an epitaph that you think another student would want written for him. Check it out to see whether he really would want it.

Three-round micro-lab (inner-outer circle): In each round, each person observes one person inside. Between the first and second halves of each round the observer gives one-minute feedback to the person in the circle.

Get videotape equipment and tape a session. View it and discuss the behavior that was taped.

Brainstorm solutions to everyday problems: pollution, overpopulation, and so forth.

Have students list "twenty things I like (dislike) about adults."

Role-play: Being a parent insisting that your child get a haircut; being a parent when his kid is coming in late; being a parent whose child has done something good; being a teacher calming a class; being a teacher explaining a commotion in the classroom to the principal; being a minority student.

Make a list of do's and don'ts for getting along with grownups.

Have grownups come in and tell how to get along with them.

Behavior change calendar: Keep track of moods, attitudes, and so forth.

Turnabout Journal: Make a list of ten things you don't like people to do to you. Keep track of how often you do them to others for one week.

Switch roles with another student: See how your behavior looks to another. (Use dyads for this activity.)

Role-play: A new student being asked to join a group; a new student being ignored.

Ranking game: List ten important attributes of friends, then rank them in order of importance (and according to other criteria).

Campaigning for "Friend of the Week": Make advertisements, cartoons, and campaign speeches. Have an election. Discuss the feelings of the winner and the loser.

The cop-out game: Two players role-play. One says, "Why can't you go to the store with me?" The other gives typical excuses. (Make up other situations.)

Make a list of all the adults you meet in a day.

Make a list of things you need that adults give you and another list of things that you give adults.

Do "Dear Abby" problems concerning adults.

Make a handbook for getting along with adults.

Write a short essay on the problem of being an adult and having a teen-age son or daughter.

Write "I urge" telegrams to your parents. Read these anonymously in the class.

Write "I appreciate" and "I resent" statements about adults and read them anonymously.

Give a compliment to someone in the group.

## Possible Discussion Topics for a Behavior Unit

A time I was angry with someone and got into a fight.

A time I avoided getting into trouble.

A time I cooperated with someone.

A time I didn't cooperate.

A time someone hit me and I didn't hit him back.

Things I do when I'm angry.

A time I spread a rumor.

A time I told someone's secret and he found out.

A time success went to my head.

A time I cut someone down to build myself up.

What I do when I'm in trouble.

How I show someone I don't like the way he's acting.

What I do that makes others feel bad (good).

How I got out of trouble.

What I like about my best friend.

The neatest thing I did with my friend.

Something my friend does that is weird.

Something I don't like about my friend.

A time I did something to someone that I don't like done to me.

A time I was honest with my friend and it hurt his feelings.

The worst thing I ever did to someone.

Something new I learned about someone in this group.

A time I really knew how someone else was feeling.

A time the class was picking on someone and I joined in.

What I can do to make someone feel good right here.

What I did when I didn't have a friend.

A time I did something somebody liked.

A time I acted without thinking first.

A time I was punished unfairly.

A time I knew I'd get in trouble but I did it anyway.

A time I did it and was glad.

A time I was just messing around and someone got hurt.

A time I decided to do the right thing but it was too late.

A time I was influenced to do something and got into trouble.

A time I had to choose between my friends and doing the right thing.

A time I knew what kind of mood someone was in without him telling me.

A good or bad habit I picked up this year.

A time I did something the teacher thought was wrong but I thought was O.K.

A time an adult surprised me by being neat.

A time I had to get along with an adult and didn't want to.

A time I tried to get along with an adult and it didn't work.

A time an adult acted like a kid.

A time I realized an adult cared.

How I show an adult I care.

A time an adult asked me to do something that was hard for me to do.

A time I wanted an adult there to tell me what to do.

What I do to get along with a teacher.

How parents are responsible for me.

How teachers show they care or don't care.

A rule I didn't understand.

A time I was punished for breaking a rule.

A time I obeyed a rule I thought was stupid.

A time it was easier to have a rule than to make a choice.

A time I had to choose between doing what I wanted or doing what my Mom (Dad) wanted.

Things I do to get along with adults.

What I like and dislike about adults.

A time I really could communicate with Mom, a teacher, or some other adult.

A time I wished I could have communicated with an adult.

A time I got my way and still pleased my teacher (parent).

A time I changed my parents' plans.

A time my suggestion helped the class.

A time I compromised with an adult.

A time I helped my family with my skills.

A time when I should have kept my mouth shut.

A time I let my anger get out of control.

A time I got angry because I cared.

Somebody who exaggerates.

A time my behavior hurt (helped) someone.

A time I made someone feel bad and was sorry.

A time I was really jealous.

A time I did something that made someone else feel like a good person.

What people do that makes me feel good.

How I helped somebody.

A person on whom I've had an effect.

The person who has had the greatest effect on me.

Something my friend (brother, parent) does that I don't understand.

A time I lied to an adult because I knew he'd say no or wouldn't understand.

A time I spoke up even though I was afraid.

A time I knew that nothing I could say would make any difference.

A time when an adult really seemed to understand.

A time that I felt adults were for (against) me.

Something I believe in that my parents don't.

A time I had a disagreement with an adult and we compromised.

How I usually get my way with an adult.

What I do when I feel that an adult has treated me unfairly.

What I do when an adult loses his temper.

How I get an adult out of a bad mood.

How I deal with adults without putting them down.

## Possible Sentence Stubs for a Behavior Unit

A time an adult and I thought the same was when . . .

My favorite subject to talk to adults about is . . .

I talk the most when I'm . . .

I'm most quiet when I'm . . .

My best friend and I quarrel over . . .

What I need most from people is . . .

## FANTASY

The world of fantasy is an excellent concern that is developable into an exciting awareness unit.

## Possible Activities for a Fantasy Unit

Make lists of superstitions.

Keep track of your horoscope and compare it to what really happens.

Fantasy trips (read *Put Your Mother on the Ceiling* by DeMille).

Finger-paint to music.

Share ESP experiences.

Role-play: A fortune-teller predicting your own future to other members of the group.

Build a bubble using thick plastic, tape and a window fan, and hold your sessions in the bubble.

**Possible Discussion Topics for a Fantasy Unit**

What it would be like to be invisible.
What I would wish for if I had three wishes.
What I would do with $1,000.
What animal, plant, or mineral I would be.
If I could be a hero, who I would pick to be.
What I did to be the hero of the game.
Which movie star I would be.
What it would be like if I were living in the year 2000.
What superstitions I believe in.
A wish someone else would like.
A nightmare I had.
A dream that I have often.
A wish that actually came true.
A wish that came true in a dream.
A dream that actually came true.

## CONDUCTING AWARENESS SESSIONS

### Discussion Topics

The next several pages contain a random listing of discussion topics that have
been used successfully with elementary (K-8) children. Many of the ideas behind the topics could pave the way for a unit of study or a class project.

When it felt good to be in a group.
What I would do to get into a group.
A time I wanted to be in the group
and couldn't.
A time I was excluded from the group
and cared (didn't care).
A time I helped someone else get into
the group.
How I felt when I was included but
my friend wasn't.
A time I disagreed with the group and
was (wasn't) afraid to speak up.
A time I was put into a group and
didn't want to be in it.
A time I was proud (ashamed) of
my group.
How I feel about working in groups.
A time someone made me feel special.
How my parents show they like me.
How I show my parents I like them.

How I show my friends that I like
them.
A time I tried to make someone feel
special and it worked (didn't work).
How I make people happy.
How people make me happy.
A time I wanted to make someone
feel good and didn't know how.
A time I gave someone something
money couldn't buy.
A time I gave someone a present
they didn't like.
Something I would do for a special
friend.
A time I gave a gift because I had to.
A time I wanted to give a gift but I
couldn't afford it.
A time I got an unexpected gift.
A time I did a favor for someone
without them asking.

How I feel when I am complimented.

A time someone in this group showed me he liked me.

Things I like about other people.

Different meanings of my smile.

A time I shared my lunch.

A time I did a favor for someone.

Someone I know who needs me as a friend.

A person I couldn't live without.

Something special that our family does.

Something I wanted and was afraid to take a risk getting.

Something I did even though I was afraid and enjoyed it.

A time I took a chance and lost.

Something I got that I had to take a risk for.

A time I trusted someone and it turned out good (bad).

A time when it was not risky for me but it was for someone else.

A time I talked a friend into taking a risk and it turned out good (bad).

A time my friend took a risk by sticking up for me.

Something I've never told anyone.

A time I said something but my actions said something different.

Something that I do that lets people know what I'm thinking without saying it.

A time I was sarcastic and hurt someone.

How I feel when someone is sarcastic to me.

A time I really tried to listen.

Something someone else in the group does that shows how he feels.

How people show that they are listening to me.

How people's bodies give away their feelings.

A time I thought somebody's non-verbal message said something it didn't.

How I act when I am moody.

A time someone had something important to say, but I didn't listen.

A time I had something important to say and no one listened.

A time I needed someone to talk to and no one was around.

A time I hid my true feelings.

A time I helped someone and it turned out badly.

A time when I was respected.

How I felt when I met a new friend.

A time I hurt someone accidentally and felt bad.

A time I heard something I shouldn't have.

A time I was lost and couldn't find my way home.

My feelings at this moment.

A time I lost someone or something I loved.

Something that I enjoy doing that most others do not.

A time I stole something or didn't return something that I found.

How I would feel if I were a blade of grass or a dandelion.

A time I wasn't asked and wanted to be.

A time I cried in front of someone and really didn't want to.

How I felt when I was left by myself for the first time.

A time I did something and was afraid to admit it.

How I feel when I think someone is using me.

A time someone laughed at me and I didn't think it was funny.

A time I was allowed to make a
choice and it didn't work out.

A time I was ashamed.

A time when I was tricked.

What respect is.

Someone I respect.

A disappointment that was hard
to hide.

A time I was embarrassed by someone younger.

A time imagination got me in trouble.

Problems I have right now.

How I felt when I said or did something really stupid.

A time when my feelings were hurt.

A time I felt good because someone
said or did something nice to me.

A time someone played a practical
joke on me.

A time I was frightened by a friend.

An embarrassing thing that happened
to me.

The time I saw something I shouldn't.

My favorite spot to be alone.

Something I thought I could do that
backfired.

If I ran away, where I would run to,
how I would get there, and what
I would do there.

How I felt when I first felt I was
growing up.

What I would have done if there was
no school today.

A fear I have that no one else has.

A time I had a problem that no one
else could help me with.

A time a friend disappointed me.

Things I do to gain or keep a friend.

How my friends and I work out our
differences.

Something I do that I don't understand.

A time I was discouraged by someone I liked.

A time I felt alone in a crowd.

Something I planned that didn't
work out.

A time when I felt cheated.

A time I got mad at myself.

A time I blamed someone else and it
was really my fault.

A time I did something really dumb.

Something I need help on.

When I made a promise to keep from
hurting someone.

Weird dreams I have had.

The worst trouble I have been in.

A time I felt "I'm O.K.—You're O.K."

A time I tried to impress someone
and it failed.

How I get my kicks (destructive
versus nondestructive.)

How I was hurt by a rumor.

Something about myself that the
group doesn't already know.

A story I have imagined.

How I can overcome a fear I have.

What boys and girls do to get each
other's attention.

A time I destroyed someone's property (how they felt, how I felt).

A time someone made fun of me and
how I felt.

A time I talked behind someone's
back.

A time I asked someone for a favor
and they wouldn't do it.

Ways people (teachers, parents, me)
are inconsistent.

What trust is.

A person I am afraid of.

A time I wanted to laugh but
couldn't.

The wildest idea I've ever had.

Prejudices I have that I don't like.

Things adults do that really bug me.

A time I had to go without something I really wanted.

A time I did something that made someone feel included.

A time I was cruel to an animal.

Good and bad feelings I have about animals.

A time I was really happy (excited).

Something I'm afraid of.

A time I pretended to be sick.

What I like to do in my leisure time.

My feelings about crime.

A time when I wanted something very badly and my parents wouldn't get it for me.

The rules I would change for me if I were my parents.

How I felt when I got hurt (bodily).

A time I laughed at something that wasn't really funny.

An important event I'll never forget.

A habit I have that I can't break.

A time I should have been afraid and wasn't.

Why people tease each other.

How I feel when I don't like someone (and what I do about it).

Something I believe about dreams.

Something I did or made well that someone else wrecked.

Feelings I had about an accident when someone was hurt.

A place I don't care about.

How I feel about working for an allowance.

What I did when I was mad at someone.

What happened when I talked back.

When I felt a TV program was not worthwhile.

A time somebody liked me and I didn't know how to handle it.

The neatest birthday I ever had.

Why I like the people I do (qualities I like in people).

What I do to scare other people.

How I felt when my best friend got mad at me.

Something I wish I hadn't done.

A time I wanted to run away (and why).

A job I have to do and wish I didn't.

Problems I have had this week.

Feelings I have about war.

Good dreams and bad dreams I have had.

How it feels to earn my own money.

A time I got into trouble and what I did.

A time someone did something and I respected him for it.

A practical joke that was played on me that turned out not to be funny.

Unexplained (supernatural) occurrences I have experienced.

How I would change school rules.

What I like and dislike about school (and why).

What makes a good friend "good?"

Something I have that I value.

If my house was burning down and I could save only one of my possessions, what it would be.

A time I lost something.

Good things about weekends.

How I know my pet likes me.

How I felt when something bad happened to my pet.

How I felt when I had a fight with my best friend.

A time I played a practical joke on someone.

Things people do that bug me.

Where I would go if I could press a magic button and go anywhere I wanted.

A time I got revenge and felt glad about it.

A time I was really frightened.

Someone I look up to (and why).

Why I need my pet.

How I feel about my favorite team.

What I would teach if I were the teacher.

What I feel about flying saucers.

A superstition I just can't overcome.

What I look for in a friend.

Little things that make me happy.

What I'd change if I were the teacher.

Getting along with my mom (dad).

What I respect (or look up to) in someone.

What I like about my favorite television program.

What's realistic and what's make-believe in television programs.

The neatest thing that happened during vacation.

What I did over spring vacation.

What I would be if I could be anything in the world.

My favorite pastime.

A time I wanted to lie but couldn't.

A really bad neighbor.

A really good neighbor.

A trick I played on someone that made me feel good.

How I felt when someone I cared about got hurt.

Plans I have for Easter vacation.

Plans I have for summer vacation.

Things my brothers and sisters get away with that I don't.

Things I do on April Fools' Day.

How I felt when I won something.

A time I got gypped.

A time I got into trouble and it wasn't my fault.

A promise that I made and knew I wouldn't keep.

A time I lied to protect a friend.

A time I stood up for a friend.

How I felt when I had to give up a pet.

How I got acquainted with a new person.

Funny things that happened to me.

Things I do with my family.

Something I like (dislike) about movies.

What age I would like to be.

A time I got into trouble with my parents.

A time that having a feeling (good or bad) got me into trouble.

Something that scared me but was funny afterward.

How I feel about my name.

How I feel about parents and teachers.

What I would become if I had a pill to change myself.

Something I wonder about.

Old times I enjoy thinking about.

Something I can do that really makes me feel good.

What I like about my family.

A time someone else got me into trouble.

A time I was asked for my opinion.

My feelings about different colors.

Three ways I've changed since last year.

How I feel about slam books.

What I want to be when I grow up.

How rumors get started.

How rumors change.

How I feel about working in groups.

A problem I solved on my own.

Feelings I get from my hobbies.

How I would fix up a room that could be any way I wanted it.

A place I've been that was really special to me (and what it was like).

How I feel about horoscopes.

How I feel about Valentines.

How I feel about school parties.

My most valuable possession.

What the year 2001 will be like.

A worry I have about the past (future).

How I feel about substitute teachers.

How I feel about unfair treatment by teachers.

Something I've never been able to do but would like to.

How I feel about people telling on others.

My favorite things to smell.

My favorite things to touch.

My favorite things to hear.

What I think of capital punishment.

What I think about going steady.

Things I enjoy doing in my spare time.

Things I do not enjoy doing around the house.

Something I wish for that would cost no money.

What I would do if my friend stole something.

Why people are shy.

**Sentence Stubs**

Completing sentences can generate much self-knowledge and takes very little time. I use sentence stubs several different ways: as openers to get a group thinking about a particular topic; as finishers to summarize what we have been discussing or to "set" a certain concept; as starters for graffiti writing (put up

butcher paper, write an incomplete sentence with a magic marker and leave it up for as long as you'd like); and as starters for thought papers, journal entries, anonymous sharing of feelings on 3 X 5 cards, and so on. The following are samples of sentence stubs (be sure to add your own):

One way I am different from everybody else is . . .
One way I am like everybody else is . . .
A person I learn a lot from is . . .
I feel encouraged when . . .
If I were taller, I could . . .
If I could have seven wishes, they would be . . .
My friend can be counted on to . . .
If I had a car I would . . .
Right now I feel . . .
My advice to the world would be . . .
My bluest days are . . .
If I could get a subscription to two magazines I would select . . .
After school, I like to play . . .
I feel put down when . . .
Secretly, I wish . . .
Right now I need . . .
If I could teach everyone in the world one thing, it would be . . .
I'm glad that I have learned how to . . .
One way I've made money is . . .
One important thing I've learned in school is . . .
The best thing about school is . . .
I always make up my own mind about . . .
Some day I would like to be a . . .
After school I like to . . .
I am important because . . .
One thing I like to do in groups is . . .
A taste I like is . . .
I like to . . .
I am happy when I see . . .
One thing I like about my friends is . . .
It's fun to . . .
It turns me on when . . .
I am happiest when . . .
A sound I like to hear is . . .
I love . . .
Something I've never told anyone about before is . . .
It pleases me to . . .
The best way I can think of to use my time is . . .
I like to hear stories about . . .

I am cool when I . . .

The thing I'd like people to admire me for is . . .

I like my family because . . .

I'd like my friends to . . .

One problem I solved is . . .

If I could spend all my time in one course at school it would be . . .

I laugh when . . .

I like myself because . . .

My favorite sound is . . .

Kids are . . .

Cooperation is important because . . .

Other people are important because . . .

Something I like to touch is . . .

One thing I like about where I live is . . .

My favorite food is . . .

My best skill is . . .

My best subject is . . .

I like myself when . . .

I like my best friend because . . .

The things that turn me on are . . .

I like my mother when . . .

The thing I like best about myself is . . .

My favorite thing is . . .

My favorite food is . . .

I feel successful when . . .

My favorite TV show is . . .

I feel strong when . . .

The greatest thing is . . .

I feel good when . . .

I really dig . . .

I feel in control when . . .

When somebody is nice to me, I . . .

The thing I like to dream about is . . .

The games I like best are . . .

One thing I could teach someone else is . . .

The thing I do best is . . .

Something I'd like to learn about is . . .

One thing I know about myself is . . .

I like being with people when . . .

One thing I do better than everybody else is . . .

I like my parents when . . .

When I grow up . . .

Someday I'm going to . . .

We're thinking about doing . . .

Next week I'm going to . . .
I love making . . .
My hobby is . . .
I enjoy reading about . . .
After school, I usually . . .

## Role-Playing

Regardless of the topic, ways can be found to use role-playing activities to involve students in thinking about what you want them to think about. The important thing to remember when you do role-playing is that the role-play is not the end product. You are not doing creative dramatics when you use role-playing. Pick kids who are hammy and let them act out whatever it is you're discussing. Then ask others to try it, emphasizing a different perception. Say, "How would your mother respond? Your best friend? What if this happened with a teacher?" One teacher I know asked a student to pick two others to be his good and bad conscience—you know, like in old Donald Duck cartoons. I watched this session, during which a child was given a situation in which he had to decide the right thing to do while his "angel" and "devil" argued about which choice he should make. After group members gave their opinions, he told the group what he actually would do. This is opportunity to get kids who usually pick antisocial choices to argue for the other point of view. Anyway, this list of role-playing situations will get you to start thinking about how to use this technique:

Getting up nerve to meet someone new.
Being the new person.
Being rejected.
Being made fun of.
Getting an unwanted haircut.
Waiting in line.
Being clumsy.
Being your friend.
Being the person in the group most different from you.
Being in the minority.
Being a person from history.
Being a teacher quieting unruly students.
Being an unruly student.
Being a parent scolding a child.
Having to go to a wake.
Everyone talking at once—not listening.
Not being dressed properly for an occasion.
Hearing someone comment about a physical problem.
Talking about your friend's problem.
Being late on the first day of school.

Reacting to something another student does as a mother or father would.

Throwing a tantrum.

Reacting to criticism.

Learning a new skill.

Learning a new sport.

Winning and losing.

Reacting to a surprise party.

Being picked last.

Being invited out or asking another out.

Girl (boy) watching.

Letting a friend down.

Making someone happy.

Being another person's feeling.

Being a person who can't speak English.

Talking to a deaf person.

Hurting someone's feelings.

Trying to help someone who is crying without knowing why they are crying.

Apologizing.

Breaking up a fight between two little kids.

Having just done something embarrassing.

Ordering in a restaurant.

Getting caught smoking.

Deciding where to line up in a spelling bee.

Going to a doctor.

Trying a risky sport.

Sneaking in late.

*Remember, the key to effective role-playing is the discussion afterward.*

## CONDUCTING CLASS MEETINGS

In Chapter 1 I alluded to the class-meeting concept developed by William Glasser. In this section, the idea of class meetings is described in some detail. Later in the chapter I have included a description of an actual experience of a friend of mine, who conducted class meetings as a regular part of his science program. At the end of this chapter is a list of interesting ideas to discuss in meetings.

The main thing to remember about class meetings is that the discussion tends to be more general than in awareness sessions. Instead of discussing "A time I was afraid," you might discuss "Being afraid—what is it? Why are people afraid? Are animals afraid?" The teacher's role is still one of accepting and listening, but it also shifts to that of "question-asker" to encourage thinking. Class meetings can be used to solve social problems involving class behavior or the behavior of individuals. If you are using class meetings as problem-solving sessions, try the following procedure:

## The Social-Problem-Solving Meeting

*Purpose:* To confront the class with problems related to the social behavior of the class or of individuals in the class; to identify reasonable solutions for social problems that the class members can live with; to develop group cohesiveness as class members think about and solve class problems.

*Process:* The group convenes with all class members seated in a circle or in a U shape with the teacher at the head. Reasonable rules of groups interaction must be established and strictly enforced before the group proceeds. Each group will have different rules, but the following ones are generally acceptable:

1. Students speak one at a time.
2. Statements that could be perceived as put-downs are not allowed.
3. All students' opinions are respected, but students are allowed, and encouraged, to disagree and present different opinions.
4. Student responses are generally directed at a particular person.
5. The emphasis is on "I" messages. Students are stopped and corrected when they make statements like, "Some people feel . . ." or "They say that . . ."
6. Students expressing factual statements that are questionable are asked to support their positions.
7. Students are encouraged to confront others about disagreements as long as it is done in a "civil" way.

Usually the social-problem-solving meeting is begun by having either the teacher or one of the students explain why the meeting is held. (Each meeting has a specific purpose.)

After the reason for the meeting is explained, the teacher encourages clarification concerning the problem by eliciting responses from class members. (Perhaps a recorder will write the important ideas on the board so that everyone can see them.)

After the problem is clearly identified, those forces that are blocking solution of the problem are identified and listed. The next step is for the group members to identify "action steps" they can take to eliminate the blocks. (The assumption is that if the blocks are eliminated, the problem will solve itself.) The most important part of a class meeting is the *commitment*. The meeting should not end until some commitment is made by the involved members about specific actions they will take.

Often something is signed, or an "oath" made or some ritual performed, to establish the commitment.

Many times all the above steps are not needed. If the leader does a good job getting members to clarify the problem, often the group will quickly jump to an obvious solution and commitments. This can happen at any stage of the discussion. It is up to the teacher-leader to decide how much discussion should be allowed before summarizing and going on to something else.

*Important Note:* The success of the class meeting depends on the students' feeling that everyone is of equal status in the group. The teacher must honor and respect all student contributions and really allow them to come up with ideas, solutions, and so forth. The group will fail if the teacher does all the talking or offers all the important ideas. The best way for the leader to facilitate this is to take the role of question-asker and mediator, rather than of an advocate of one position or another.

Here are some key questions that the teacher can ask to facilitate the group process:

1. What is the problem?
2. Are there some parts of the problem we are ignoring or running away from?
3. Is there something about our class that has changed and resulted in the problem?
4. What are the alternatives open to us?
5. What are the consequences of each alternative?
6. Are there any risks involved in deciding a certain way?
7. Is there something we're protecting?
8. Are we being honest about the problem?
9. What are some other ways of thinking about what happened?
10. Did anyone see the situation differently?
11. How can we make sure our solution works?
12. What should happen if someone breaks his commitment?
13. Whose responsibility is it to solve this problem?
14. Are we being concerned about the feelings of the people involved?

*The following article was written by a friend of mine who is a junior-high-school science teacher. Keith likes science and likes kids. When he was exposed to many of the ideas in this book, he wanted to put them into practice in his science classes without turning his subject into group counseling. His discussion is a clear guide to anyone in a similar position. It offers another alternative for putting affective education into action.*

## CLASSROOM MEETINGS
### by Keith Copeland

William Glasser has suggested in his book, *Schools Without Failure,* an affective-education approach that utilizes classroom meetings. I initially used the technique in my homeroom—using the ten-minute homeroom time and borrowing ten minutes from the first-period class the students had with me. Later, I did expand to other classes as productive situations spontaneously developed from routine class discussions. I found it necessary to establish a definite time limit (about twenty minutes worked best for me) to eliminate malingering and to curb rambling. It was also apparent that students are sincerely responsive to each other and enjoy the meetings immensely. Originally we did not form a circle, with the result that people in the front seats participated more frequently. We then mutually planned a rapid and consistent pattern of desk movement to allow for circle formation with minimal confusion. I found it well worth the time required for the change, as face-to-face communication was made possible. Most important, I was able to sit among the students, avoiding the directive, instrumental role, and become a participant.

I did establish a summary check list, using the class role sheet, for recording frequency of responses. The notations were done following the meeting rather than during the conversations. I could thereby determine tendencies of dominance and reluctance, judge individuals' enthusiasm for certain topics, and recognize patterns of responses. For example, I noticed that one boy always answered immediately following a contribution by another boy. It may be possible to relate personal peer choice, as in a sociogram, to conversational trends. These techniques lead to more realistic appraisal of leadership and functional roles adopted by classmates. The following are simple comments made on individual file sheets:

R.'s comments are usually quite lengthy.

B. is not very tolerant of the opinions of girls.

R. wanted to go to his locker during class. He was refused. During the meeting he pushed his chair to the side and did not participate. This was unusual, for R. would dominate all meetings if given the chance.

I talked to S. very much on a personal basis, but she never volunteers in meeting. May have something to do with seating arrangement.

M. has a hard time holding back when he wants to talk. He is very much interested in class opinion, and suggests topics for discussion. Even asked opinion of his haircut in meeting. He comes on tough in manner, but talks with humility and concern. A puzzle.

L. bubbles over, very interested. Other times is bored to the point of disruption. No topical reason for this???

J. on several occasions would jump into the discussion with statements of skepticism.

K. is quiet in class, but talks during meetings. Is now opening up more to those not known well.

R. talks very loudly. Seems strained.

F. interrupts constantly. Little restraint in derogatory opinions.

C. is coming out of her shell, talks once every meeting; asks to do errands now.

W. is always volunteering and does not seem to worry about what people are going to think about her stories. Very confident.

The Glasser model includes three types of meetings, classified according to purpose: the open-ended meeting, the social-problem-solving meeting, and the educationally diagnostic meeting. Although I tried all three types, my students preferred the open-ended meeting, in which they could propose topics. They usually selected subjects related to school events that lead to current problems in their lives. Popular items were fears of changing schools, anticipation of ridicule, and the inevitability of punishment. They were open about relating personal incidents within the topic, such as when they were paddled, moved, or retained in a grade. The question "What was the most terrible thing that has ever happened to you at school?" brought many volunteers that had previously been rather uninvolved.

I limited use of the problem-solving meeting, as I was reluctant to use this as a punitive measure. We did have a discussion on class rules in order to establish students' preferences democratically. Although this was a particularly productive means of maintaining cooperation, I limited its use to five or six times a year. It may be important to confine discussions to whole-class problems, rather than dealing with interpersonal conflicts or annoyances caused by one individual.

It is also necessary to avoid using the class meeting as an opportunity to manipulate the opinions of students, even when concerned with room-management problems. The following are examples of behavior-modification questions I used:

1. How would you feel if your father came to class to give a talk and everyone was noisy?
2. If someone gave you all the money you ever needed, would you still go to school?
3. What could be done for people who hate school?
4. How do you feel about people who get on the honor roll?
5. Can we tell lies sometimes?
6. Is it O.K. to cheat sometimes? When?

The third type of meeting, the educationally diagnostic, did not suit my purposes. Consequently, I modified it to result in value clarification discussions. We began with the public interview, which proved to be our most popular event. I think the students' enthusiasm derived from the opportunity to ask me questions following each interview. Many students conspired on trick questions and were well prepared each time. We also enjoyed the rank ordering of three life events, for great controversy often developed concerning our choices. These are a few of the items we ranked:

*What would you rather be?*
A nurse.
A secretary.
A teacher.

*What would you rather be?*
A farmer.
A construction worker.
An auto worker.

*Which disease is worst?*
Cancer.
Heart attack.
Tuberculosis.

*What would you do if the teacher had spinach on his tooth?*
Ignore it.
Tell him.
Laugh.

*Which would you rather do?*
Read
Listen to the radio.
Watch TV.

*Where would you rather go?*
To church.
To the dentist.
To visit relatives.

*What would you do if you saw someone steal?*
Report it.
Ignore it.
Tell him.

*Which would you rather have?*
A mouse.
A parakeet.
A frog.

*Which would you rather fall in?*
Mud.
Moss.
Manure.

Occasionally, following activity, we would engage in agree-disagree voting, indicated by hand raising. It was interesting to note changes in opinion due to peer pressure and to watch the formation of consulting groups who voted as blocs. At other times, no discussion was allowed, which led to great hesitance and many stragglers. Others were rapid and unwavering in their choices. The following are some of the questions I used effectively:

1. Would you kill someone in terrible pain?
2. How many of you get an allowance?
3. Would it be O.K. with you if your parents adopted a black child?
4. Do older brothers and sisters get more breaks?
5. Do you exaggerate when you brag?
6. Are you for capital punishment?
7. Do you know any sissies?
8. Have you ever cried because your feelings were hurt? This year?

9. Would you like to be President?
10. Are you in favor of men staying home and women working?
11. Do you think it should be legal to drink at eighteen? At sixteen? At fourteen?
12. Is it O.K. for men to cry?
13. Is it O.K. for women to cry?
14. Do prisons reform or help most inmates?
15. How many of you would like to work a half day while in high school?
16. Should the driver's-license age be eighteen?
17. Do you spend most of your money on food? On clothes?
18. Should girls ask boys for dates?
19. Are teachers nice to you?
20. Do you ever throw out trash?

Many of the problems I had with class meetings were a result of my inexperience with the method and were gradually resolved as the students and I learned together the function and limitations of our conversations. Other difficulties reflected personal variations among the students and required gradual intervention on my part. In every group, there were certain students who enjoyed hearing themselves talk and who tried to dominate the meetings. We began by requiring brief hand-raising signals for desire to speak, which were recognized by a nod from the teacher. This was eliminated later as we developed some feeling for being a group. I also encountered a few students who made hurtful, derogatory comments to each other. I would ignore much of the baiting but would respond with an apology to the victim of a particularly cutting remark. If more pressure was needed, I would ask the individual why he made such a statement or would reflect the remark to the group for discussion. Less critical, but more common, were students who tended to talk at great length and in extensive detail. I would often find it necessary to interject the question, "And how did it turn out at the end?" to terminate an extensive narration. The most persistent problem was that of students who listened but did not talk until the meeting was ended and I was available for an individual conference. Many students did not respond to the group but would pursue the topic with me privately. I would comment on how interesting their ideas were and ask them to share them with the group next time. These people, many of them girls, needed much reassurance of an accepting atmosphere. During instructional time, I might comment to a student that I would like to hear more from him, or that I was expecting to hear his ideas on the next subject that I would identify. This enabled them to prepare an idea, even though it may have been too demanding for the very shy.

As I deliberately tried to modify the behaviors of the students, I found equal changes necessary in my own verbal manner. It was absolutely necessary for me to avoid a judgmental tone, which was particularly difficult when the class was aligning itself with the antithesis of my values or when factions were developing on a critical issue. I tried to phase out my own influence once the system of discussion had been established. I remained a calming factor on the group but allowed them to direct themselves. During the earlier group meetings, I had come prepared to share snappy topics and exciting experiences. I found this less necessary as we progressed.

I suspect that introducing class meetings is most effective if accompanied by other changes in class atmosphere. We instituted a suggestion box for student gripes and began the Person of the Day activity. We featured, on the bulletin board, a member of the class, who arranged a display of items he chose to share with the group. These included pictures, trophies, awards, hobbies, his life history, and so forth. We designed a questionnaire giving family information and interests. I began this project by preparing the first display on my own life, which led to great curiosity about my experiences and opinions.

We were more able, through use of these techniques, to relate as individuals, rather than just fulfill functional roles, and still accomplish the business of the day. I was disappointed, however, to find that the gains we made in establishing trust, rapport, and cooperation had little transfer to other classes. I had many of the same students in directed study for another class and experienced great difficulty with their behavior, especially evasiveness and belittling of others. I am, therefore, convinced that establishment of affective-education programs must be on a school-wide basis for maximum effectiveness.

## CLASSROOM MEETING QUESTIONS*

These questions are designed to encourage students to think. The word "Primary" following a question indicated that it is most appropriate for very young children.

1. What is a friend? If you moved to a new town, how would you go about making new friends?
2. What is a teacher? Have you ever had a teacher who is not in school? How do you know when you have a good teacher?
3. What is a school? How do you know if a school is good or bad? What could students and teachers do to make this school better?
4. If you could not be a human being anymore, what animal would you choose to be and why? What problems would you have? What advantages would you have?
5. What is a uniform? Who wears uniforms? If the School Board passed a ruling that students had to wear uniforms to school, how would you feel about it and why?
6. If the energy crisis became crucial and you were permitted to have only *one* electric appliance in your house, which one would you choose? Why?

---

*I thank Marilyn Tannebaum and Frank Cushing for most of these questions.

7. If you were suddenly left without parents, how could you go about making a living for yourself?

8. How would things be different if the earth were made of cement?

9. What are rules? Why do we have rules? What rules do you think a school needs?

10. What ideas do you have to help adults and children get along better together?

11. What is health? How can you tell if a person is healthy? What can you do to keep yourself healthy? Why do you keep your fingernails clean? Why do you brush your teeth?

12. What is loneliness? Why are some people lonely?

13. What would you do if you were asleep at home and someone woke you up and said there was a fire in the kitchen? What would you do first? Second? Third? What is a good rule to remember in event of a fire? If your sister becomes frightened and begins to run, what should you do? What do you do if someone is on fire and begins to run? Should we call the fire department first or get everyone out of the house first? Then what should we do?

14. Can we help anyone to attend class regularly? How can we help someone who has been absent? If somebody is absent in our class, does it hurt you any way? How do you like going to this class?

15. What would you do if you lost your lunch? What would you feel? If you eat someone else's lunch, are you sure the food is clean? Would you know how it was fixed and under what conditions? Why is it bad to eat food when you don't know how it was prepared?

16. Why do we need health examinations at school when we're feeling okay? What is a health examination? What does the nurse do? The doctor? What are they trying to find out? How can your health affect your school work? How can you help yourself remain healthy?

17. What would you do if your family acquired a large amount of money (a million dollars)? What would you do that would be different than now? What things would you do that are the same as now? What kind of people would you have as your friends? Where would you live and what kind of house would it be? What would you do with the money?

18. What would you do if you had a chance to run the school for one day? What do you think your biggest job would be? How would you handle discipline problems? What would you do in case of emergencies, such as accidents on the playground?

19. How do you feel about remaining after school for punishment? How do people disturb you in the classroom? How should kids be punished?

20. What is a perfect school day to you? What suggestions do you have that might make school ideal for you? How would you spend most of your time during the day? Why?

21. If you were given the task of fencing your back yard, how would you go about doing it? What mathematical concepts would you use? What kind of fencing would you use? How would you figure the cost of the fencing?

22. If you had $150 to spend, how would you spend it? Should money be spent wisely and carefully? What would you buy first? What is a miser? A spendthrift?

23. If you could turn yourself into any animal on earth, what would you be? Would you like to be a gentle deer or a fierce tiger? Would you like to be an animal that helps man or one that hurts him? Do you think some animals remind you of certain people? Do you think animals would bother people if people didn't bother them? Do you think people react in the same way if someone bothers them?

24. If you found a $5.00 bill on the street, what would you do? Would you hide it and say nothing? Would you tell your mother? Would you tell your friends? Would you try to find the owner? If you could keep it, how would you spend it?

25. Would you rather be little again or just the way you are now? What can you do that your little brother or sister can't do? Do you think you have more fun than your little brother or sister? Do you think you'll like being older than you are now? Why? What are you looking forward to doing when you get older?

26. If you had three wishes, what would they be? Would you wish for things that cost money? Who would you want to make your wish come true?

27. What does being sad mean to you? How do you act? What things sadden you? How do you make other people feel when you are sad?

28. What does honesty mean? Should children be honest? Should children and adults tell the truth all the time? Should one be punished for being dishonest? How do you feel when you have not told the truth?

29. Why do people have children? Are you happy your parents had you? Are you an only child? What are the advantages of being an only child? Would you like to be an only child? What are the disadvantages of being an only child?

30. What does it mean when someone says you are nervous? What are some mannerisms that show that boys and girls are nervous? How do you feel when you are nervous? What are some things you have to do in school that make you nervous?

31. What is love? How can you tell when someone loves you? How can you show someone that you love them? Are you in love?

32. If you could have all the money you wanted, how would you spend it?

33. What is happiness? What person would you like to make happy today? How do you act when you're happy? What can you do to make someone happy?

34. If you had a choice to live where it is either mostly hot or mostly cold, where would you live? Why?

35. Why do you come to school? What can you do to enjoy school life more? How can you show your teacher that you are learning?

36. If you had a magic pencil what would you have it do? What would school be like if we had magic pencils? [Primary]

37. What is your favorite TV show? Which character would you like to be and why?

38. What's the worst punishment you have gotten or could get? If you were a parent, how would you punish your child?

39. If your town made a law saying that only one kind of pet was allowed, which would you choose? How would you take care of it?

40. Do animals dream? What might they dream about?

41. If you could have famous people for your parents, whom would you choose? How do you think your life would be the same or different with other parents?

42. If you awoke to find you were the last person on earth, how would you feel? What problems would you have?

43. What is a President? Would you like to be President? What would you do if you were President?

44. What would you do if you had a friend no one liked? Play with him? Walk to school with him? How could you help him have more friends?

45. What is a crayon? What is your favorite color? What would you do if you were a crayon? What would you do if you were drawing a picture and your crayon wouldn't do what you wanted it to? Suppose your crayon could talk? [Primary]

46. What is a circle? Make a circle with fingers, hands, and a body—is it really a circle? What are some circles in our room? What is your favorite circle? What would the world be like without circles? Could we ride bikes? Bounce balls? [Primary]

47. What is a television? What if the picture were upside down? What if there were no sound? What if you had to pay to watch TV?

48. If you could be on *Sesame Street,* what would you do? If you could bring someone or something home with you, what would you choose? What would you do with him or it? [Primary]

49. What is a ghost? Are ghosts friendly or scary? Which would you be? Where would you live? What would you do? [Primary]

50. What animals have tails? Why? What if you had a tail? What if you had four legs? [Primary]

51. If you made up an animal, what would you call it? What would it look like? Where could it live? How could you take care of it? How would you play with it?

52. What is a tree? Do all trees look alike? How do trees help us? Where would you want to be if you were a tree? What if there were no trees? What would we do for a Christmas tree? For wooden toys? For houses?

53. [I used an old, stuffed toy monkey, small in size, with the fuzz worn off

his stomach and back. His head was wrapped with gauze bandages. I held it in my hands or on my lap during the discussion.]
What do your eyes tell you about this toy? What kind of an animal is this? Why is the fur worn off his stomach? Why do you suppose his head is bandaged? What do your thoughts tell you about the person who owns this monkey? Why do we keep old, worn-out things? Do you have any toy that is a "best-loved" toy for you? [Primary]

54. If you could invite someone special that you admire for Thanksgiving dinner (someone outside of your family), whom would you ask to come? If you could ask someone from the past (someone who is not living), who might that be?

55. What makes a house a home? Could a motel be a home? Could a tent? A shack? Could you ever have two homes?

56. Why do we go to church? What does the church do with the money people give? Why do parents take their children to church or Sunday School?

57. How do children learn to talk? How old is a baby when he learns to talk? When he says, "da-da" does he mean "daddy," or is he just playing around with his voice? What was the first word you learned? Could you find out for our next meeting?

58. What is pollution? Where did it come from? How can you and I help clean up the world? What are grownups doing now to help stop pollution?

59. Why is there a tooth fairy? Have you ever seen her? What did she look like? How does she know who lost a tooth? [Primary]

60. What is fire? How can a fire start? What are some bad effects of fire? What are some good things fire does for us? What can we use to put out different kinds of fires? How can we call the fire department?

61. What is the scariest thing that ever happened to you? Where were you? What did you do? If it happened again, would you still be scared? Would you do anything different if it happened again?

62. What is food? What is your favorite food? What food do you really dislike? If you did the shopping for one day's meals, what would you buy? Are all foods good for you? What are some foods that aren't very good for you? What do you do when you don't like the food you're eating?

63. What is a shot? Who gives them? What part of your body do you get shots in? What is a shot for? What kinds of shots have you had?

64. Have you ever been in a bad mood? How did you get that way? How did you get out of it? How can you help your mom when you come home from school and she is in a bad mood?

65. How can we help our classroom become a more cheerful place to be?

66. Why do people get married?

67. Why do people get divorced? What is divorce? How do you get one?

68. What does it mean when someone tells you that you are bad? Who decides what is good? Do you feel like a good person?

69. Why do people lie? Do people believe you when you tell them something? When do you lie? Is lying bad?

70. What is kindness? Do you know anyone who is kind? Why are some people mean to others? Are you a kind person?

71. If you didn't go to school, what would you do with your life? Why do we have schools? Why do people work? Is some work fun?

72. Did you know that a long time ago only boys could go to school? What do you think of this? What is woman's liberation? Does it affect you?

73. If a child becomes ill, what do you do? What if no teacher were near? Who would go to the nurse? If you were in charge, what would you have the other children do? What if this happened on the playground? What would you do if the child were bleeding? What if the child were vomiting? What would you do if the teacher became ill?

74. What is cheating? Do you know anyone who cheats? Do you ever cheat? Why do people cheat? Would you trust a person who cheats? Why not?

75. Should we do away with fact learning and memorizing in school? Do you know anyone who didn't ever have to do fact learning or memorizing? (Such as poems, words to songs, lines for plays, multiplication games, conduct, certain rules, rules for games.)

76. What do you think your school would be like if only second-grade students came to it and all the other grades went to different schools?

77. Do you think that you could start settling your own problems without being able to ask your older brothers and sisters to hit someone with whom you are having an argument?

78. Do you like to be hit by someone bigger than you? Do you ever hit people?

79. How do you think other children feel who are hit by someone bigger and older than they are?

80. Do you think there would be more or less fighting if there were only children of your own age at this school?

81. Would it be possible to act as if we didn't have older brothers and sisters going to this school?

82. Why do teachers send your report cards home?

83. What are good grades? Do you know what each grade means? Do you think your grades show what you are doing?

84. What do your parents do and say when you bring home your report card?

85. Would you rather not have report cards? What if your parents could know how you are doing another way? Would you like that better than report cards? Why?

86. What is a fire drill? Why is a fire drill necessary? Is a fire drill a waste of time? Do teachers think that fire drills are a waste of time? Why is following directions important? Should we practice (drill) although we know it is not happening?

87. What would you do if the teacher was absent and the school caught on fire? What would you do if no substitute teacher were there? What are the rules during a fire drill?

88. Why do we call each other names? Does it hurt the other person when you call him a name? Does it make you feel better? How do you feel when someone calls you a name? What can you do about it? What are nicknames? Do you have one? Do you like it?

89. If you could change your classroom, how would you make it different? Why? What do you think other people would say about the change?

90. If you could do anything in school, what would you like to do? Why? How would you feel when you do this?

91. Why do you think we have a dress code? Why couldn't we come barefoot? Why couldn't we wear bathing suits? Why no fishnet hose? Do you think dress codes are good?

92. Why do people steal? Do they need money? Food? Is that why some grownups steal? How about the ones from whom they steal—do they need that money or food? Is there anything that we could do to help children who steal?

93. Would you like to be an only child, with no brothers or sisters? Would you be lonely? What could you do if you were lonely? Would you have more or less things than you have now? Would you be happier? Sadder?

94. If Mother and Daddy had to go away for a few days and left you to take care of the house and baby, what would you do? Could you take care of the baby? The house? Could you fix food for you and the baby?

95. If you could have any job when you grow up, what would you like to do? Would you want a job that would make you rich? Would you want a job in which you could help people? How many hours a day would you like to work? How many days a week would you like to work? Which skill would you need to learn right now so that you could do that job well?

96. What is prejudice? How can prejudice be like lying? Does prejudice only mean not liking people with a different skin color? Where have you most often heard people with prejudices speaking? Who were they? Why do you suppose people are prejudiced? Have you ever met anybody you didn't like at first? Could you dislike anybody you didn't know? How may we stop prejudices from arising? Are there people you don't like? Why?

97. What is the moon like? Why do people want to go there? Would you like to go to the moon? Why or why not? What do you think you would find there?

98. What is air? Can you see air? How do you know it exists? What does air do?

99. What is arithmetic? Why do we learn it? How do we use it later in life?

100. If you were the President, what things would you do to make the United States a better place in which to live?

101. Suppose you could change our report-card system—what would you do?

102. How could your progress in school be recorded or reported other than on report cards?

103. What problems do many of you have with math or reading or writing? Why do so many of you fail to turn in your work? What can your teacher do to make math (or any subject) more interesting?

104. How much homework should a teacher give each week? Should any homework be given? In what subject should it be given? Should homework be given for over the weekend?

105. Which kind of teacher do you like better? A strict teacher or an easy one? Is a strict teacher necessarily a mean one? With which teacher do you feel you learn more? Which kind of teacher do you like?

106. Why do you come to school? If you could, would you stay home? Do you feel that school is helpful? What do you like about school? What do you dislike about school?

107. What would you do if you saw your best friend pull the fire alarm when there was no fire? Would you tell the teacher? Would you say nothing? Would you tell his parents?

108. What would you do if you went to the cafeteria and they were serving food you don't like? Would you eat the food? Would you go hungry and save your money? Would you give it to a friend?

109. Does punishment help you to do better? Why are you punished? What is punishment? What type of punishment do you get at home? At school? What type of punishment do you hate most? Is punishment fair? What can you do to prevent future punishment?

# 5

## WHAT IFS

The following pages contain a list of the most common kinds of problems that come up in groups from time to time. Each problem is stated in the form of a "What if" statement. The likely causes of the problem are listed in the left-hand column and some possible solutions are listed in the right-hand column.

The suggestions offered represent the experiences of many teachers who have been leading groups for at least two years. If you are having a problem that is listed here, and if one of the possible causes listed seems to fit your situation, then try one or more of the solutions offered. Remember, though, that each situation is unique. While the possible causes listed here are common, your problems may stem from very different causes—ones that aren't mentioned here.

1.   What if a Child Always Talks About the Same Thing?

*Possible Causes*

a. He may really care about the thing and it may represent more to him than is apparent on the surface. He may be a child who has few successes, and this may be one of the few areas in which he really feels good about himself.

b. Much of his life may be upsetting, and this one thing may offer him security.

c. He may be saying he doesn't feel secure enough in the group to share more of himself.

d. His wealth of experiences to draw from may be so limited that he can't really think of anything outside this one area.

e. He may have developed an attention-getting pattern such that all the other kids expect him to talk about the same thing.

*Possible Solutions*

a. Accept all his contributions, no matter how much of a drag it becomes. After you have accepted his contribution, say, "I really like what you said about your horse (car, sport, or whatever) but I wonder if you could think of something else, unrelated to that, that goes with our topic."

b. If his comment is unrelated to the discussion at hand say, "That's interesting, but can you tell us how it relates to our discussion? Can you think of something that is more related to our discussion?"

c. Sit by him and let him know non-verbally, that you accept him and notice him.

d. When he does say something different, reinforce him strongly. Say, "Bill, I like when you tell us more about you than just about your horse (car, sport)."

2. What If a Child Tells You a Topic Is Too Personal—an Invasion of Privacy?

*Possible Causes*

a. You may, in fact, be getting into an area that several students feel is too personal, and he has the guts to say something about it.

b. He may not mean it. He may be testing you or trying a negative attention-getting behavior.

c. Because of his personal life, this area may be too personal for him and he may be afraid you will force him to talk about it.

d. He may be uncomfortable in the group and simply not trust you.

*Possible Solutions*

a. Reflect his feelings that he is upset by the topic and then go on with the discussion, ignoring him and letting him decide whether he wants to participate.

b. Reexamine the topic and the overall feeling in the group. Perhaps you have given the students the feeling that these discussions are very "heavy." After you reflect the students statement, ask the group what they think about it. Encourage different comments.

c. Remind the whole group that no one has to talk about anything if he doesn't want to.

3. What if a Child Speaks Too Softly Or Too Loudly?

*Possible Causes*

a. You may be having your circle in an area that is too noisy. Some children normally have quiet voices that *can* be heard if there is quiet; some need to speak very loudly to overcome the background noise.

b. By habit, the child may always speak very quietly or very loudly. There are many psychological reasons for this, none of which are important in terms of the circle.

c. The child may have a physical problem, such as a speech or hearing impairment.

d. The soft-spoken child may feel very insecure in the circle and may think that what he says will not be acceptable to the group. He may find it difficult to risk.

*Possible Solutions*

a. Examine the physical setup within your group and around it. Have the children sit closer together, or if possible, move to a quieter spot in the building. Enforce rules within the group to avoid too much cross-talking that is not relevant.

b. Say directly to the child, "I really want to hear you, but you'll have to speak louder. Could you try it again?" or "I like the things you say, but sometimes you really talk loud. Could you try and use a quieter voice?"

c. Ask the person to reflect what someone else has said, talking in the same voice they use.

d. Ask the group, "How many of you heard Gary?"

*Possible Causes*

*Possible Solutions*

e. Respond nonverbally, using hand and facial motions to say, "quieter" or "louder."
f. Reflect the child's statement in the opposite tone of voice.
g. Check to see whether the student has a physical problem.
h. Let the child know you like what he says and consider him a valuable member of the circle.

4.   What If a Child Says Something Like "I Hate Circles" or "This Is Boring"?

*Possible Causes*

a. He may really hate the group.
b. The child may know he can get attention that way and may really need the attention. He may feel he won't get it if he just sits and participates regularly.
c. The child may be upset about something else but is projecting it onto you or the group.

*Possible Solutions*

a. Accept his statement, reflect it back to him ("You feel the circle is really boring,") and then continue with the circle.
b. If the negative child makes any positive contribution, reinforce it. Don't use sarcasm. Don't say, "Oh, I thought you hated circles."
c. If you feel he's upset about something else, say, "Bill, are you really saying that to us?" or "You seem to be upset about something. Would you like to talk about it?"
d. If you feel the total group is supportive, ask them for their opinions. Do they agree or disagree? Don't do this if everyone feels as he does.
e. After the circle, meet with the student alone to discuss the problem. Offer him some alternatives, like being leader, picking a day's topic, sitting out for a while, or being official rememberer.

## 5. What If a Child Is Noticeably Disliked by the Group?

*Possible Causes*

a. The child may have some habit or overt behavior that bothers other students. Often this type of child has a poor self-concept and tries to compensate by being a clown or a critic or by engaging in other obnoxious behavior.

b. The child may simply be very different from the others (racially, economically, or physically). The other children may be anxious about this difference and, instead of talking about their own fears or inadequacies, use this "different" child as a scapegoat.

c. He may have serious emotional problems that require professional help. The other students simply can't cope with him.

d. The child may require much more attention because of his emotional problem and other students may resent this.

*Possible Solutions*

a. You must remember that everything a child does springs from his feelings about who and what he is. If the child is encouraging this dislike by his own behavior, try to reinforce him as a good person. Set up a strength bombardment activity with the whole group. Set it up so that his chances of being put down will be minimal. Organize some activity in which he is put in a position of high esteem. Make sure he can succeed at it. Physically deal with his need to feel accepted by sitting next to him, touching him encouragingly, and letting him know that you're glad he is here. Set up an activity in which something he is good at becomes apparent.

b. Do some group role-playing in which the isolated child has a chance to play a very different role in the group.

c. Do some warm-up activities that build group cohesiveness.

d. Do a unit on tolerance with the whole group. At some point in the group have *all* members mention something about themselves that is hard to tolerate. In this way, the isolated student will see that he is not the only one who has behavior problems. Following the unit on tolerance, conduct a social-problem-solving meeting about the *real* problem. The student should not be attacked, but people should feel free to tell him what he does that is the problem.

*Possible Causes*

*Possible Solutions*

e. Set up a private meeting with this child. Follow the seven steps laid out by William Glasser. Get the child to understand that he is doing something in the group that is causing the difficulty. Reinforce him by telling him you like him, but get him to make a commitment to changing his behavior.

6. What If a Child Has Very Different Values from Those of the Leader and Other Students?

*Possible Causes*

a. The home-life experience of the child may be very different from yours or the other students'. He is what he is.

b. His values really aren't that different, but he feels a need to test you to see whether you really mean all that stuff about acceptance.

*Possible Solutions*

a. Don't ever deny or put down his values; assume he means what he says. If he says he gets a good feeling from busting heads, accept it, but get him to discuss how he feels, not to give details about the behavior. It is important to remember that the best way to change him is to let him know you accept his having a certain value and then let him hear others tell about their value.

b. If his value statements are very strong or offensive, you may have to say more. The following statement is reasonable. "Bill, I accept that you feel that way about (fighting, stealing, lying), but I must tell you I feel very strongly against it. I wonder if you have ever been on the other side of the coin." or, "Bill, I believe you feel that way, but I must tell you that most of us feel differently. I wonder if you could tell us more about the reason you feel so strongly."

c. Have a personal conference with the student.

d. Discuss the problem with the principal or school psychologist.

7.  What If a Child Consistently Copies Another's Contributions?

*Possible Cause*

a. The child may be saying: "I'm afraid to risk getting ridiculed or rejected by teachers or peers."

*Possible Solution*

a. Deal with his feelings. Reflect them. Tell the student, "You feel good about choosing a horse like Mary did because you think it's nice. You feel good because you said something." Make an independent statement of direction: "You feel ––– because you said something. It is good that you said that because we want to know what makes you feel good. We are interested in the feelings you have."

8.  What If a Child Tells You What He Thinks You Want To Hear?

*Possible Cause*

a. He may be saying: "I'm afraid to risk because this is not an accepting climate." Remember, he is saying something you want because he is afraid to risk. In time he will try to express his own feelings, but he will close up if he is rejected.

*Possible Solutions*

a. Relax and accept what he says. Give him time to begin expressing his own feelings.
b. If many students are doing this, bring it up in the group.
c. Discuss a topic about it: "a time I told somebody what I thought they wanted to hear."

9.  What If a Child Talks and Talks and Won't Finish His Story?

*Possible Cause*

a. He may be saying: "I have to get mine while I have the floor or I will never have another chance."

*Possible Solutions*

a. Make sure everyone gets a chance. This is why it is best to keep the groups small. If the children can be convinced that it is important that they all get an opportunity to speak, in time they will help control the group so that each does get a turn. At first make sure they clearly understand you accept the responsibility for giving them all a chance to speak by asking them

*Possible Cause*

*Possible Solutions*

and then waiting for them to speak. Do not rush them. If you do not have time in one day for all to have a chance to speak, clearly state that those who didn't speak today will have a chance tomorrow, and then remember.

b. When he stops to breathe, reflect what he has said and thank him.

10. What If Kids Talk About Teachers or Others not in the Circle in a Gossipy, Negative Way?

*Possible Causes*

a. They may not be clear about the rules of the circle regarding such issues.

b. You may have lost control of your group.

c. There may be a serious problem with someone not present that has gotten the students very upset.

*Possible Solutions*

a. You can't stop a child from saying someone's name the first time, but once it has been said, stop the group and remind them of the reason for not discussing negative things about people in the circle.

b. Reflect what the child has said and gently point out that while we are concerned about his feelings, we really don't want the person not here to be discussed.

c. If numerous students want to discuss a problem, table the discussion and tell them you will get more information about the problem and then discuss it. Perhaps you can get the person they are upset with to come to class and tell his side.

d. Regardless of what else is done, *get control* of the group. If you say something shouldn't be discussed, then make sure they don't discuss it.

11.  What If No One in the Circle Will Say Anything?

*Possible Causes*

a. Somehow they may have the idea
   that the circle is too heavy. They
   may be uncomfortable and feel
   that talking involves too great a
   risk.
b. They may feel they will be put
   down in some way.
c. They may not understand what
   the circle is about.

*Possible Solutions*

a. Reread the part of this book
   called "Beginning Awareness
   Sessions."
b. Use the sentence-stub approach
   to loosen them up.
c. Involve them in some gamelike
   activities to build group cohesiveness. Use games that don't require
   verbal participation. (Read: *Will
   the Real Teacher Please Stand Up?*)

12.  What If a Child Confesses to an Illegal Act or Shares Something Ex-
     tremely Personal In The Circle?

*Possible Causes*

a. He may feel extremely guilty
   about what he has done and may
   want someone to know. The general tenor in the circle encourages
   sharing, so he may feel secure in
   saying it in the circle.
b. You may have developed a climate
   of trust about the circle that
   makes the child feel that disclosing possibly damaging information will be accepted and won't
   be retold outside of the circle.
c. He may have a need to get attention and may be consciously trying
   to shock people in the circle
   in order to meet that need.

*Possible Solutions*

a. The most important thing to remember is that as soon as you realize
   what has happened in the circle,
   you should get away from the
   topic of conversation quickly. Ignore the comment or reflect it
   briefly, accepting it and going on.
   Don't act shocked by what has
   been said. It's important that
   after the circle is over you talk with
   the child about what has happened.
   Let him know how serious you
   consider what has been said and
   suggest different courses of action
   with him depending on what he
   said. The problem for you is your
   responsibility to the school and to
   the child. Whatever you do, don't
   promise him that you won't repeat
   what he has said. If you promise
   that, you're in a bind if the child's
   welfare becomes endangered.
b. A situation like this is an opportunity to discuss the question of
   privacy with the whole circle. You

*Possible Causes*

*Possible Solutions*

might have them talk about whether or not they should tell what happens in the circle outside and how they feel about what they say being retold outside the circle.

13. What If It Seems Like the Children Are Interested in the Discussion but No One Starts Talking?

*Possible Causes*

a. Your directions may have been un-clear. You may not have given enough examples, so they're not sure what kind of responses are appropriate.

b. Without knowing it, you may have picked something too risky for them to talk about.

c. The group may simply be in a lethargic mood: the weather, the lighting, or similar factors may be involved. Examine those conditions to decide what to do.

*Possible Solutions*

a. Repeat the question or reintroduce it in a different way. If you introduced it directly, try reintroducing it using voting questions or a sentence stub or some other indirect method.

b. Give more examples of what you mean. You may have to give four or five examples to get them started.

c. Reword the topic or the idea for discussion in a way more appropriate to their level.

d. If it seems like it's too personal and they don't want to talk about themselves, restate the question so they can talk about people in general or someone they know rather than themselves. Later on you can go from this into their own lives.

14. What If a Group Discussion or Activity Completely Bombs Out and No Matter What You Try To Do You Can't Get Them To Talk?

*Possible Causes*

a. It may be poor planning. What you've scheduled for the session may not be consistent, clear, or relevant to the group.

*Possible Solutions*

a. Let the silence go for several minutes. Let all the children experience the silence so that at least you can talk about that.

*Possible Causes*

b. It may be such a bad day or the kids may be in such a mood that doing anything with them on this day wouldn't work.

*Possible Solutions*

b. Have a list of warm-up exercises at your disposal, and if five or ten minutes have gone by and nothing is happening, tell them, "We're just not in a mood to discuss something today so let's just play a game." Then bring out a warm-up game like Concentration.

c. Bring up your own favorite topic that always seems to work.

d. Discuss what's happening right now in the circle. Go around and have each person make a statement about why everything is bombing today. Then talk about it.

15. What If Kids Say "We Did That One Already" When You Introduce An Activity or Topic for Discussion?

*Possible Causes*

a. They may have done it before and don't think you can do something twice and still have it be meaningful.

b. Some of them may have done it and find this a way to get attention and to torpedo what's happening in the group.

*Possible Solutions*

a. Explain that this topic is similar to previous topics but show by your examples how it's different.

b. Point out that the last time they talked about this or did this activity they were younger and very different in the way they thought about things.

c. Accept their comments that they have already done it and just tell them, "O.K., that's the way you feel, but we're going to do this again today, so try to get into it."

d. Use the analogy of books or movies and how you sometimes see a movie or read a book five or six times and get more out of it each time. The same can be true with some kinds of circle experiences.

16. **What If There Is a Child in Your Group That No One Will Sit Next To?**

*Possible Cause*

a. There may be some physical problem with the child, such as an odor or some physical deformity. Or it may be general peer pressure because this child is an isolate.

*Possible Solutions*

a. You, as the leader, can sit next to this child and model accepting behavior for the group.

b. You can give the students assigned places so that they don't have a choice of where to sit.

c. Something you should do regardless of the others: privately check with the nurse or the principal about the child and see what can be done to eliminate the problem.

17. **What If the Child Talks Only to the Person Next to Him?**

*Possible Causes*

a. The person next to him may be his good friend and he enjoys talking to him.

b. He may be a very shy child who would like to participate but who can only get up the courage to talk to one other person.

c. The child may be very verbal and unable to wait his turn and so may talk to the person next to him.

*Possible Solutions*

a. Look at the child who is talking and say, "Do you have something you'd like to share with us?" Don't do this in a negative, sarcastic way, but sincerely, indicating that you really care what the person has to say and you think the whole group cares, too.

b. Change the seating so that the two children aren't sitting next to each other.

c. Talk to the whole group about the problem of cross-communication and about how the circle is a time for having a general conversation with ten or fifteen people. Explain that it's different from when you're with one person talking about a private thing.

d. Use nonverbal communication methods to tell the child his behavior is inappropriate.

## 18. What If a Battle of the Sexes Occurs?

*Possible Causes*

a. The ratio of boys and girls may be uneven, and either group may feel threatened because they are underrepresented.

b. If you are dealing with sixth graders, the age level of the children may make the social-acceptance norm against the opposite sex.

c. The structures of the children's families may reinforce a pattern of negative feeling toward the opposite sex.

d. One or two peer leaders may be responsible for the feeling and may have organized the whole group to respond this certain way.

*Possible Solutions*

a. Require that the children sit boy-girl, boy-girl. If you let them know that you mean business, they'll almost certainly go along with it.

b. The chain interview technique will increase interaction between boys and girls. Do the chain interview and tell the person that if you're a boy you have to ask a girl and if you are a girl you have to ask a boy.

c. Dump the problem on the group. Talk to them about boy-girl relationships and ask them what they're going to do about it. One good technique in this area is to relate their experience (not liking boys or girls), to what they see going on in the school with older children. Just ask them to describe what they see eighth-grade boys and girls doing, and if they think they'll ever do that. Go from that into a discussion of getting along with members of the opposite sex.

## 19. What If a Child Feels So Negative About the Circle or About Himself That He Just Doesn't Want To Participate?

*Possible Causes*

a. Something may have happened in the group or may been said to him that makes him feel rejected.

b. He may be testing you to see how far you'll go to accept him; he may really want you to urge him to participate.

*Possible Solutions*

a. Talk to the child privately and see whether you can get him to come to the circle and sit by you if you promise him you won't call on him. All he has to do is sit there and listen—not participate.

b. Positively reinforce him at every

*Possible Causes*

c. He may feel that the risk involved in being in the circle is too great and he'd rather continue to see himself as a failure and an isolate than take the risk.

*Possible Solutions*

opportunity. If he comes to the circle, look at him directly and say, "I'm really glad you decided to come today." Do the same thing when he comes to your class, and so on.

c. Get into the strength bombardment activity quickly and make sure that he gets his share of strengths early so that he realizes that people think there are nice things about him.

d. Do a large group activity in the circle that has people working in dyads so that he has a partner with whom he can develop a good relationship.

e. Try to get him to allow you to interview him publicly in the group and ask him the kinds of questions in the interview that will make him look good and feel good about himself. Then have the others remember his answers.

# 6

# EVALUATING AWARENESS SESSIONS

There are many ways to evaluate what is happening in your group sessions. There are things you can do to evaluate the process of learning itself—to evaluate the knowledge students have that they didn't have when you began. You can measure changes in student attitudes, social behavior, and intellectual achievement on the assumption that positive changes in student attitudes will show up in better schoolwork.

## PROCESS EVALUATION

Every now and then you want to know how the sessions are going. Do students enjoy them, do they think they are learning from them, and are they, in your eyes, behaving differently than before?

You can conduct an evaluation session by discussing an evaluative topic, such as "the best and worst thing about groups," "something I learned from an awareness session," or "what group meetings are really all about."

You can do a quickie evaluation by throwing out a sentence stub, like "I liked the session when . . ." or "Discussions bomb out when . . ." You can involve the students in group activities that will be evaluative. Following are descriptions of several possible evaluative activities. In addition to these activities, try a physical nonverbal continuum in which kids line up from the person who likes awareness sessions the most to the one who likes them the least, or from the best listener to the worst listener. Have them rank three or four sessions from their favorite to their least favorite. Have them explain their choices. Use thought papers as evaluative devices. Every week or month, have them write about awareness groups, either privately or for sharing.

After a particular unit ask, ten to fifteen questions that students can raise hands to respond to. For example: "How many of you think you are more tolerant now than you were two weeks ago? How many liked the blue eyes-brown eyes game? How many understood it? How many thought you were good listeners during the dyad activity? How many thought your partner listened to you? How many actually said stuff that you really felt?"

The fish-bowl evaluation technique can be a powerful one. Get five or six participants to sit in an inner circle and have them discuss some aspects of the program: discipline, participation, effectiveness of different activities, and so on. People in the outer circle can listen and can enter into the discussion by coming into the inner circle or by changing chairs with someone already in the circle. The teacher can stay out in order to observe student behavior. He can, however, enter into the discussion by throwing out a question for discussion.

### Group Collage

*Purpose:* To evaluate where the group is at the present time; to assess what we have learned about each other.

*Process:* Today's session is an evaluation session of the awareness activities. Begin the session by whipping around the following sentence stubs: "the best thing about the group is . . ." "something I'd like to change about the group is . . ." "the reason we do the awareness thing is . . ."

After they have completed the whips, bring out the following materials: a large piece of paper, some crayolas, scissors, magic markers, white glue, and some magazines. Put all the materials in the middle of the group and tell them that they are to work together to create a collage that represents the group—*without* talking. Keep them going on the collage until the end of the session. If time permits, tell them to decide on a group name and put the name of the group on the collage. If time doesn't permit, take a second session to complete the task. Put the completed collage in some visible place.

As the group works on the task, observe their interactions. Do there seem to be less isolates than there were in September? Do they work with each other in a positive way or a negative way? Are many students taking leadership roles? Is agressive behavior present? Focus on children who have particular problems. How are they participating?

## Remembering

*Purpose:* To remember the last several sessions; to examine student and teacher expectations after a particular unit.

*Process:* Begin the session by asking for several volunteers to remember what they have done during the last several sessions. Following the general reviewing, ask each member to remember something another person said during the sessions. Encourage people to comment on why they remembered a particular thing. Was it because the same thing happened to them, or because it was particularly funny, or what?

When at least one thing has been remembered about each person, use the last ten minutes to get statements from the group about the group. Ask, "What do you like best and least about these activities? What would you like to do more of? Why do you think we have these sessions?" Encourage any kind of evaluative comments. Finish the group by having each person do a "here-and-now face" about the process. To do a here-and-now face, students draw a round face on a piece of scratch paper and add a smile, a frown, or a neutral mouth. They can spruce it up if they wish. Each member should also write one sentence about his face explaining why he felt that way about the group at this time. These faces should be anonymous. Collect the faces and evaluate yourself based on the responses. Questions for yourself: Do they seem to know why they do the activities? Do they take the activities seriously? Do they see you as being nonjudgmental?

### Studying Yourself

*Purpose:* To get the students to accept the idea that it is worthwhile to study one's own life; to review what we have accomplished so far in our group.

*Process:* Begin today's session by having students whip the following sentence stub around the circle: "I always used to be . . . but now I am . . ." After they have shared their ideas, ask each one to share one thing he likes about being his current age and one thing he liked better about being younger.

Ask the following questions and discuss them after the sharing: "What have you learned so far in the group? What is the subject matter in the group? Is it worth studying? What would you like to learn about yourself and other people?"

Try to get students to make value statements about learning more about how they feel and act and how others feel and act. Continue this discussion a second day if it catches on. Make a list of student responses to the fourth question and develop units around some of them.

### Thought Paper

*Purpose:* To evaluate orally and in writing the progress of the group.

*Process:* Begin the session by asking the students to make "I learned" statements about the awareness sessions for the whole year. This should take about ten minutes. Don't question any of the statements; just accept them.

Hand out sheets of paper and have the group members write thought papers about their experiences in awareness sessions. The title could be "The Best Group Experience I Had This Year" or "How Awareness Discussions Have Helped Me" or "My Personal High and Low of the Group." Tell them it isn't necessary to sign them but they can if they want to. Read a few of the thought papers to the group, then file them in student folders. If a student doesn't want his paper read, tell him to put "Don't Read" at the top.

If this activity seems to generate good response, elaborate on it. Read all papers that don't say "Don't Read," and discuss student reactions to them. Hand out 3 X 5 cards and have students complete "I appreciate" statements for the class in general or for other kids.

### How I See Myself

Give out copies of the following form every few months and ask students to complete them for you. This is *private* information that can be very helpful to you, but it must not be misused. After they have completed the self-concept form, have them discuss "when I like myself best."

## SELF-CONCEPT FORM

Please check the proper square for the first ten items. Check "Like Me" if the statement is mostly true for you. Check "Unlike Me" if the statement is hardly every true for you. Answer the last five questions with one or two sentences each.

|  | Like Me | Unlike Me |
|---|---|---|
| 1. I often wish I were someone else. | _____ | _____ |
| 2. I am liked by most kids. | _____ | _____ |
| 3. There are a lot of things about me I would like to change. | _____ | _____ |
| 4. I'm proud of my school work. | _____ | _____ |
| 5. No one pays much attention to me. | _____ | _____ |
| 6. I understand myself. | _____ | _____ |
| 7. I have a low opinion of myself. | _____ | _____ |
| 8. I like to be called on in class. | _____ | _____ |
| 9. I'm not very nice looking. | _____ | _____ |
| 10. People can usually depend on me. | _____ | _____ |

11. List two things you are proud of. _____
_____

12. What will you be doing in five years? _____
_____

13. What is one thing you would like to change about yourself? _____
_____

14. Do you think you are liked by most other kids? _____ Yes _____ No.
Explain your answer. _____
_____

15. What situations do you feel confident in? _____
_____

Not confident? _____
_____

## Self-Concept

This activity involves using another self-concept test (see page 223). Begin the session by saying, "We have been having these activities for about X weeks now. Hopefully, all of you have learned something about yourselves: how you react in different situations, what you believe, and so on. Hopefully, you have learned a little about the other people in this group as well. Today I want you to complete this form by yourself and then give it to me.

# How Do You Feel About Yourself as a Leader?

### Use this page to evaluate
### yourself as a group leader
### every twelve weeks of work.

On the following continuums, place yourself where you feel you are right now. Circle the nearest numeral.

| | | |
|---|---|---|
| "Carl Rogers, you got nothing on me" (Super listener.) | 1    2    3    4    5    6    7<br>**REFLECTIVE LISTENING** | "Just shut up kid, and I'll tell you the right answer." |
| I can accept anything a child says. | 1    2    3    4    5    6    7<br>**ACCEPTANCE** | It's my way or not at all. |
| "Would you like to tell us more about that?" (Great question.) | 1    2    3    4    5    6    7<br>**QUESTIONING TECHNIQUES** | "Why do you feel bad?" (Rotton question.) |
| All sessions fit together smoothly. | 1    2    3    4    5    6    7<br>**CONTINUITY** | What'll we do today, kids? |
| Who's in charge here? (All share leadership.) | 1    2    3    4    5    6    7<br>**STUDENT INTERACTION** | All eyes are on me kids. (I am the leader.) |
| Under control. Kids know the limits and abide by them. | 1    2    3    4    5    6    7<br>**GROUP CONTROL** | Chaos: "I can't hear myself relate." |
| I take risks by sharing myself. | 1    2    3    4    5    6    7<br>**OPENNESS** | "You think I'm gonna tell those kids how I feel? Never." |

Total the number circled and check your score on the following basis:

1.  If you scored 7-14, you are a super group leader. People love to talk to you. Invite someone in to see your group.

2.  If you scored 15-21, you are doing a very good job—especially if you've only been going for twelve weeks. You might try focusing your attention on the one skill you feel you are poorest at.

3.  If you scored 22-28, you are a good solid leader. Practice your skills. Tape a group and listen to it.

4.  If you scored 29-35, you need some help, but you are trying. Attend a workshop. Team up with another teacher. You need some nonthreatening feedback.

5.  If you scored 36-49, you're in trouble. You probably haven't been enjoying your group. Seriously, you need help. Talk to your principal, another teacher, or someone in the building to set up a plan for improving your group. Maybe leading these groups just isn't for you.

## MY FEELINGS

Please check the box that is most like how you feel about each item.

1.  If it is a big problem or you worry about it a lot, check the first box.
2.  If it is a medium problem check the second box.
3.  If it is a problem, but a little one, check the third box.
4.  If it is not a problem for you, or no big thing, check the last box.

| MY FEELINGS | A big problem for me | Sometimes a problem for me | A small problem for me | Almost never a problem for me |
|---|---|---|---|---|
| **About Me and My Group** | | | | |
| 1.  I wish I would talk more in the group. | | | | |
| 2.  My teacher doen't like me. | | | | |
| 3.  The kids in my group don't listen to me. | | | | |
| 4.  I'm nervous when I talk in the group. | | | | |
| 5.  The group is boring for me. | | | | |
| **About Me and My School** | | | | |
| 1.  I want to learn to read better. | | | | |
| 2.  I don't like school very much. | | | | |
| 3.  I wish my teachers were friendlier. | | | | |
| 4.  Sometimes I wish I could quit school. | | | | |
| 5.  I am not doing as well as I can in school. | | | | |
| **About Myself** | | | | |
| 1.  I wish I were nicer looking. | | | | |
| 2.  I think other boys and girls are better than me | | | | |
| 3.  I often feel lonesome. | | | | |
| 4.  I worry all the time. | | | | |
| 5.  I wish I could control myself more. | | | | |
| **Getting Along with Others** | | | | |
| 1.  I wish I had more friends. | | | | |
| 2.  Grownups make fun of me. | | | | |
| 3.  I fight too much. | | | | |
| 4.  Most people don't understand me. | | | | |
| 5.  I wish I knew why people get mad at me. | | | | |
| **Things in General** | | | | |
| 1.  I wish I had more hobbies. | | | | |
| 2.  It's hard for me to talk about my problems. | | | | |
| 3.  I am worried about growing up. | | | | |
| 4.  I wish I were smarter. | | | | |
| 5.  I wish I were better in games and sports. | | | | |

This is a way for me to get your opinion of yourself so I can know more about you. These forms are private and I'm the only one who will see them. Try and be as honest as possible on this form. If the item is a big problem, put a check in the first box; if the item is no problem for you check the last box; and so on. Now turn your back on the group and complete the form."

After all students have completed the form, let them ask questions or make statements about the test or the group. Reflect all responses. Any of the questions could become data for a discussion or activity.

### Group Decision Making

*Purpose:*  To experience the fish-bowl strategy; to increase the amount of feedback students get on their behavior, allowing you to evaluate the perceptiveness of the students concerning other people's behavior; to provide practice in decision making.

*Process:*  Begin by saying to the group that you will need six volunteers for this activity. The six will join you in the circle of chairs inside the larger circle of nonvolunteers.

Tell the others they are to be observers who will tell what they see later. When everything is set, announce to the others in the inner group, "We are all in a fallout shelter* and, in addition to us, there are others. We have to decide whether they can join us or not. We only have room for three more. We have to decide who shall join us and who shall not. Those who don't join us will most certainly die. All of us must agree on who joins and who doesn't." Here is a list of the other people:

1. An eighth-grade boy who isn't very intelligent and who gets poor grades, but who is easy going and good with his hands.
2. A very beautiful seventh-grade girl who is a good student, but who is very stuck up and thinks she is perfect.
3. A fifty-five-year-old teacher. He is the meanest teacher in the school. Kids usually don't like him, but his students always do the best on exams.
4. The captain of the eighth-grade football team. He is also a bully and is always pushing smaller kids around.
5. An eighth-grade girl who is supernice to everyone, good at making things, smart, pretty, and good at making decisions. The problem with her is that she is determined not to come unless we take her sister, too. Her sister is a thief, is on drugs, lies to everybody, and has been in trouble with the police for severely stabbing a girl who called her a name.
6. A 35-year-old mother of one of the students, who is really good when she is sober, but who is drunk half the time. She can make things, she can cook, she is smart, and she likes kids—except when she is drunk.

---

*This activity is an adaptation of an idea used at National Training Labs to help adults look at how they manage stress.

7. A boy of fourteen years of age who is super in every way imaginable except that he has an incurable disease and will die in one year.

Let the group argue about who to keep and who to throw out. You should play a very passive role throughout the discussion. When there are ten minutes left, stop the discussion and have the observers tell what they saw and heard. (You will probably have to take a second discussion to complete the processing of this.) After everything has been talked out, have the observer rank the group members (including you) from the most helpful at making the decision to the least helpful. Then discuss why they ranked the way they did. Ask observers to name the kinds of roles people played (leader, clown, mother, and so forth).

As students are engaged in giving feedback, observe them for any perceivable changes in attitude or skill since the group began.

### Feedback: Activity 1

*Purpose:* To become aware of the perceptions that group members have of each other, with regard to some particular idea. (This is both a good evaluative session and a way to increase the students' awareness of how the other people in the group perceive them.)

*Process:* Start off by saying, "We've been together a long time and we've learned a lot of things about each other. Today I'm going to give you a chance to demonstrate what you've learned about the people in this group. We're going to play a game about it. You can't talk during the game, and I want you to line up so that at one end of the line is the person who likes school the second most, then the third most, and so on, until, at the other end of the line, is the person who hates school the most. You can't talk, though. You have to do it silently. You might argue with each other about how to line up, but you have to do the arguing without talking."

After you have explained the directions, let them live with the chaos of trying to get in line—eventually, they'll do it. Whey they have finally succeeded, have them sit down and have a discussion about how they decided. Ask them, "How did you decide where to go and where to put someone else? What information did you have about the people in this class?" Spend the rest of the session encouraging them to relate information that they have about other people in the group that would lead them to make a decision about whether they like or dislike school. Get them to generalize about how we learn other things about people.

### Feedback: Activity 2

*Purpose:* To enable group members to give and get feedback from others as to how they are perceived in the group. (This is a continuation of the session that began with the physical continuum, although it can be done separately.)

*Process:* Start the session by having each student draw a circle on a piece of paper and divide it into 4 segments. After all have done so, tell them that they are to pick a partner—or you might want to assign them partners. Have the pairs sit facing each other, close together, separated in the room from the other dyads. Tell them they have two things to do. Their first job is, while they are looking at their partner, to fill in each of the four quadrants of the paper with an adjective that they think describes their partner. When they finish, there should be four different adjectives on each student's paper, describing that student's partner.

After each member has completed the task, the group should spend the next ten minutes discussing why they put certain words down for their partner. Each member of the dyad should share his reasons.

Allow them to complete the process, with you also participating, if possible. After the activity is completed, bring them back into the circle and have them discuss what happened. Was it easy? Hard? How did they decide what to put down? Did they agree with what their partner put down for them or would their own opinion be quite different? Were they surprised that their partner thought they were a certain way? Continue the discussion till the end of the period.

## OUTPUT OR END-PRODUCT EVALUATION

Evaluation is finding out whether you've gotten to the place you wanted to go. To find out, you have to know where you want to go. After you have evaluated your program, you should have information that will help you decide (a) whether you are going where you want to go; (b) how far you still have to go; and (c) whether your present route for getting there is the best one.

I have worked for three years in research projects designed to evaluate affective-education programs and have learned many methods for predicting the changes in student and teacher behavior that result from programs like the one described in this book. The rest of this section will describe the methods I have used for evaluating affective-education programs.

### The Sociogram

*Assumption:* Given a particular program designed to increase group cohesiveness, sensitivity to others, and so forth, there ought to be significantly fewer isolates at the end of the program period than at the beginning.

*Technique:* The sociogram is a method for finding out who is most popular, who is least popular, and so on. Tell the students to write down the names of three other students they would like to have as friends, would like to work with on a committee, or would like to play with. It doesn't matter what the actual question is, but if you are using a control group for comparison, make sure both groups get the same directions.

Collect the papers and make a diagram that shows who picked who. (I don't know any clever technique for making the diagram. It always takes me about an hour to figure out what system I used the last time to chart the responses.) When you have finally figured it out you should have a diagram that looks like this:

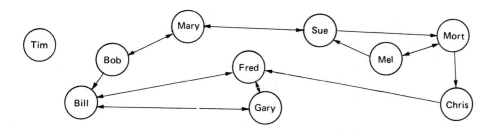

The arrows tell who picked whom. The information you get from this is: who gets picked most, where the cliques (members of which always pick each other) are, who doesn't get picked at all (isolates), and so on.

If your program is effective, you will have significantly fewer isolates or near-isolates in May than you had in September, when compared to a group that didn't use the program.

## Social Acceptance Scale

*Assumption:* After using an affective education program for a given period of time, there will be significantly fewer students seen as unaccepted by their classmates.

*Technique:* The social acceptance scale is similar to the sociogram. Give out a roster to everyone in the class and give them the following directions: Place a 1 next to the name of anyone you would like for a *best* friend; place a 2 next to the name of anyone you would like for a friend; place a 3 next to the name of anyone you wouldn't want for a friend but who is O.K.; and place a 4 next to all other names. Obviously, the 4s are the students who aren't accpeted by the class. If the program is effective, there will be fewer 4s in May than there were in September.*

---

*A note to research enthusiasts: I do know about validity, reliability, T tests, control groups, co-variance analysis, and so forth. I assume people evaluating affective education programs will consider those well-established principles of research, outlined in such exciting books as Ferguson's *Statistical Analysis in Psychology and Education.*

## Self-Concept-Self-Report Instruments

*Assumption:* Given a program designed to improve students' self-concepts, students will score significantly higher on a post-group self-concept test than on a pre-group test. When you add a control group, the comparison shifts to a comparison of differences between groups.

*Technique:* Right now, self-concept tests are the main way researchers are getting data on how students feel about themselves. Essentially, the self-concept, or self-esteem, test is a list of statements that a student reads and responds to by indicating which represent the way he feels. For little kids, pictures are used to get the same data. There are several self-concept instruments that are widely used. Some of the most widely known include: the Coopersmith Self-Esteem Inventory (Stanley Coopersmith, *The Antecedents of Self-Esteem*); The Real-Ideal Self Scale (developed by Donald Dinkmeyer, author of *Encouraging Children to Learn*); and the Hofmeister Self-Esteem Questionnaire (developed by Dr. James K. Hofmeister of Boulder, Colorado). There is a good list of other self-concept tests contained in Part Two of *Improving Educational Assessment and an Inventory of Measures of Affective Behavior,* published by A.S.C.D. and edited by Walcott Beatty.

The problem with using self-concept tests that ask students to tell the truth about their opinions of themselves is obvious: If they lie, the test is invalid. So, if you want to get accurate data this way, deal with the problem by discussing it beforehand with the kids, as well as by making the test anonymous.

Many people design their own self-concept instruments. The problem with this is that drawing conclusions from a test that has not been normed on a large sample, or the reliability of which has not been established, is risky. Of course, in all of this evaluation business, you need to know why you are evaluating—to get funds, to impress parents, to find out for yourself how it's going, or to get a doctorate in educational administration.

I recently came across an instrument called the "JIM Scale," developed by Dr. Jack Frymier at Ohio State University, that impressed me as the most rigorous measure of student affect around. (The acronym JIM stands for Junior Index of Motivation.) What really impressed me about this scale was the extensive reliability and validity testing that went into the final choice of items. I think instruments like the JIM Scale will finally make programs with affective objectives as acceptable to "hard data" researchers as cognitive programs.

One of the best ways to demonstrate the effectiveness of an affective-education program is to collect unobtrusive data about your population and then to analyze it in conjunction with your hypotheses regarding behavioral change. Improvement in such matters as attendance, truancy, tardiness, discipline referrals, fighting, broken windows, graffiti, and kids standing in the hall can give strong support to your claims that affective education works. In a project in which I worked, it was demonstrated that conducting circle discussions as part of an overall attempt to make a school more responsive to students did in fact have a significant positive effect on several unobtrusive measures. This kind of data is being used more frequently in educational research today.

## COGNITIVE GROWTH

Students involved in activities similar to the ones in this book learn lots of cognitive stuff, and this learning can be measured. For example, if you are going to be studying some of the principles of effective social interaction, you can test the students' understanding of those principles by using good old-fashioned pencil and paper tests, along the lines of the following examples (listed after the test items are some sample objectives that could be part of your program—objectives that can be measured using traditional cognitive evaluation devices):

**Sample Test Items**
(for measuring students' understanding of the basic principles of social interaction)

**True or False:**

1. Few people have the same feelings in childhood.
2. Boys find it hard to cry because they have been taught that "boys don't cry."
3. Being tolerant requires that you like everyone the same.

**Multiple choice:** After working hard on his science project, the teacher gave Billy an "F." Billy is likely to:

1. Pout and feel bad.
2. Thank the teacher for her honesty.
3. Have a lowered sense of self-esteem.
4. Decide to really get the teacher.

**Essay:** Why do you think people fight with each other?

**Sample Objectives**
The best objectives are real behavioral ones, like the following:

1. Students will participate in sessions because they think they are worthwhile rather than because they are missing math.
2. Students will ask for the opportunity to make public statements about their opinions.

3. Students will have more words with which to describe their feelings.
4. Students will use significantly more clarifying questions, "I" messages, and so forth.
5. Given the task of describing a given behavior pattern, students will give more comprehensive descriptions, more consistent descriptions over time, and so forth.
6. Regarding any given decision, students will identify more options after the course than before.

Of course, the simplest way to find out whether the sessions are effective is to just ask the children, "Are these activities helping you?"

## SUMMARY

Evaluation is a very important part of an ongoing affective education program. The most important evaluation occurs when you and your students talk about how things are going and how you could make them go better.

Perhaps the best evaluation is to ask the kids whether they are learning anything from these activities and whether they like them. Below are a few comments from some sixth-grade students about a program they participated in.

- I found out about what people would like to do when they get bigger.
- The circle is being able to talk free and say things we feel about different things.
- In the circle you can discuss your problems.
- The circle is talking without hurting no one.
- I learned that by talking we were learning at the same time. We had to listen and hear what the people had to say.
- I found out how we can work things out.
- I have also learned to judge matters which really don't have a thing to do with social studies.
- I learned that Kathy Schmid is nicer than I thought and that she is a thoughtful person.
- I learned more about people in our room. I learned that some aren't as lucky as others.
- It's fun to get into a circle.
- I learned that people in this room take turns in talking together.
- From the circle I learned that people can talk things out without arguing and settle things calmly. I also learned from the circle that our class can really try and accomplish what they have in mind. We can respect the rights of other people to talk without someone interrupting him or her.
- I learned about a million things about my friends and teacher. I wish we could be in a circle more often, you can learn things about your friends that you never knew before.

- I learned about the kids in my room and I learned the sports they liked.
- I learned that there are all kinds of people.
- I learned lots of good stuff.
- I learned that we can work hard if we tried.
- I learned something about all of the people in our class.
- Everyone wanted to say something.
- I learned that a circle is kind of fun and I like being in a circle. People have feelings too and that some people are good at something I can't do.
- I learned to respect others and what they like and dislike.
- I learned about the people in the circle and that we can carry on a conversation without having twenty-six other conversations going on.
- I learned that it is kind of fun being in the circle because we have lots of fun and sometimes it's exciting and interesting.
- I learned to respect others and what they like and dislike.
- You can learn a lot by talking to each other. Some say you can't, but you can if you listen.
- I learned that when we had people from the Board of Education that we got to have sewing because we talked things over.
- I learned that if you really try and accomplish a good goal that you can get a good grade.

# APPENDIX A
# BIBLIOGRAPHY

Allen, M. S. *Morphological Creativity*. Englewood Cliffs, N.J.: Prentice-Hall, 1962.

Allinsmith, Wesley, and Goethals, George W. *The Role of Schools in Mental Health.* New York: Basic Books, 1962.

Allport, G. *Becoming.* New Haven, Conn.: Yale University Press, 1955. *Association for Supervision and Curriculum Development Yearbooks: Humanizing Education: The Person in the Process. Improving Educational Assessment & An Inventory of Measures of Affective Behavior. Perceiving, Behaving, Becoming. To Nurture Humaneness.*

–––. *Pattern and Growth in Personality.* New York: Holt, Rinehart and Winston, 1961, Chapter 12, "The Mature Personality."

Alschuler, Alfred. *Teaching Achievement Motivation.* Middletown, Conn.: Education Ventures, 1971.

Argyris, C. *Personality and Organization.* New York: Harper & Row, 1963.

Ashton-Warner, Sylvia. *Teacher.* New York: Simon and Schuster, 1963.

Assagioli, Roberto. *Psychosynthesis.* New York: Hobbs, Dorman, 1965.

Bach, Richard. *Jonathan Livingston Seagull.* New York: Macmillan, 1970.

Barron, Frank. *Creativity and Personal Freedom.* New York: Van Nostrand Reinhold, 1968.

Bennis, Warren. *Planning of Change.* New York: Holt, Rinehart and Winston, 1969.

Berman, Louise. *New Priorities in the Curriculum.* Columbus, Ohio: Merill International Education Service, 1968.

Bessell, Harold. *Methods in Human Development.* San Diego, Calif.: Human Development Training Institute, 1970.

Bettelheim, Bruno. *Love Is Not Enough.* Glencoe, Ill.: Free Press, 1950.

Borton, Terry. *Reach, Touch and Teach.* New York: McGraw-Hill, 1971.

Bradford, Gibb, and Bradford, Benne. *T-Group Theory and Laboratory Methods.* New York: Wiley, 1964.

Briggs, Dorothy. *Your Child's Self-esteem: The Key to His Life.* Garden City, N.Y.: Doubleday, 1970.

Brown, George I. *Human Teaching for Human Learning.* San Francisco: Esalen Institute, 1971.

Bruner, Jerome. *On Knowing.* New Haven, Conn.: Harvard University Press, 1962.

Buber, Martin. *Between Man and Man.* New York: Macmillan, 1965.

Bugenthal, J. *Challenges of Humanistic Psychology.* New York: McGraw-Hill, 1967.

Combs, Arthur, and Snygg, Donald. *Individual Behavior,* rev. ed. New York: Harper & Row, 1959.

Coopersmith, Stanley. *Antecedents of Self-esteem.* San Francisco: W. H. Freeman, 1967.

Cullum, Albert. *The Geranium on the Windowsill Just Died but Teacher You Went Right On.* New York: Quist, 1971.

–––. *Push Back the Desks.* New York: School Book Service, 1966.

DeMille, Richard. *Put Your Mother on the Ceiling.* New York: Walker, 1967.

Dennison, George. *The Lives of Children.* New York: Random House, 1969.

Erikson, Erik H. *Childhood and Society,* rev. ed. New York: Norton, 1964.

Frazier, Alex. *Learning More about Learning.* Washington, D.C.: Association for Supervision and Curriculum Development, 1969.

Fromm, Erich. *The Art of Loving.* New York: Harper & Row, 1956.

Getzels, J. W., and Jackson, P. W. *Creativity and Intelligence.* New York: Wiley, 1962.

Ginott, Haim. *Between Parent and Child.* New York: Macmillan, 1965.

–––. *Between Parent and Teen-ager.* New York: Macmillan, 1969.

–––. *Teacher and Child.* New York: Macmillan, 1972.

Glasser, William. *Schools Without Failure.* New York: Harper & Row, 1969.

Gordon, Thomas. *Parent Effectiveness Training.* New York: Wyden, 1970.

Gordon, William J. J. *Synectics: The Development of Creative Capacity.* New York: Harper & Row, 1961.

Greenberg, H. M. *Teaching with Feeling.* Indianapolis, Ind.: Pegasus, 1970.

Greer, Mary, and Rubenstein, Bonnie. *Will the Real Teacher Please Stand Up.* Pacific Palisades, Calif.: Goodyear, 1972.

Gunther, Bernard. *Sense Relaxation: Below Your Mind.* New York: Macmillan, Collier Books, 1968.

Hampden-Turner, Charles. *The Radical Man.* Cambridge, Mass.: Schenkman, 1970.

Harris, Thomas. *I'm OK–You're OK.* New York: Harper & Row, 1969.

Hassett, J., and Weisberg, A. *Open Education: Alternatives within Our Tradition.* Englewood Cliffs, N.J.: Prentice-Hall, 1972.

Heller, Joseph. *Catch-22.* New York: Simon and Schuster, 1961.

Hentoff, Nat. *Our Children Are Dying.* New York: Viking Press, 1966.

Herndon, James. *How to Survive in Your Native Land.* New York: Simon and Schuster, 1971.

Holt, John. *How Children Fail.* New York: Pitman, 1964.

–––. *What Do I Do Monday?* New York: Dutton, 1970.

Horney, Karen. *Neurosis and Human Growth.* New York: Norton, 1950.

Jackson, Philip. *Life in the Classroom.* New York: Holt, Rinehart and Winston, Inc., 1968.

Jersild, Arthur. *When Teachers Face Themselves.* New York: Horace Mann Lincoln Institute Service Teachers College; pap. text ed., 1955.

Jones, Richard M. *Fantasy and Feeling in Education.* New York: New York University Press, 1968.

Jourard, Sidney. *Disclosing Man to Himself.* Cincinnati: Van Nostrand, 1968.

Juster, Norman. *The Phantom Tollbooth.* New York: Random House, 1961.

Kelley, Earl. *Education for What Is Real.* New York: Harper & Row, 1947.

Koch, Kenneth. *Wishes, Lies and Dreams.* New York: Random House, 1971.

Kohl, Herbert R. *The Open Classroom.* New York: Random House, New York Review, 1970.

–––. *36 Children.* New York: New American Library, 1967.

Kozol, Jonathan. *Death at an Early Age.* Boston: Houghton Mifflin, 1967.

Krathwohl, David R.; Bloom, Benjamin S.; and Masia, Bertram B. *Taxonomy of Educational Objectives.* Handbook II: Affective Domain. New York: David McKay, 1964.

Laliberte, N. *One Hundred Ways to Have Fun with an Alligator, or 100 Art Projects.* Blawvelt, N.Y.: Art Education Inc., 1969.

LaShan, Eda. *Conspiracy Against Childhood.* New York: Atheneum, 1967.

–––. *What Makes Me Feel This Way.* New York: Macmillan, 1972.

Lederman, Janet. *Anger and the Rocking Chair.* New York: McGraw-Hill, 1969.

Leonard, George. *Education and Ecstacy.* New York: Delacorte, 1968.

Lyon, Harold. *Learning to Feel, Feeling to Learn.* Columbus, Ohio: Merrill, 1971.

Maltz, Maxwell. *Psycho-Cybernetics.* Englewood Cliffs, N.J.: Prentice-Hall, 1960.

Maslow, A. *Motivation and Personality,* 2nd ed. New York: Harper & Row, 1970.

–––. *Toward a Psychology of Being,* 2nd ed. New York: Van Nostrand, 1968.

May, Rollo. *Love and Will.* New York: Random House, 1968.

Miles, Matthew. *Learning to Work in Groups.* New York: Teachers College, Columbia University, 1959.

Moustakas, C. *The Authentic Teacher.* Cambridge, Mass.: Howard Doyle, 1966.

———. *The Self: Explorations in Personal Growth.* New York: Harper & Row, 1956.

Murphy, G. *Human Potentialities.* New York: Basic Books, 1958.

Neill, A. *Summerhill: A Radical Approach to Child-Rearing.* New York: Hart, 1960.

Otto, Herbert, and Mann, John. *Ways of Growth.* New York: Viking Press, 1969.

Perls, Frederick S. *Gestalt Therapy Verbatim.* Moab, Utah: Real People Press, 1969.

Polanyi, Michael. *The Tacit Dimension.* Garden City, N.Y.: Doubleday, Anchor Books, 1966.

Postman, Neal, and Weingartner, Charles. *Teaching as a Subversive Activity.* New York: Delacorte, 1969.

Purkey, William. *Self-concept and School Achievement.* Englewood Cliffs, N.J.: Prentice-Hall, 1970.

Raths, Louis; Harmin, Merrill; and Simon, Sidney. *Values and Teaching.* Columbus, Ohio: Merrill, 1966.

Reisman, D. *The Lonely Crowd.* New Haven, Conn.: Yale University Press, 1969.

Rogers, Carl R. *Freedom to Learn.* Columbus, Ohio: Merrill, 1969.

———. *On Becoming a Person.* Boston: Houghton Mifflin, 1970.

Ryan, Kevin, ed. *Don't Smile Until Christmas.* Chicago: University of Chicago Press, 1970.

Saint Exupéry, Antoine de. *The Little Prince.* Translated by K. Woods. New York: Harcourt, Brace & World, 1943.

Sax, Saville, and Hollander, Sandra. *Reality Games.* New York: Macmillan, 1972.

Schrank, Jeffery. *Teaching Human Beings: 101 Ways to Subvert Your Classroom.* Boston: Beacon Press, 1972.

Schutz, William. *Joy.* New York: Grove Press, 1968.

Shostrom, Everett. *Man The Manipulator.* Nashville, Tenn.: Abingdon, 1967.

Silberman, Charles. *Crisis in the Classroom.* New York: Random House, 1970.

Silverstein, Shel. *The Giving Tree.* New York: Harper & Row, 1964.

Simon, Sidney; Howe, Leland; and Kirschenbaum, Howie. *Values Clarification: A Handbook of Practical Strategies.* New York: Hart, 1972.

Spolin, Viola. *Improvisations for the Theater.* Evanston, Ill.: Northwestern University Press, 1963.

Stanford, G., and Stanford, B. *Learning Discussion Skills Through Games.* New York: Scholastic Book Service, 1969.

Stevens, Barry. *Don't Push the River.* Moab, Utah: Real People Press, 1970.

Sutich, Anthony J. *Readings in Humanistic Psychology.* New York: Free Press, 1969.

Von Hilshimer, George. *How to Live with Your Special Child.* Washington, D.C.: Acropolis, 1970.

Weinstein, G., and Fantini, Mario. *Toward Humanistic Education.* New York: Praeger, 1970.

Williams, Margery. *The Velveteen Rabbit.* Garden City, N.Y.: Doubleday, 1958.

Young, L. *Life Among the Giants.* New York: McGraw-Hill, 1966.

# APPENDIX B
# AFFECTIVE FILMS

The films listed here can be used as motivational films or as sources of data for awareness sessions. These particular films were picked because I have used them or know someone who has. For a very good book that discusses using films to teach affective concepts read: *Teaching Human Beings* by Jeff Schrank.*

All films are 16mm sound productions, unless otherwise indicated.

*The Adventures of* †. John Hubley, 1957 (10 min., color). Man, represented by the asterisk symbol, grows from infancy to adulthood in this animated film about the wonders of life and living.

*Alexander and the Car with a Missing Headlight.* Weston Woods, 1966 (14 min., color) Recounts Alexander's experiences with the creatures and people he meets on sea and on land as he drives his car around the world.

*Amblin.* United Productions of America, 1968 (24 min., color). A story about the relationship between two young hitchikers in the desert.

*The Bicyclist.* Brandon Films, 1959 (15 min., color). A safety film presented from the viewpoint of a red bicycle, owned first by a boy who obeyed the traffic rules and then by one who brought himself and the bicycle to a bad end because he failed to observe the rules.

*Black and White: Uptight.* Bailey Film Associates, 1969 (35 min., color). This film discusses the myths that perpetuate prejudice against Negroes in our society and the subtle ways in which hate is learned. Examples are given in which government, business, and black and white people are working together to eliminate misunderstanding.

*Black Thumb.* King Screen Productions, 1970 (9 min., color). A black man tending the garden behind a suburban home is assumed by a white salesman to be a handyman. The black man is the owner. What kind of prejudice produced that assumption?

*Blindness.* National Film Board of Canada, 1965 (28 min., B & W). Uses dramatized incidents to show how a young, active man learns to accept the fact that he will never see again.

*The Bold Men.* Wolper Productions, N.D. (50 min., B & W). The story of adventurers, daredevils, scientists, and explorers—men who risk death because, for them, adventure is a satisfying way of life. Excitement ranges from riding a killer whale to diving for salvage from the Andrea Doria.

*Boundary Lines.* International Film Foundation, 1948 (10 min., color). An animated film analyzing the ancient symbolism of lines that men have used to express their ideas and of the imaginary lines that people have drawn to divide them from one another—lines of fear, possession, greed, and color.

*The Boy Who Couldn't Walk.* Films Inc., 1964 (10 min., B & W). The story of Glenn Cunningham, who was so badly burned as a child that he was told he would probably never walk again. The film shows his efforts to overcome his handicap and his ultimate success.

*Brotherhood of Man.* Anti-defamation League of B'nai B'rith, 1946 (11 min., color). An animated film based on the pamphlet "The Races of Mankind," by Ruth Benedict. Explains that there are no basic differences between the races of the world.

†*Building Class Involvement.* Media Five, 1972 (28 min., color). This film demonstrates three different activities that encourage students to work together to develop techniques for obtaining information through questioning. These activities are recommended for building student involvement in a way that is fun for both teacher and students.

---

*Jeff Schrank has developed many media kits to enhance affective education programs. He can be contacted by writing: The Learning Seed Company, 145 Brentwood Avenue, Palatine, Illinois 60067.

*The Cabinet of Dr. Caligari.* National Cinema Service, 1920 (53 min., B & W). A haunting, expressionistic fable of a monster and his creator that presents sanity as being merely relative: who is mad—the doctor, the young narrator, or the audience?

*A Chairy Tale.* National Film Board of Canada, 1957 (10 min., B & W). A fairy tale in the modern manner, told without words, about a youth and a common kitchen chair. When the young man tries to sit on the chair, it declines to be sat upon. There is an ensuing struggle, first for mastery and then for understanding.

*Children of the Sun.* Association Instructional Materials, N.D. (10 min., color). This animated film presents the story of a happy child—his fun, pleasures, and growing up—in contrast to the life of a hungry, unhappy child. The needs of children and the importance of UNICEF aid are expressed.

*Children on the Move.* Smart Family Foundation, 1964 (22 min., B & W). Presents some of the problems involved in frequent or occasional moves from one location to another, with emphasis on the mental adjustments required of children.

*A Christmas Fantasy.* National Film Board of Canada, 1963 (8 min., color). Impressions of the lights of Christmas as they transform a winter's night, the wonder on children's faces, and the lyrical music of harp, celesta, and flute all combine to recreate the magic mood of Christmas.

*Civil Rights Movement—The Personal View.* Encyclopaedia Britannica Educational Corp., 1966 (25 min., B & W). Reveals attitudes of fear, hate, and suspicion between Negroes and whites. Explores the problem of community race relations, focusing on a well-to-do Negro professional family living in a predominantly white neighborhood.

†*A Class Meeting on Class Meetings.* Media Five, 1972 ( 28 min., color). Class meetings, their goals and objectives, are discussed by a sixth-grade class with three years of class meeting experience. This film demonstrates the dramatic results that class meetings can produce as these sixth graders think about intellectual questions, listen to others, and search for reasonable alternatives to problems.

*Color of Man.* University of California, 1954 (10 min., color). Points out man's relationship with his environment by showing how different climatic conditions have affected human activity and development. Explains that hereditary differences, as exemplified by skin color, are illustrative of the adaptability of man to the forces of nature.

*Cosmic Zoom.* National Film Board of Canada, 1971 (10 min., color/B & W). A look at relativity, from infinitely big to infinitely small.

*A Day in the Night of Jonathan Mole.* National Film Board of Canada, 1959 (33 min., B & W). A fantasy pointing out the fallacies upon which prejudice thrives and the inadequacy of law to eliminate discriminatory employment practices.

†*Dealing with Discipline Problems.* Media Five, 1972 (30 min., color). Filmed on location at three of William Glasser's model "schools without failure," this film demonstrates proven techniques for handling many of the most common school discipline problems. In twelve different real-life situations, individual teachers reveal how they achieve discipline by putting the success concepts of reality therapy into everyday practice. The teachers themselves supply the commentary on what they are doing and what they hope to accomplish, often suggesting alternative ways for handling the same situation. Problems covered range from the uncomplicated to the very difficult: classroom disruption, uninvolved students, violation of playground rules, truancy, fighting. Suggested background films: *Glasser on Discipline, The Reality of Success.*

*The Detached Americans.* Carousel Films, 1965 (33 min., B & W). Examines the widespread problem of apathy in the United States, presenting incidents in which Americans stood by and refused to heed the cry for help. Points out some of the reasons for this reaction, especially as found in family relationships.

*The Dot and the Line.* MGM, 1965 (9 min., color). A cartoon about a straight line who falls in love with a dot who, in turn, is in love with a squiggle.

*Dream of the Wild Horses (le Songe des Chevaux Sauvages).* Contemporary Films, 1962 (9 min., color). A cinematic poem uses slow motion and soft-focus camera to evoke the wild horses of the Camargue district of France, showing them as they roam on the beach.

*Drugs and the Nervous System.* Churchill Films, 1967 (16 min., color). Demonstrates the effects of drugs on the body organs and the serious disruption of the nervous system caused by airplane glue, stimulants, depressants, and hallucinogens.

*The End of One.* Learning Corporation of America, N.D. (7 min., color). A film allegory that uses seagulls to depict man's greed and seeming indifference to life.

*Exchanges I.* ACI Productions, 1967 (10 min., B & W). Presents a dramatization about a Negro youth and a white girl who encounter each other while riding on a train; illustrates how a simple exchange between people is complicated by prejudice.

*Feeding Time.* Films, Inc., N.D. (14 min., B & W). An old home is devoured in an orgy of metallic indigestion. Human microorganisms scurry about, tending the steel dragon. A film comment on the changing face of life . . . the disposable home . . . and perhaps disposable people.

*Flatland.* Harvard University, 1965 (11 min., color). An allegory about a square who discovers the third dimension but is jailed by the two-dimensional inhabitants of Flatland when he preaches multidimensionality.

*4 Artists Paint 1 Tree.* Walt Disney Productions, 1964 (16 min., color). Shows four Disney artist-animators painting the same subject, a live oak tree, according to each one's individual impressions, perspective, and philosophy of art, resulting in four vastly different paintings.

*The Girl and the Sparrow.* Films, Inc., N.D. (14 min., color) A young girl captures a sparrow and puts it in a cage. She teases it and eventually falls asleep. In her dreams she is chased and harassed by eagles, bears, and wolves. When she awakes, she releases the sparrow, realizing that all creatures have the right to live.

† *Glasser on Discipline.* Media Five, 1972 (28 min., color). A new approach to an old problem: school discipline. Using typical discipline problems as examples, Glasser reveals some surprisingly practical solutions, including five basic steps for achieving effective discipline in any school. Recommended viewing for teachers, staff, students, and parents.

† *Glasser on Schools.* Media Five, 1972 (10 min., color). A thought-provoking introduction to Glasser's no-failure approach to education. It explains what led to Glasser's concept of "schools without failure," reviews familiar school problems and tells why they exist. The film convincingly shows that failure in life too often results from failure in school. Glasser relates reality therapy and schools without failure, offering practical ways to let every student succeed.

*The Golden Fish.* Columbia Pictures, 1962 (20 min., color). A story about a little boy who wins a goldfish in a game of chance and takes it home to become a friend of his canary. The pets almost succumb to a predatory alley cat.

*The Hangman.* Contemporary Films, 1964 (12 min., color). Based on Maurice Ogden's poem, this animated film conveys, in the simplest terms, the message that we are all responsible human beings—and are liable to have to answer for it one day. Narrated by Herschel Bernardi.

† *The Identity Society.* Media Five, 1972 (28 min., color). William Glasser explains the major cultural shift that is permanently affecting our lives and schools. He looks closely at today's students—why they seem so dramatically different and why many of them are restless and unresponsive when it comes to their education.

*I Never Went Back.* Charles Cahill and Associates, 1964 (16 min., color). Demonstrates the serious emotional, social, and economic consequences of the high-school dropout problem, tracing the history of several dropout cases.

†*Interviewing Class Meeting Guests.* Media Five, 1972 (28 min., color). William Glasser introduces two class meetings that demonstrate techniques for interviewing class-meeting guests. A sixth-grade class meets to formulate questions for a visiting parent, then interviews the parent, whose unusual hobbies trigger a fascinating discussion.

*Leaf.* Pyramid Film Producers, 1962 (7 min., color). Portrays the spirit of autumn in the wilderness by following a lone golden autumn leaf as it separates from the tree, tumbles onto the rocks below, and is blown down a riverbed by a draft of warm canyon air.

*Lemon.* John Ratliff, 1973 (29 min., color/B & W). Available from: Office of the Superintendent of Public Instruction, Springfield, Illinois. This is a film about a Title III project in which affective education was the main goal. It is a funny, technically excellent film that looks at one attempt to humanize and personalize education at the middle school level.

*Little White Crimes.* National Film Board of Canada, 1967 (28 min., B & W). Examines ethics and the pressures affecting attitudes in business (as well as in life) as demonstrated by the experiences of a successful young businessman who uses questionable methods to solve problems brought about by an overextension of resources.

*The Lottery.* Encyclopaedia Britannica, 1969 (25 min., color). An eerie tale of one small town's answer to the population explosion. Based on Shirley Jackson's short story.

*Madeline.* International Film Bureau, 1955 (10 min., color). The story of the youngest of twelve little school girls who march all over Paris in two straight lines. She becomes the envy of her companions when she goes to the hospital for an operation.

*The Monkey Who Would Be King.* Encyclopaedia Britannica Films, 1957 (11 min., color). The story of a monkey who wins the crown of the animal kingdom upon the lion's retirement and of his resulting difficulties and responsibilities.

*Night on Bald Mountain.* Contemporary Films, 1933 (9 min., B & W). A film in shadow pinboard animation that creates an eerie mood in an attempt to illustrate Moussorgsky's "Night on Bald Mountain."

*Nothing To Do!* Journal Films, 1962 (10 min., color). Expresses the need for children to find positive ways to spend their time, as exemplified by the experience of children living in different environmental situations.

*Occurrence at Owl Creek Bridge.* Contemporary Films, 1964 (27 min., B & W). A dramatization about the last minutes in the life of an American Civil War soldier who stands on a bridge waiting his hanging. Filmed in France.

*Parable.* Protestant Council of the City of New York, 1964 (22 min., color). A parable in pantomime about a white-faced clown who joins a circus parade, takes upon himself the burdens of the lowly, the abused, and the humiliated, and is rewarded with death in a harness as a human marionette.

*People Are Different and Alike.* Coronet Films, 1967 (11 min., color). Illustrates that all people need friendship and love, food, and a place to live and that they all want an education, fun, and happiness as well.

*The Purse.* National Film Board of Canada, 1966 (12 min., B & W). Uses a dramatization about the discovery of a lost purse containing a large sum of money to raise questions about conscience and its motivations, about principles of honesty and integrity, and about the effect on others of our own lapses.

*The Question.* McGraw-Hill, 1969 (10 min., color). In this animated film, a little man seeks the answer to the meaning of life and eventually finds it in love.

†*Questions for Thinking.* Media Five, 1972 (28 min., color). This film explores what schools are doing, not doing, or could be doing to encourage students to think. As William Glasser explains: "Education runs on questions. Four basic types can be easily identified and classified. These range from completely closed questions intended to elicit memorized responses, all the way to totally open-ended questions that make students (and teachers) think. Recognize and achieve a balance among these, and you can encourage more thinking, along with the traditional learning and memorizing."

†*The Reality of Success.* Media Five, 1972 (28 min., color). This film suggests a simple process by which every teacher and counselor can reach the child who, up to now, has been considered a time-consuming problem. William Glasser explains how the seven basic steps of reality therapy can help a student start succeeding in school.

*The Red Balloon.* Brandon Films, 1959 (34 min., color). A fantasy about a boy who makes friends with a balloon, "tames" it, plays with it in the streets of Menilmontant and Montmarte, and tries unsuccessfully to elude a gang of urchins who endeavor to destroy it.

*The Red Kite.* National Film Board of Canada, 1966 (17 min., color). Relates how, subsequent to buying his daughter a red kite on an impulse, a man begins to ruminate about the significance of life.

*Run!* Brandon Films, 1962 (16 min., B & W). An allegory about the destructive tendencies in high-pressured modern society and in self-centered modern man. Shows a harried man, panicked and unthinking, as he runs blindly through life until he falls into a grave that he has dug for himself.

†*School Without Failure.* Media Five, 1972 (46 min., color). This film shows William Glasser's no-fail concepts at work in a public elementary school in Palo Alto, California. It demonstrates class meetings, student-parent-teacher conferences, cross-age tutoring, enrichment programs, team teaching, and student involvement in curriculum planning. At this school, everyone is involved—students, teachers, parents, and administrators.

*The Searching Eye.* Eastman Kodak Co., 1964 (16 min., color). Turns a small boy's walk along the beach into a cinematographic treat in which ordinary objects reveal unsuspected worlds of intense visual experience. Uses time-lapse, underwater, aerial, micro- and stop-action photography.

*Shyness.* National Film Board of Canada, 1953 (23 min., B & W). Discusses abnormal shyness in children—its causes and the ways, through greater understanding by parents and teachers, this problem may be dealt with. After portraying the lonely existence of a typical shy adult, the film presents the case histories of three children.

*State of the Earth.* NBC Educational Enterprises, 1969 (18 min., color). A nonverbal essay on the quality of American life. Uses brief vignettes to evoke mood and bring up subtle questions about existence in a complex society.

*Steps Toward Maturity and Health.* Walt Disney Productions, 1968 (10 min., color). Uses animation and live action to point out how the responsibility of caring for one's body passes from nature to parents and then to the individual. Points out that the ultimate health and maturity of a person depends on his or her social, mental, and physical bearing.

†*A Success-Oriented Classroom.* Media Five, 1972 (28 min., color). This film presents an uncut sixteen-minute visit to a classroom in one of William Glasser's model "schools without failure." Dr. Glasser explains that class meetings are just one part of a school without failure. What happens during the rest of the school day is also important and is the subject of the film.

†*The Teachers' View.* Media Five, 1972 (28 min., color). Staff members from various schools without failure gather to share their experiences in beginning class meetings and enrichment programs. A discussion of common difficulties and solutions provides valuable encouragement for a school staff working toward a school without failure.

*The Unanswered Question.* Brandon Films, 1967 (5 min., B & W). "What is Brother-hood?"—a question people in all walks of life are either unable to or refuse to answer—is the question posed in this brief film.

*Understanding Stresses and Strains.* Walt Disney Productions, 1968 (10 min., color). Discusses the mental side of the health triangle, emphasizing how the pressures and worries of life can damage a person's health.

*Unicorn in the Garden.* Columbia Pictures Corp., 1953 (7 min., color). In this cartoon, the wife of a meek little man who sees a unicorn in his garden attempts to have her husband committed to an insane asylum, with surprising results.

†*Why Class Meetings?* Media Five, 1972 (28 min., color). This film gives a detailed ex-planation of why class meetings are an integral part of a success-oriented school. William Glasser discusses the importance of the circle and explains the techniques used in the meeting, including how the leader can remain nonjudgmental and still retain control.

*Why Man Creates.* Kaiser Aluminum and Chemical Corp., 1968 (29 min., color). Demon-strates the nature of the creative process and discusses the variety, richness, and importance of creative vision.

*World of '68.* Pyramid Film Producers, 1969 (5 min., color). A brief re-living of the fateful events of 1968—the deaths of Martin Luther King and Robert F. Kennedy among others.

†NOTE: The descriptions of Glasser films were written by Media Five Film Producers in Los Angeles, California.